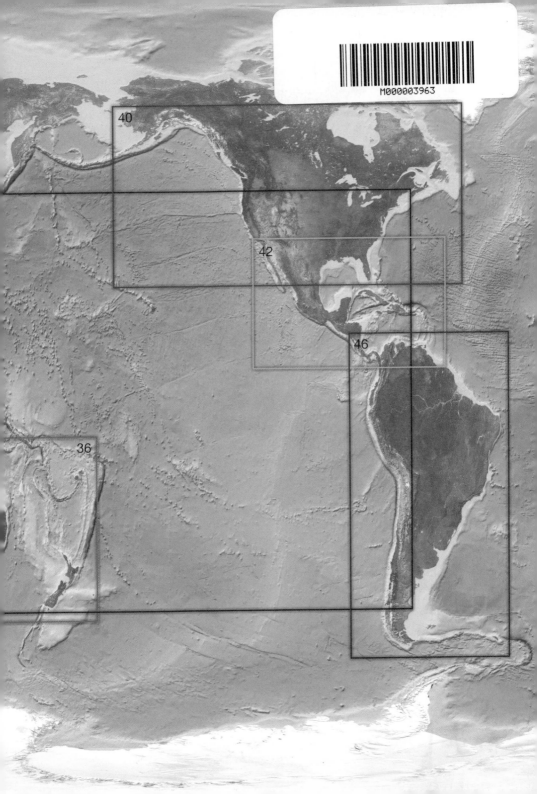

Personal Log

name

address

home phone

mobile phone

e-mail

passport no

doctor

doctor phone

blood group

next of kin

allergies

vaccinations   valid until

THE STORMRIDER SURF
JOURNAL

● ATLAS ● PLANNER ● LOG

LOW PRESSURE

FLAME BOWLS, VEZO REEFS, MADAGASCAR

THE STORMRIDER SURF
JOURNAL

Contents

ATLAS

PLANNER

Indonesia

June

SOUTH-PROVINCE NEW CALEDONIA
●●●●●○○●○●●○○
+ Virgin spots
+ Variety of beach & reef breaks
+ Exotic yacht trip
+ Low crowd factor
− Most spots only accessible by boat
− Easily blown out
− Very expensive
− Not super-consistent

Nouméa sits on the edge of the largest lagoon in the world making it a big kite and windsurfing destination. The outer reefs conceal waves that are the equal of anywhere else in the South Pacific, but the problem is they break on reef passes between 5-20km offshore, which is too far for even the most hardcore of paddlers! Stretched along a 700km fringing barrier reef riddled with passes and bands, only an expensive charter yacht or spending a couple of hours commuting each day will make it possible to explore this potentially great region.

YEMEN
●●●●●○○●○●●○
+ SW monsoon guaranteed surf
+ Powerful, virgin beachbreaks
+ Very warm water
+ Unique desert environment
− Messy windswell surf
− Lack of points and reefs
− Remote, difficult access
− Visas, permits and high costs

Yemen has an ill-founded reputation for feisty tribes, intent on war, kidnapping and terrorism in this fundamental Islamic nation. Instead, the adventurous will discover a warm-hearted and friendly people for whom pride, hospitality and honour are the pillars of life. Only a handful of people have ridden the waves breaking along Yemen's long south-facing Indian Ocean coastline. A 2003 trip led by US-expat Jay Quinn found surf before British journalist Stuart Butler unveiled 6-8ft barrely wedging lefts and a Surfing US team shot some A-grade barrels on the remote island of Socotra.

GISBORNE NEW ZEALAND
●●●●●○○●○●●○○
+ Many right pointbreaks
+ Clean mid-season swells
+ Hollow, powerful beachbreaks
+ Untouched coastline
− Small and crappy summers
− Semi-crowded main spots
− Chilly winter temps
− Some difficult access

With nearly 3,500km (2190mi) of coastline, there are plenty of areas to check on the North Island. Many of New Zealand's best competitive surfers come from the Gisborne area, because it is generally consistent, cleaner and just as powerful as the surf on the west coast, although it's usually a bit smaller. A wide swell window means more choice for wind/swell combos, firing up some great reefs and points. These quality spots, conveniently hidden amidst the sunniest and most untouched part of New Zealand, gives rise to Gisborne's reputation as the surf capital.

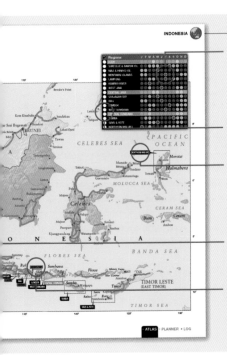

When to Go Table
Easily compare regions using monthly traffic lights. A white ring represents the corresponding month in the *Planner Section*.

White tick boxes
For recording your trips.

180 x Featured Regions
Located with black markers on the 13 Continental/Oceanic Maps. These regions appear in the *Planner Section*.

120 x Also Consider Regions
Located with a grey marker and listed in the *When to Go Tables*.

36 x Hotspots
Located with a coloured marker. Break reports for these spots appear in the *Planner Section*.

*If you know which continent or country you would like to visit locate potential surf zones in the **Atlas Section** and compare seasons using the **When to Go Table**. For further information on a specific zone use the white dot to determine which month it appears in the **Planner Section**.*

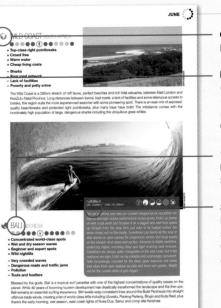

Colour-coded globe
Links to *Atlas Section*.

Monthly Traffic Lights
● Likely to be good conditions
● Variable conditions
● Likely to be bad conditions
Wetsuit key is on back flap

180 x World Surf Regions
Pluses & Minuses, Summary, Season, Wetsuit

36 x Hotspots
Detailed break report and a full set of Stormrider symbols for a widespread selection of world-class surf breaks.

*Alternatively browse the **Planner Section** for the month in which you wish to travel. Select a destination and locate it in the **Atlas Section** using the colour coded globe found to the left of the region name. From here you can find nearby regions with similar seasons by comparing on the **When to Go Table**.*

Using Your Journal

Trip Log and Wave Log have been specifically designed to allow personalization and freedom when recording trips and surf sessions. Utilize the symbols or simply overwrite them to use the pages as a standard lined journal.

Use the star symbols to rate your trips and waves.

Select your boards from the quiver adding details like model, length, fins etc.

Fill in the blank symbols using the easy to draw **Stormrider Symbols** shown in the key on the front cover flap or design your own symbols and abbreviations.

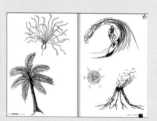

*The **Sketchbook** is made with wood-free, recycled cartridge paper, perfect for drawing maps, sketching pictures, painting watercolours and gluing in photos, clippings or mementos of your journey.*

Trip Log

Where	MALUKU
When	Jan 10th - 22nd 2011
Who	Neil, Lee, Marco, Erik, Ant, Oscar, Bobby, Dave
How	Sama Sama Boat
Rating	Waves 9, food, 9, people 9...overall 9!
Notes	So good to be back on the Sama Sama again. Explore trip in pacific Indo...found half a dozen new spots but highlight was the super consistent and fun seranade. Volcanos, waterfalls, dolphins, great fishing and snorkling. Surf was smallish but no people and lots of quality reefs....dream trip!
Gear	FCS K2.1 foam core, M3's. GoPro Hero3 + board mount
Quiver	Pukas 6'6" Rawson Firewire 8'6" Flexfire

Where	CAPE COAST - WESTERN GHANA
When	April 12th - 22nd 2010
Who	Boris, Simon, Toby, Florian

Wave Log

13 / 1 /2012 Serenade, MALUKU

▼	time	Last day surfing Serenade where overnight rain brought
	size	colder fresh water from the river, turning the lips greeny
	swell @ 10sec	yellow. The outside section wasn't really working, but 4-6ft
	wind @ 3km	sets concentrated on the inside section and wide. Only 6 of
	tide	us since Benji cut his foot yesterday. Got 30 waves in 2hrs
	crowd	before captain threatened to sail away without us. Stoked -
	waves	8 out of 10!
	gear	6'6" KS2's

13 / 9/20 12 LE PENON, HOSSEGOR, FRANCE

	time	2-4pm
	size	OVERHEAD ON SETS
	swell	NW @ 12
	wind	E @ 10KM/H
	tide	SPRING HIGH INCOMING
	crowd	10-20 GOT BUSIER LATER
	waves	GOOD TO VERY GOOD
	gear	FIREWIRE 8'6 FLEXFIRE

7

MALDIVES - MAY-JUNE 2013

Couldn't say no when Antoine asked if we were interested in a couple weeks atoll-hopping in the Maldives looking for some new spots in the further corners of the archipelago. I convinced Oscar and Dave from work to get aboard and hooked up with 2 of Ant's French mates, Jacques and Arnaud. The plan was to start in North Male surfing some of the famous breaks then travel by local dhoni to some other nearby atolls. At the last minute, Antoine decided it was too sketchy to go by dhoni, but he had managed to secure a proper safari boat for a cheap price. Nothing about the Maldives is really cheap, but we were happy that we would get proper food and sleep in aircon cabins, instead of boiled rice and hammocks! It turned out to be one of the finest culinary trips of our lives as the amazing fishing provided a steady stream of tuna sushi, steaks and stews. The surfing wasn't quite so amazing and we were dogged by strong monsoonal winds and a lack of swell from the right direction. This didn't stop

Where
When
Who
How
Rating
Notes
Gear
Quiver
Where
When
Who

First surf off the plane no sleep. 30+ surfers in the Jailbreaks line-up and cross-onshore when we paddled out, but most of the crowd was beginners flailing on the inside so the shoulder-high peak was quite empty. By the time we left there was only Oscar, Dave and me left in the water. Scored 10 or so waves with half a dozen great ones. Long walls and shallows on the inside at low tide when it closed-out a lot. Fun session at an iconic wave that I've always wanted to surf, but it left me wanting more in the way of size and power. Luckily we had to wait around for the French guys to arrive on an afternoon flight so we got a late arvo session that was a bit bigger (headhigh) and seemed to be less sectiony with the mid tide. There was only 4 Brazilians out and a local surf guide so plenty of waves to go round. Jacques and Arnaud were stoked and caught everything that moved while we hung on the wider section to get the good ones through the inside that would stand up better. A solid 6.5 rating which isn't bad in a 2ft SE swell! Dinner was a sign of things to come with a great spread of chicken

May 20 2013 — Jailbreaks
time ◔
size ◑
swell ◐
wind ◕
tide ◑
crowd ◐
waves 10
gear 5'10" Twin

May 20 2013 — Jailbreaks
time 3h
size S
swell SE
wind SW
tide M
crowd 7
waves 6.5/10
gear Q

LOG

APPENDIX

ATLAS

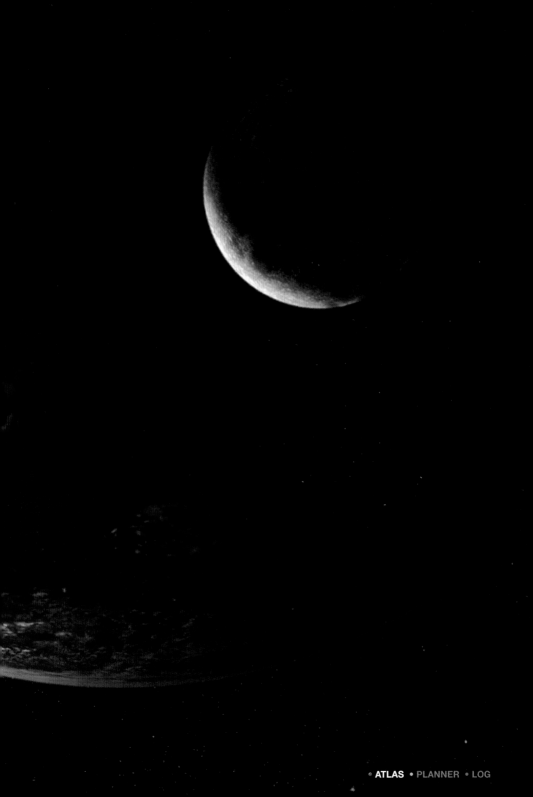

World Political

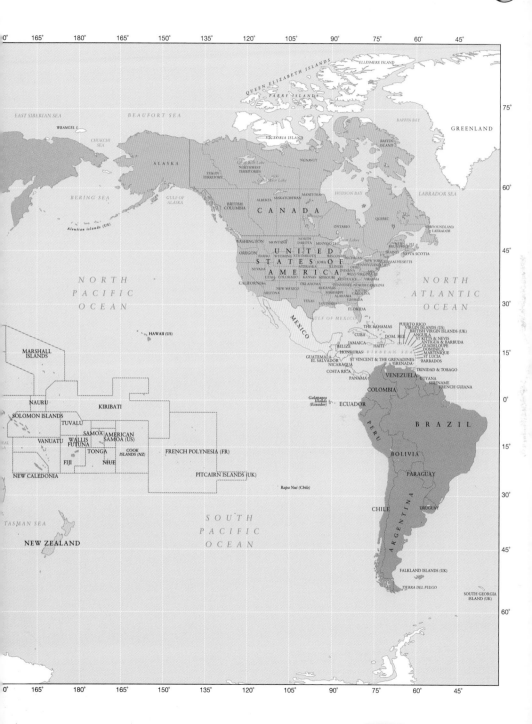

World Swell Generation

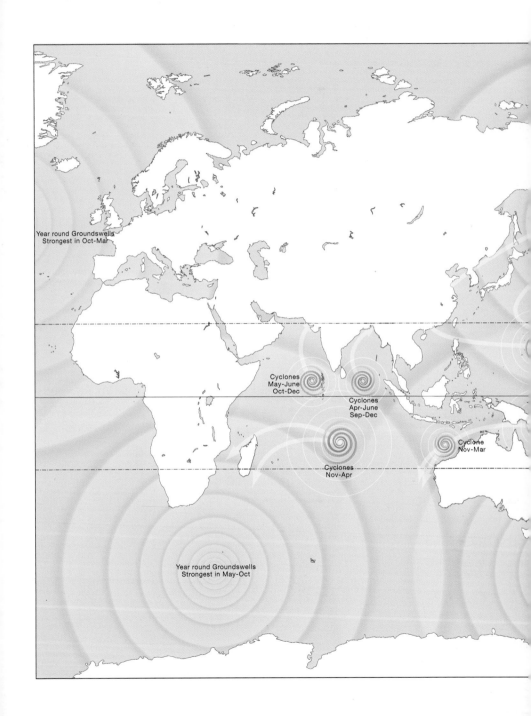

Year round Groundswells
Strongest in Oct-Mar

Cyclones
May-June
Oct-Dec

Cyclones
Apr-June
Sep-Dec

Cyclone
Nov-Mar

Cyclones
Nov-Apr

Year round Groundswells
Strongest in May-Oct

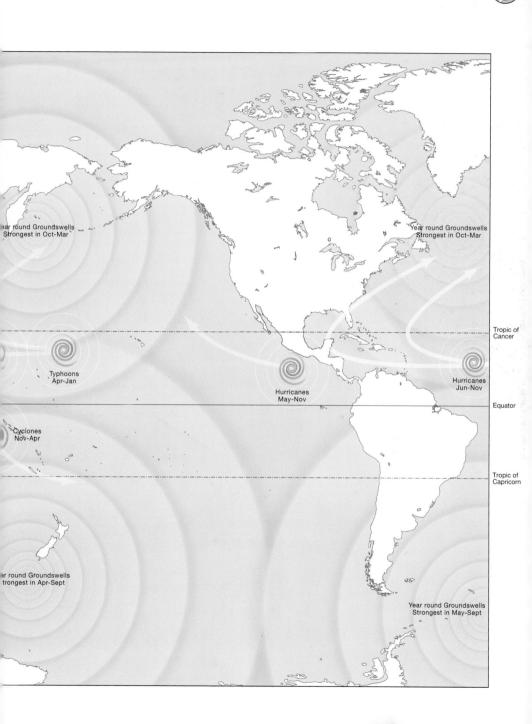

ear round Groundswells
Strongest in Oct-Mar

Year round Groundswells
Strongest in Oct-Mar

Tropic of
Cancer

Typhoons
Apr-Jan

Hurricanes
May-Nov

Hurricanes
Jun-Nov

Equator

Cyclones
Nov-Apr

Tropic of
Capricorn

ear round Groundswells
trongest in Apr-Sept

Year round Groundswells
Strongest in May-Sept

World Winds and Ocean Currents

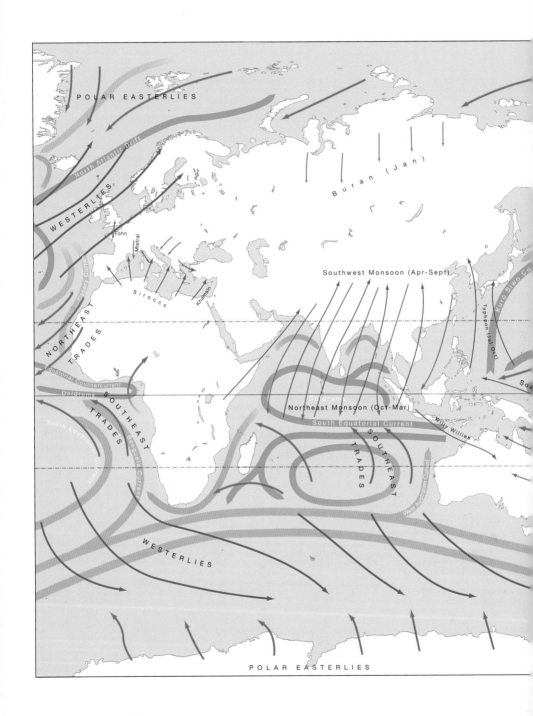

POLAR EASTERLIES

North Atlantic Drift

WESTERLIES

Fohn

Mistral

Sirocco

Khamsin

Canary Current

NORTHEAST TRADES

Equatorial Countercurrent

Doldrums

SOUTHEAST TRADES

South Equatorial Current

Benguela Current

Buran (Jan)

Southwest Monsoon (Apr-Sept)

Doldrums

Northeast Monsoon (Oct-Mar)

South Equatorial Current

SOUTHEAST TRADES

Kuro Siwo Current

Typhoon (Jul-Oct)

Willy Willies

West Australian Current

So

WESTERLIES

POLAR EASTERLIES

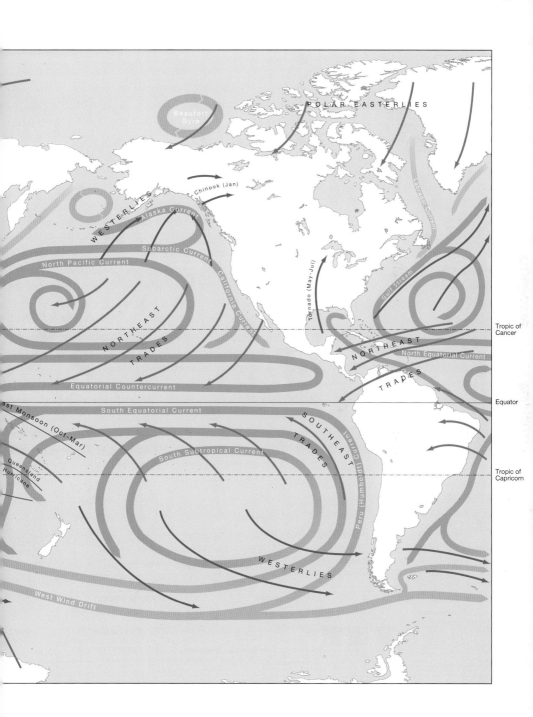

World Tides

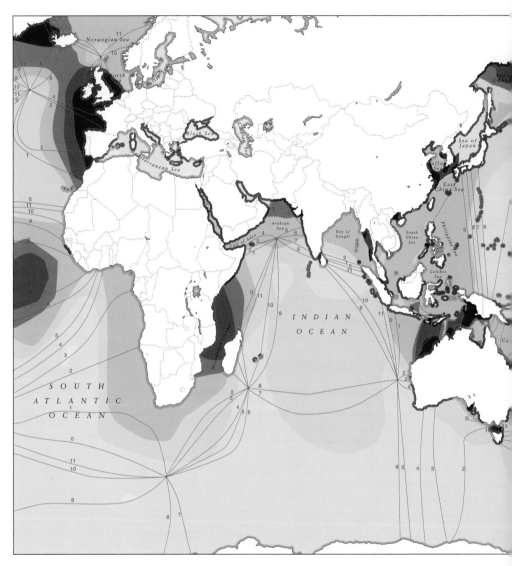

TIDAL RANGE

Micro-tidal | Meso -tidal | Macro -tidal

<0.4m | 0.4-0.8m | 0.8-1.2m | 1.2-1.6m | 1.6-2m | 2-4m | >4m

TIDAL TYPE

	Semi-diurnal	Diurnal
	Even – 2 daily tides Similar range	1 daily tide
Mixed	Odd – 2 daily tides different range	1 or 2 daily tides

TIDAL NODES

● **Amphidromic Points**
Indicate where the tidal range is almost zero.

Co-tidal lines
Join places where high tide occurs simultaneously.
Numbers denote co-tidal hours from Greenwich.

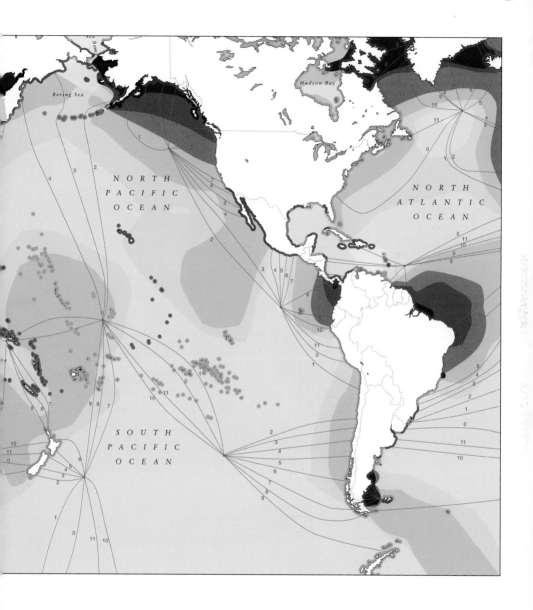

World Time Zones

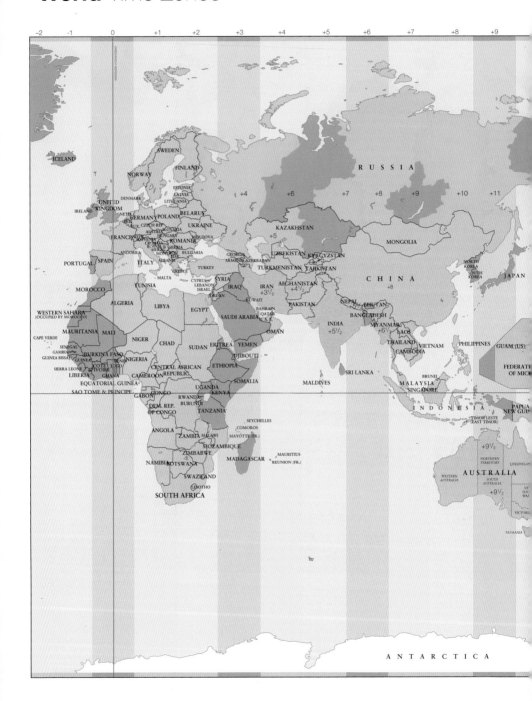

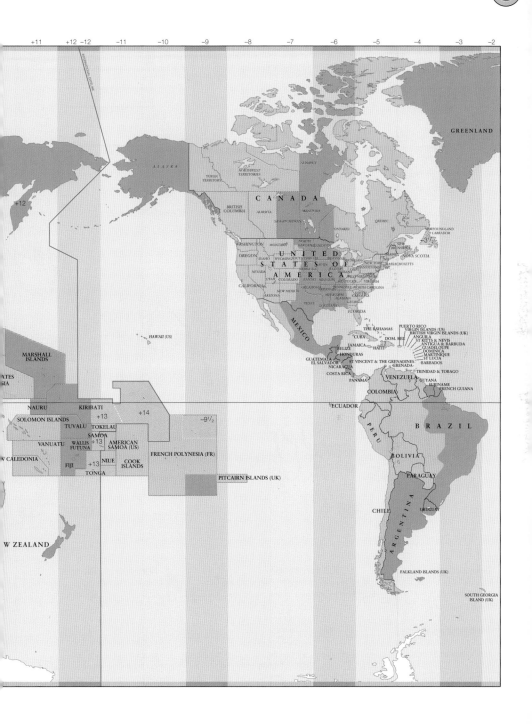

+11 +12 −12   −11   −10   −9   −8   −7   −6   −5   −4   −3   −2

GREENLAND

+12

ALASKA

CANADA

YUKON
TERRITORY

NORTHWEST
TERRITORIES

NUNAVUT

BRITISH
COLUMBIA

ALBERTA

SASKATCHEWAN

MANITOBA

ONTARIO

QUEBEC

NEWFOUNDLAND
& LABRADOR

−3½

WASHINGTON

MONTANA

NORTH DAKOTA

MINNESOTA

MAINE

NEW
BRUNSWICK

NOVA SCOTIA

OREGON

IDAHO

WYOMING

SOUTH DAKOTA

WISCONSIN

MICHIGAN

VERMONT

NEW HAMPSHIRE
MASSACHUSETTS

UNITED

STATES   OF

NEVADA

UTAH

COLORADO

NEBRASKA

IOWA

ILLINOIS

INDIANA

OHIO

PENNSYLVANIA

NEW YORK

RHODE ISLAND
CONNECTICUT

CALIFORNIA

AMERICA

KANSAS

MISSOURI

KENTUCKY

WEST
VIRGINIA

VIRGINIA

NEW JERSEY
DELAWARE
MARYLAND

NEW MEXICO

ARIZONA

OKLAHOMA

ARKANSAS

TENNESSEE

NORTH CAROLINA

SOUTH
CAROLINA

HAWAII (US)

TEXAS

MISSISSIPPI

ALABAMA

GEORGIA

MEXICO

FLORIDA

MARSHALL
ISLANDS

THE BAHAMAS

PUERTO RICO
VIRGIN ISLANDS (US)
BRITISH VIRGIN ISLANDS (UK)
ANGUILLA
ST KITTS & NEVIS
ANTIGUA & BARBUDA
GUADELOUPE
DOMINICA
MARTINIQUE
ST LUCIA
BARBADOS

CUBA

DOM. REP.

JAMAICA

HAITI

ATES
IA

BELIZE

HONDURAS

GUATEMALA
EL SALVADOR

NICARAGUA

ST VINCENT & THE GRENADINES
GRENADA

NAURU

KIRIBATI

COSTA RICA

PANAMA

VENEZUELA

TRINIDAD & TOBAGO

GUYANA
SURINAME
FRENCH GUIANA

SOLOMON ISLANDS

+13

+14

COLOMBIA

ECUADOR

TUVALU

TOKELAU

−9½

PERU

BRAZIL

VANUATU

WALLIS
FUTUNA

+13

SAMOA

AMERICAN
SAMOA (US)

BOLIVIA

W CALEDONIA

FIJI

+13

NIUE

COOK
ISLANDS

FRENCH POLYNESIA (FR)

PARAGUAY

TONGA

PITCAIRN ISLANDS (UK)

CHILE

URUGUAY

A R G E N T I N A

W ZEALAND

FALKLAND ISLANDS (UK)

SOUTH GEORGIA
ISLAND (UK)

Surf Migration

ARCTIC OCEAN

Decades of Discovery

Pre-War

1950s and 60s

1970s

1980s

1990s

2000s

Duke Kahanamoku
was surfing's ambassador and figurehead of the 20th Century, demonstrating the art of board-riding in California, New Jersey, Australia and New Zealand, attracting large crowds of onlookers and inspiring many to take up a board and contribute to global surf culture.

US Servicemen built a vital surfing link to the furthest flung countries and mid-ocean islands of strategic importance. The Canaries, Azores, Iceland, Morocco, Japan and all the Pacific islands where the US military are present, saw the first surfboards arrive with army, navy and air force personnel, who often left their boards behind for the locals to build their own scene.

Lifeguards spread the word through the seasonality of their work, living a truly endless summer. The Australian Surf Life Saving Association was instrumental in the propagation of rescue surfboards around the world and the lifeguards would pass on their skills to a new and willing membership.

This map is a general representation of discovery periods and the first surfers may only have surfed a small portion of the country's coastline. There may still be coastline within a shaded region that remains undiscovered/unsurfed. Unshaded coastline is not covered in the **Stormrider Surf Guides**, but may have some existing surf culture/history.

ARCTIC
OCEAN

Beaufort
Sea

Bering Strait

ALASKA

Hudson Bay

Bering Sea

BRITISH
COLUMBIA

ONTARIO

WASHINGTON   MINNESOTA   NOVA SCOTIA
OREGON   NEW ENGLAND
                    MICHIGAN OHIO
N O R T H   MID ATLANTIC   N O R T H
                              THE SOUTH
P A C I F I C   TEXAS   A T L A N T I C
O C E A N   FLORIDA   O C E A N

HAWAII   MEXICO   BAHAMAS
                                          CUBA   DOMINICAN
MARSHALL   JAMAICA   REPUBLIC
ISLANDS   HAITI PUERTO RICO
                          LINE   BRITISH VIRGIN ISLANDS
MICRONESIA   ISLANDS   GUATEMALA   ANTIGUA AND BARBUDA
                                  EL SALVADOR GUADELOUPE ST MARTIN & ST BARTHÉLÉMY
                                  NICARAGUA   MARTINIQUE
SOLOMON   COSTA RICA   BARBADOS
ISLANDS   PANAMA   VENEZUELA   TRINIDAD AND TOBAGO

VANUATU   COLOMBIA
           WESTERN AMERICAN
           SAMOA   SAMOA   GALAPAGOS   ECUADOR
NEW CALEDONIA FIJI   PERU
           TONGA   BRAZIL
                   FRENCH POLYNESIA

                              RAPA NUI
                                          CHILE
S O U T H
P A C I F I C   URAGUAY
O C E A N   ARGENTINA

Tasman Sea   NEW ZEALAND

Explorers have added an important ingredient to the cultural melting pot, striking out into the unknown, searching for the perfect wave, which may be just around the next headland. Blake, Troy, Boyum, Naughton and Peterson are just a few of the names who have pushed the frontiers and taken the road less travelled.

• ATLAS • PLANNER • LOG

Europe

50°   40°   30°   20°   10°

0   500 Miles
0   500km

Reykjavik
REYKJANES PENINSULA
ICELAND

Norwegian Sea

Europe North

Faroe Islands

Shetland Islands

Bergen

Haugesund
Stavanger

Inverness
SCOTLAND • Aberdeen
Glasgow • Dundee
Londonderry • Ayr • Edinburgh
IRELAND • Belfast • Tynemouth
Tralee • Dublin★ **ENGLAND** *North Sea*
Cork Liverpool • Preston
Manchester
WALES Nottingham
Birmingham
Swansea
Bristol **London** Amsterdam **NETH.**
Southampton Antwerp The Hague
Guernsey Brussels★ **BEL.** Cologne
Jersey Ghent Liège
Brest Lille

Europe Continent

Rennes **Luxembourg LUX.**
Bay Nantes **Paris**★
of Tours **FRANCE** Nancy
Biscay La Rochelle Poitiers Dijon
La Coruna El Ferrol Limoges Lausanne ★**SWI**
Pontevedra Oviedo Bordeaux Geneva Bern
Santander Valence Milan
Porto Zamora Bilbao Toulouse Turin
PORTUGAL Valladolid **ANDORRA** Nîmes Genoa
Salamanca Marseille **MONACO**
Peniche Abrantes **SPAIN** Zaragoza
★**Lisbon** Toledo • **Madrid** Barcelona Corsica
Setubal Badajoz Sassari
Seville Cordoba Valencia Sardinia
Cadiz Malaga Murcia Carbonia Oristano
GIBRALTAR Cagliari
Tetouan Algiers
Casablanca **Rabat** Oran ★ Skikda Annaba
Safi Fes Oujda Tlemcen **Tunis**★
Meknes Sougueur **TUNISIA**

SÃO JORGE TERCEIRA
SÃO MIGUEL
Azores

MADEIRA
Madeira

FUERTEVENTURA LANZAROTE
Canary Islands
TENERIFE
GRAN CANARIA

Marrakech
Agadir **MOROCCO**

A L G E R I A

ATLANTIC OCEAN

40°

30°

20°   10°   0°   10°

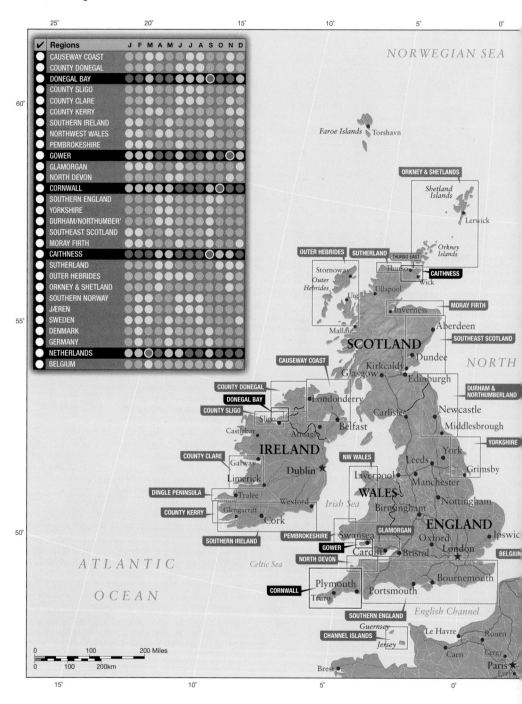

Regions ✔	J F M A M J J A S O N D
CAUSEWAY COAST	
COUNTY DONEGAL	
DONEGAL BAY	
COUNTY SLIGO	
COUNTY CLARE	
COUNTY KERRY	
SOUTHERN IRELAND	
NORTHWEST WALES	
PEMBROKESHIRE	
GOWER	
GLAMORGAN	
NORTH DEVON	
CORNWALL	
SOUTHERN ENGLAND	
YORKSHIRE	
DURHAM/NORTHUMBER'	
SOUTHEAST SCOTLAND	
MORAY FIRTH	
CAITHNESS	
SUTHERLAND	
OUTER HEBRIDES	
ORKNEY & SHETLAND	
SOUTHERN NORWAY	
JÆREN	
SWEDEN	
DENMARK	
GERMANY	
NETHERLANDS	
BELGIUM	

NORWEGIAN SEA

Faroe Islands • Torshavn

ORKNEY & SHETLANDS
Shetland Islands
Lerwick

OUTER HEBRIDES   SUTHERLAND
THURSO EAST   Orkney Islands
Stornoway   Thurso   CAITHNESS
Outer Hebrides   Wick
Uig   Ullapool
Malaig   Inverness   MORAY FIRTH
SCOTLAND   Aberdeen
Dundee   SOUTHEAST SCOTLAND
Glasgow   Kirkcaldy   NORTH
CAUSEWAY COAST   Edinburgh
COUNTY DONEGAL   Carlisle   DURHAM & NORTHUMBERLAND
DONEGAL BAY   Londonderry   Newcastle
COUNTY SLIGO   Middlesbrough
Castlebar   Sligo   Belfast   YORKSHIRE
Armagh   York
COUNTY CLARE   Galway   NW WALES   Leeds   Grimsby
Limerick   Dublin ★   Liverpool   Manchester
DINGLE PENINSULA   Tralee   Wexford   WALES   Nottingham
COUNTY KERRY   Glengarriff   Irish Sea   Birmingham   ENGLAND
Cork   GLAMORGAN
SOUTHERN IRELAND   PEMBROKESHIRE   Swansea   Oxford   Ipswic
GOWER   Cardiff   London ★   BELGIUM
NORTH DEVON   Bristol
Celtic Sea   Bournemouth
CORNWALL   Plymouth   Portsmouth
Truro   English Channel
SOUTHERN ENGLAND
IRELAND
ATLANTIC   Guernsey   Le Havre   Rouen
OCEAN   CHANNEL ISLANDS   Jersey   Cergy
Caen   Paris ★
Brest   Evre

| 0 | 100 | 200 Miles |
| 0 | 100 | 200km |

SOUTHERN NORWAY

Namsos
Stenkjær
Steinkjer
Umea
Ornskoldsvik
Vaasa
FINLAND
Trondheim
Kristiansund
Ostersund
Kramfors
Tampere
Harnosand
Alesund
Molde
Oppdal
Sundsvall
Gulf of Bothnia
Lahti
Vyborg
Maloy
Fokstua
Ljusdal
Pori
60°
Eikefjord
NORWAY
Lillehammer
Bollnas
Rauma
Honefoss
Gjovik
Hamar
Falun
Turku
Helsinki
Bergen
Odda
Drammen
Uppsala
Norrtalje
G. of Finland
Sauda
Kongsberg
Vasteras
Hango
Tallinn
Haugesund
Skien
SWEDEN
Stockholm
Hiiumaa
Raph
Tartu
Stavanger
Evje
Karlstad
Orebro
Sodertalje
Saaremaa
Parnu
ESTONIA
Sandnes
Uddevalla
Wanern
Norrkoping
Kuressaare
Valmiera
JÆREN
Trollhatan
Linkoping
Ventspils
G. of Riga
LATVIA
Kristiansand
Skagerrak
Vattern
Vastervik
Visby
Gotland
Jelgava
Riga
Jekabpils
Gothenburg
Jonkoping
Liepaja
Panevezys
DENMARK
Alborg
Saeby
Vaxjo
Kalmar
Kretinga
LITHUANIA
Thisted
Randers
Kattegat
Ljungby
Oland
Klaipeda
Silale
Vilnius
55°
Viborg
Arhus
Helsingborg
BALTIC SEA
Kaunas
DENMARK
Copenhagen
Kaliningrad
RUSSIA
Marijampol
Esbjerg
Odense
Malmo
Bornholm
SWEDEN
Gdansk
Marijampol
GERMANY
Tonder
Slupsk
Elblag
Bialystok
Flensburg
Kiel
Rodby
Stralsund
Tczew
Szczecinek
Torun
Brest
NETHERLANDS
Neumunster
Rostock
Stettin
POLAND
Wilhelmshaven
Hamburg
Schwerin
Bydgoszcz
Heerenveen
Bremen
Achim
Luneburg
Berlin
Poznan
Warsaw
NETHERLANDS
Uelzen
Lodz
Radom
The Hague
Amsterdam
Enschede
Hanover
Pabiance
Lublin
Rotterdam
Salzgitter
Zielona Gora
Kielce
Dortmund
Halle
Wroclaw
Antwerp
Dusseldorf
GERMANY
Leipzig
Liberec
Katowice
50°
BELGIUM
Siegen
Usti nad Labem
Gliwice
Cracow
ussels
Liege
Wetzlar
CZECH REP.
Pardubice
Ostrava
Uzhhoro
arleroi
Frankfurt
Prague
Olomouc
Zilina
Kosice
LUXEMBOURG
Mainz
Tachov
Plzen
Nurnberg
Zlin
Luxembourg
Trier
Brno
SLOVAKIA
Metz
Mannheim
Ceske Budejovice
Vienna
Bratislava
Miskolc
Nancy
Buhl
Stuttgart
Linz
Debrecen
Strasbourg

SEA

5°   10°   15°   20°   25°   30°

5°   10°   15°   20°

ATLAS • PLANNER • LOG

Europe Continent

✔ Regions	J F M A M J J A S O N D	✔ Regions	J F M A M J J A S O N D
LA MANCHE		ERICEIRA	
BRITTANY		LISBON	
VENDÉE		ALENTEJO	
GIRONDE		ALGARVE	
LANDES		ANDALUCIA	
COTE BASQUE		EASTERN SPAIN	
PAIS VASCO		SOUTHERN FRANCE - W	
CANTABRIA		SOUTHERN FRANCE - E	
ASTURIAS		SARDINIA	
GALICIA		NORTHERN ITALY	
MINHO & DOURO		CENTRAL ITALY	
BEIRA LITORAL		SOUTHERN ITALY	
PENICHE		SICILY & CALABRIA	

Africa

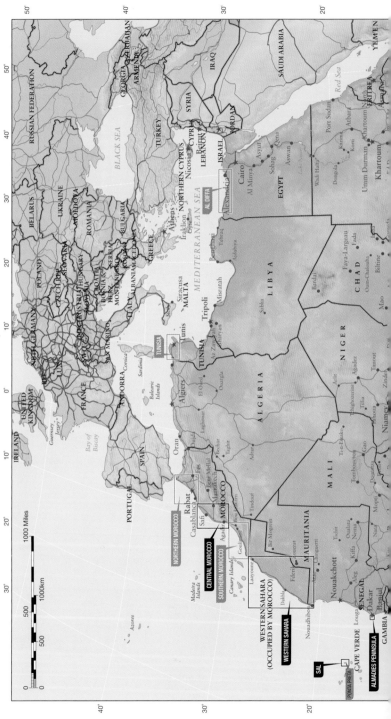

Map labels:

KENYA · SOUTHERN KWAZULU NATAL · WILD COAST · EAST LONDON · DURBAN · CAPE ROCK · INHAMBANE PROVINCE · LESOTHO · ST. FRANCIS BAY · GARDEN ROUTE · CAPE PENINSULA · WESTERN CAPE · SWAKOPMUND · SKELETON COAST · LUANDA & BENGO · POINTE-NOIRE · NORTH GABON · SÃO TOMÉ · SAO TOMÉ & PRINCIPE · TOGO & BENIN · GOLD COAST · IVORY COAST · NW LIBERIA

Region	J	F	M	A	M	J	J	A	S	O	N	D
AL DIFFA												
TUNISIA												
NORTHERN MOROCCO												
CENTRAL MOROCCO												
SOUTHERN MOROCCO												
WESTERN SAHARA												
SAL												
ALMADIES PENINSULA												
NORTHWEST LIBERIA												
IVORY COAST												
GOLD COAST												
TOGO & BENIN												
SAO TOME												
NORTH GABON												
POINTE NOIRE												
LUANDA AND BENGO												
SKELETON COAST												
SWAKOPMUND												
WESTERN CAPE												
CAPE PENINSULA												
GARDEN ROUTE												
ST. FRANCIS BAY												
EAST LONDON												
WILD COAST												
SOUTH KWAZULU NATAL												
DURBAN												
INHAMBANE PROVINCE												
KENYA												

Indian Ocean

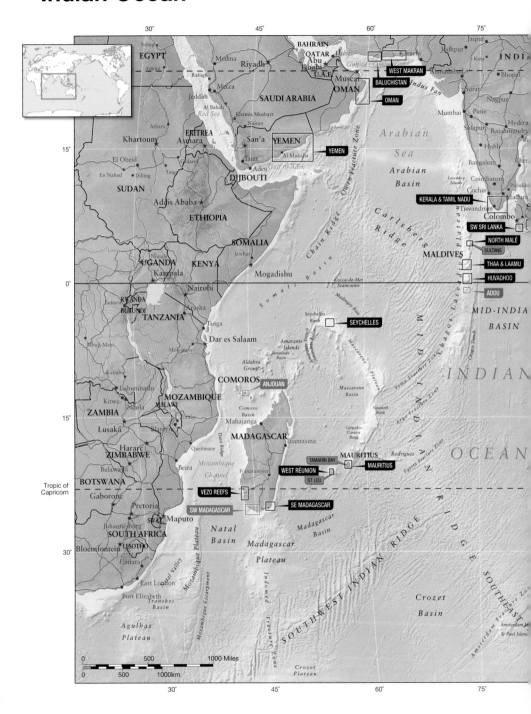

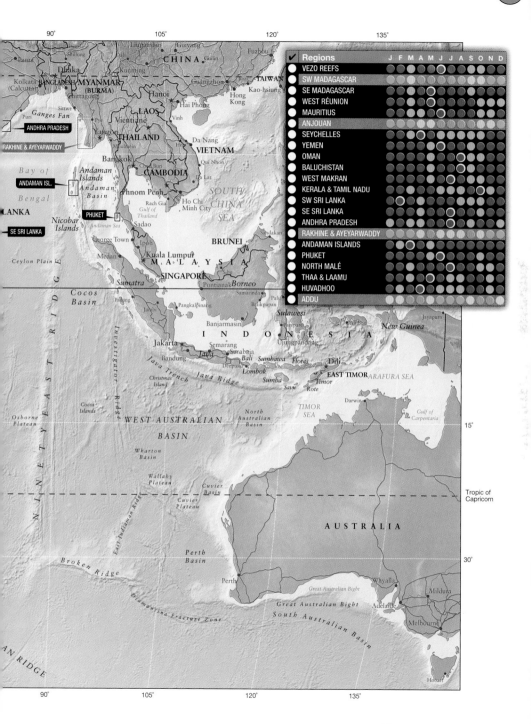

Regions	J	F	M	A	M	J	J	A	S	O	N	D
VEZO REEFS												
SW MADAGASCAR												
SE MADAGASCAR												
WEST RÉUNION												
MAURITIUS												
ANJOUAN												
SEYCHELLES												
YEMEN												
OMAN												
BALUCHISTAN												
WEST MAKRAN												
KERALA & TAMIL NADU												
SW SRI LANKA												
SE SRI LANKA												
ANDHRA PRADESH												
RAKHINE & AYEYARWADDY												
ANDAMAN ISLANDS												
PHUKET												
NORTH MALÉ												
THAA & LAAMU												
HUVADHOO												
ADDU												

ANDHRA PRADESH

RAKHINE & AYEYARWADDY

ANDAMAN ISL.

SE SRI LANKA

PHUKET

East Asia

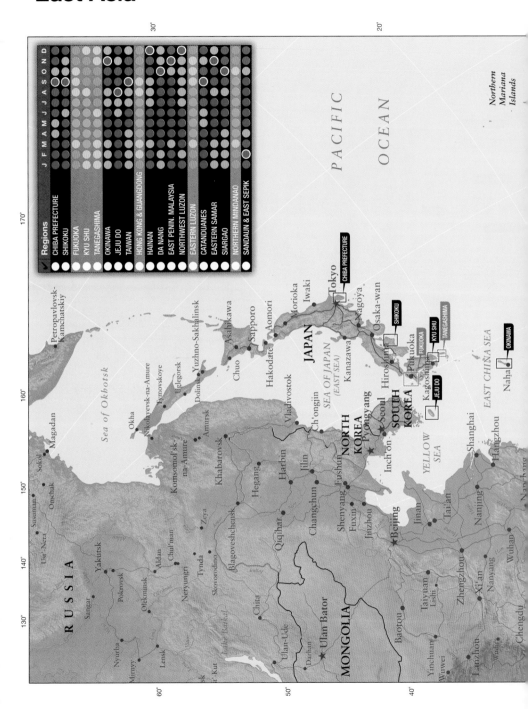

Regions	J	F	M	A	M	J	J	A	S	O	N	D
CHIBA PREFECTURE												
SHIKOKU												
FUKUOKA												
KYU SHU												
TANEGASHIMA												
OKINAWA												
JEJU DO												
TAIWAN												
HONG KONG & GUANGDONG												
HAINAN												
DA NANG												
EAST PENIN. MALAYSIA												
NORTHWEST LUZON												
EASTERN LUZON												
CATANDUANES												
EASTERN SAMAR												
SIARGAO												
NORTHERN MINDANAO												
SANDAUN & EAST SEPIK												

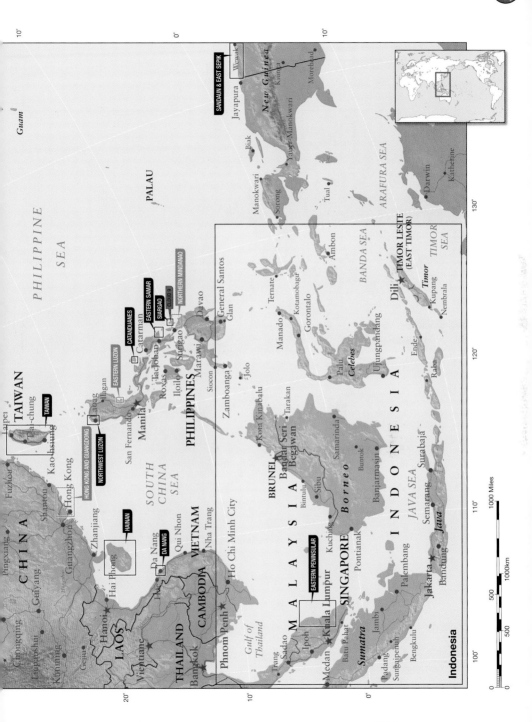

ATLAS • PLANNER • LOG

Indonesia

Australasia

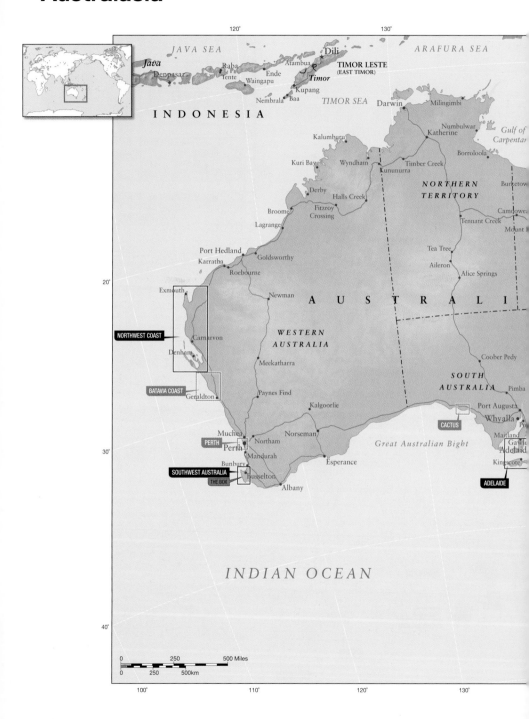

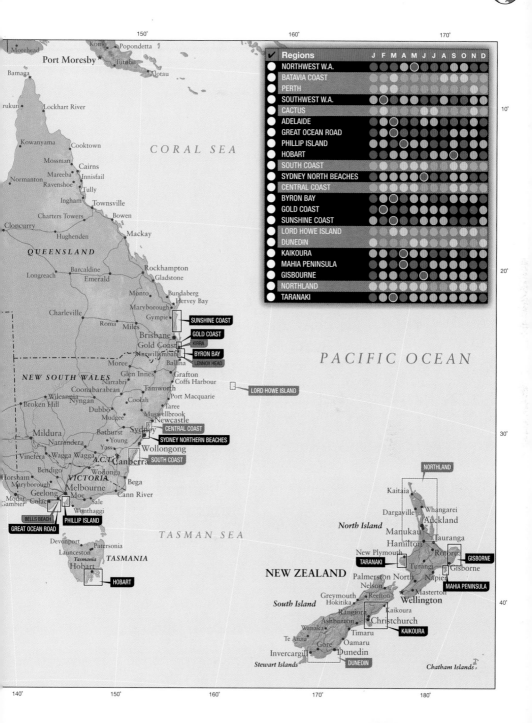

Regions	J	F	M	A	M	J	J	A	S	O	N	D
NORTHWEST W.A.												
BATAVIA COAST												
PERTH												
SOUTHWEST W.A.												
CACTUS												
ADELAIDE												
GREAT OCEAN ROAD												
PHILLIP ISLAND												
HOBART												
SOUTH COAST												
SYDNEY NORTH BEACHES												
CENTRAL COAST												
BYRON BAY												
GOLD COAST												
SUNSHINE COAST												
LORD HOWE ISLAND												
DUNEDIN												
KAIKOURA												
MAHIA PENINSULA												
GISBOURNE												
NORTHLAND												
TARANAKI												

ATLAS • PLANNER • LOG

Pacific Ocean

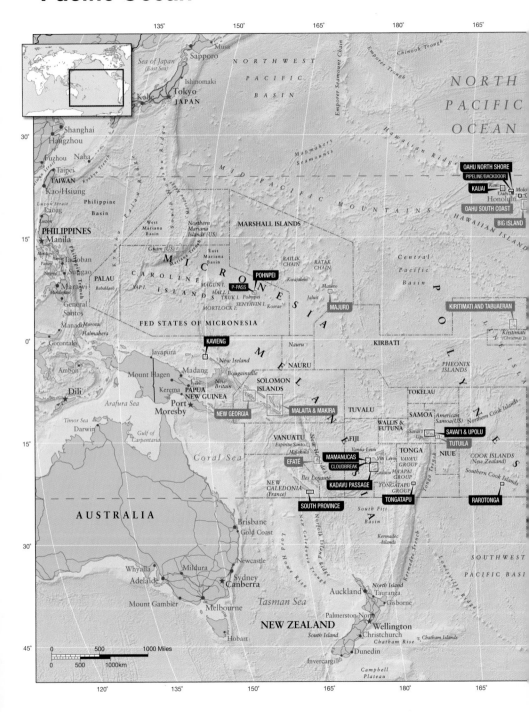

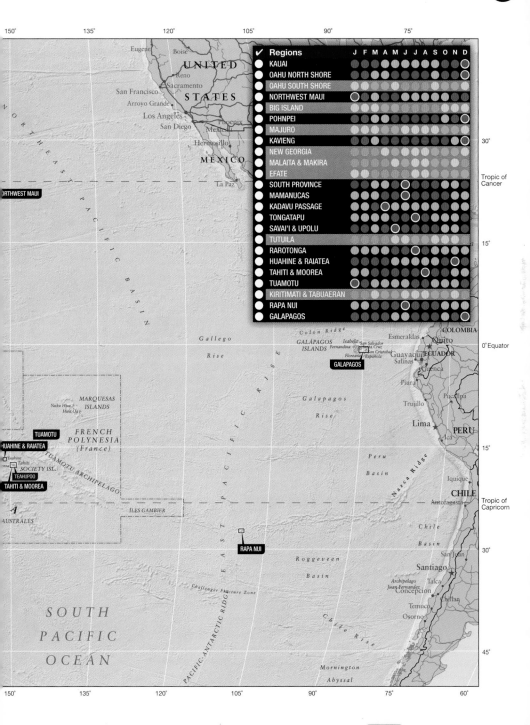

✓	Regions	J	F	M	A	M	J	J	A	S	O	N	D
●	KAUAI												
●	OAHU NORTH SHORE												
●	OAHU SOUTH SHORE												
●	NORTHWEST MAUI												
●	BIG ISLAND												
●	POHNPEI												
●	MAJURO												
●	KAVIENG												
●	NEW GEORGIA												
●	MALAITA & MAKIRA												
●	EFATE												
●	SOUTH PROVINCE												
●	MAMANUCAS												
●	KADAVU PASSAGE												
●	TONGATAPU												
●	SAVAI'I & UPOLU												
●	TUTUILA												
●	RAROTONGA												
●	HUAHINE & RAIATEA												
●	TAHITI & MOOREA												
●	TUAMOTU												
●	KIRITIMATI & TABUAERAN												
●	RAPA NUI												
●	GALAPAGOS												

ORTHWEST MAUI

TUAMOTU

HUAHINE & RAIATEA

TAHITI & MOOREA

TEAHUPOO

GALAPAGOS

RAPA NUI

North America

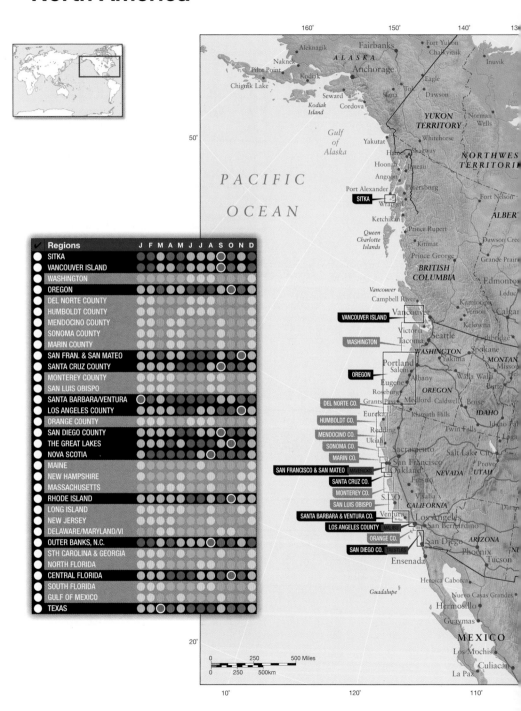

Central America

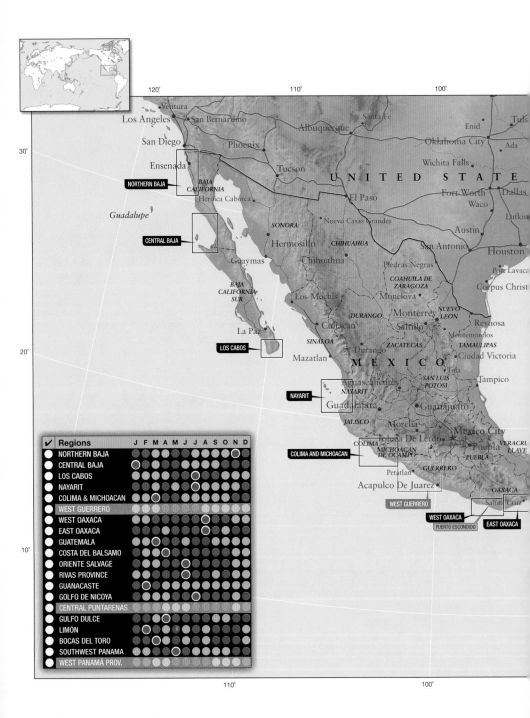

✔	Regions	J	F	M	A	M	J	J	A	S	O	N	D
○	NORTHERN BAJA												
○	CENTRAL BAJA												
○	LOS CABOS												
○	NAYARIT												
○	COLIMA & MICHOACAN												
○	WEST GUERRERO												
○	WEST OAXACA												
○	EAST OAXACA												
○	GUATEMALA												
○	COSTA DEL BALSAMO												
○	ORIENTE SALVAGE												
○	RIVAS PROVINCE												
○	GUANACASTE												
○	GOLFO DE NICOYA												
○	CENTRAL PUNTARENAS												
○	GULFO DULCE												
○	LIMÓN												
○	BOCAS DEL TORO												
○	SOUTHWEST PANAMA												
○	WEST PANAMÁ PROV.												

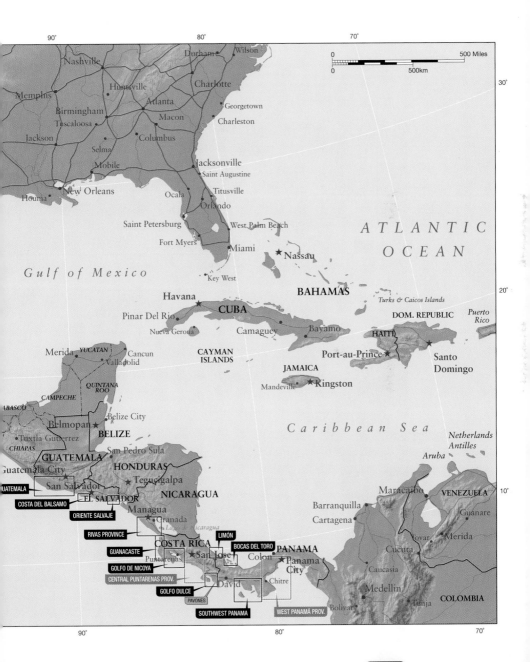

Caribbean

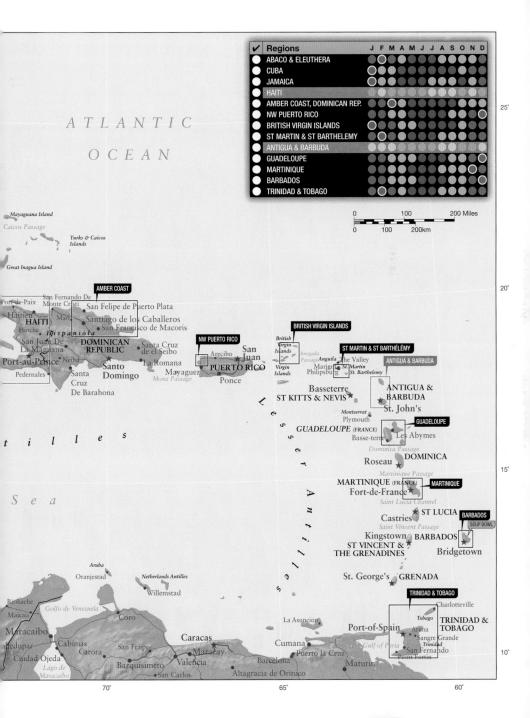

South America

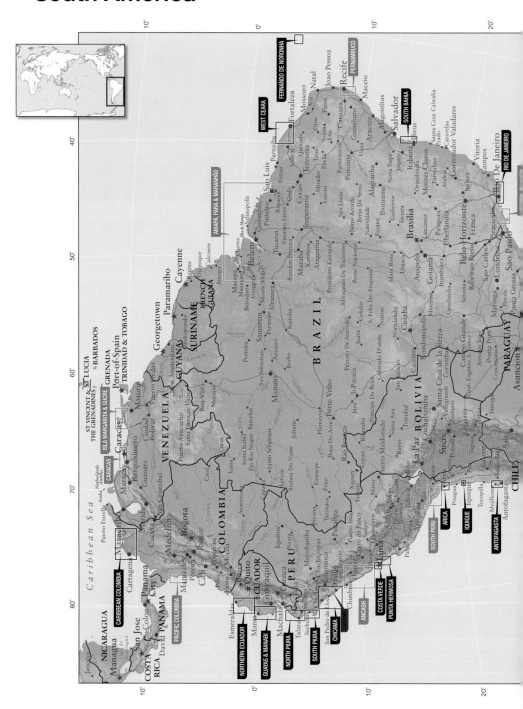

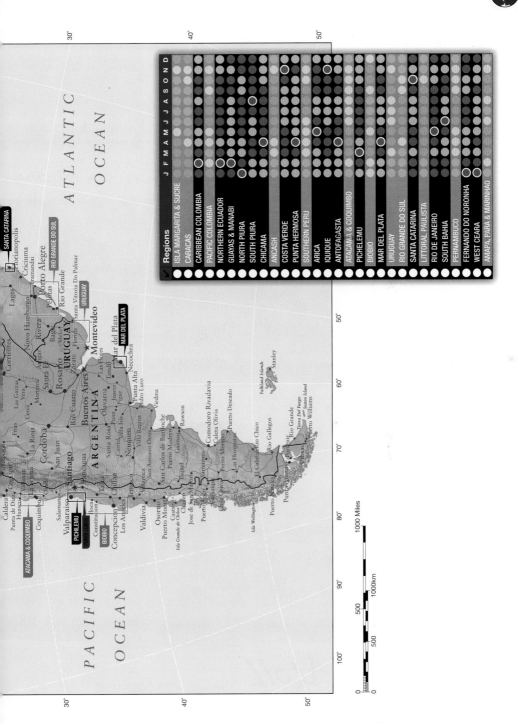

Honky's

**Chaaya Island Dhonveli Resort
Maldives**

Have your big wave boards gathered dust?

**Kandui Villas
Mentawai Islands**

If you answered YES to any of these questions—

YOU NEED A SURF TRIP!

**Namotu Island Resort
Fiji**

WaterWays
SURF ADVENTURES

P: 1 (310) 584 9900
E: sean@waterwaystravel.com
waterwaystravel.com

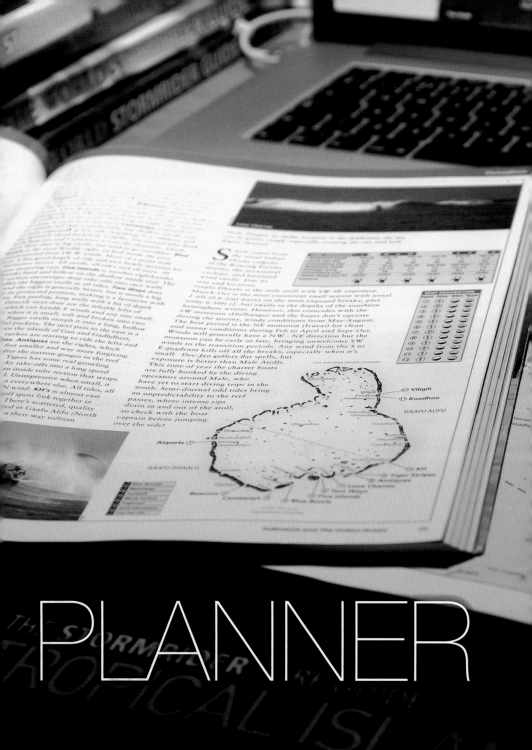

PLANNER

January

LANZAROTE CANARY ISLANDS

LA SANTA

TIMO JARVINEN

+ Powerful waves
+ Lots of spots
+ Dry climate
+ Dramatic scenery

− Sharp, shallow lava reefs
− Windy conditions
− Fierce localism
− Thefts and car crime

The Canaries reputation for being the Hawaii of the Atlantic is well earned, as these volcanic islands have much in common with their Pacific cousins. NE trade winds fanning heavy reef waves, breaking close to shore in clear blue water, full of fierce locals, under a burning hot sun seems a fair description of both surf zones. The truth is there are many differences, like the climate and water temperature, but when it comes to the waves, Lanzarote certainly has powerful, challenging surf reminiscent of Oahu's North Shore.

CENTRAL BAJA MEXICO

OPEN DOORS

DUSTIN HUMPHRIES

+ Quality right pointbreaks
+ Natividad tubing waves
+ Miles of uncrowded surf
+ South-facing spots offshore

− Lack of lefts
− Surprisingly cold water
− Bad roads and remote Natividad
− Basic accommodation

Baja California is a long, narrow peninsula extending south of San Diego, barely linked to the Mexican mainland by a thin strip of land. This arid, rocky finger has long been a playground for surfers from "Upper California" seeking righthand pointbreak perfection, without the urban crowds that dominate the US line-ups. Central Baja is where the main highway heads inland and the huge Bahia Sebastian Vizcaino hides a treasure trove of rights. The offshore island breaks include the heaving barrels of Open Doors on Isla Natividad.

TUAMOTU FRENCH POLYNESIA

SECRET SPOT

BEN THOUARD

+ Year-round swells
+ Juicy reef passes
+ World-class fishing and diving
+ Luxury boat travel

− Occasional flat spells
− No shelter from trade winds
− Large distances between breaks
− Extremely expensive surf trip

The vast majority of the world's 400 atolls are located in the Pacific and the Tuamotu include 77 of them, which cover a territory as vast as western Europe. This dusting of islands is also called The Labyrinth, or the Archipelago of the Rough Sea and has remained essentially uncharted due to the difficulty of navigating the local waters. With a sturdy boat and some good charts, there are some awesome reef passes to be found by the rich and adventurous.

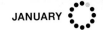
CUBA

+ Uncrowded outside Havana
+ Exploration possibilities
+ Boca de Yumuri pointbreak
+ Perfect winter climate

− Short, inconsistent swell season
− Onshore winds
− Difficult travel logistics
− Expensive accommodation & food

BOCA DE YUMURI

STUART BUTLER

Beyond the postcard clichés of *mojitos*, salsa dancing and cigars, Cuba has consistent surf in warm, tropical and largely empty water. Cuban surfing is usually a winter-only affair with the northeastern coast gathering up only the biggest Atlantic swells as they filter between gaps in the Bahamas. Big storms can also churn out of the Gulf of Mexico and send stormy swell marching towards the northwestern corner of the island, around Havana. A third and much rarer swell generator comes from hurricanes, which can produce massive waves for the south coast of Cuba.

ANCHOR POINT
LAT. 30.544990° LONG. −9.725268°

PATRICE TOUHAR

A medium to large, long period NW swell is what's needed to light up this world-class right, first surfed by Aussies in the 1960's. From the steep take-off at the outside peak, a seemingly endless succession of speed walls and cutback hooks present themselves. Occasional emerald green rooms appear on the sandy sections down the point. It's easier to come in at one of the coves and walk back to jump off at the end between sets. Works on all but high tides, unless it's huge, which is when it may be possible to ride back to Taghazout. In town there are a couple more waves like the uber-mellow Hash Point for those too lazy to walk out to Anchor or the fickle but zippy barrels off the rocks of Panoramas. With all the recent growth in Taghazout, pollution is a real problem after heavy rain for the crowds of people escaping the northern winter.

CENTRAL MOROCCO

+ Swell consistency
+ Long righthanders
+ Beginner-friendly area
+ Great winter weather

− Frequently messy line-ups
− Strong N winds
− Anchor Point crowds
− Pollution after rain

Despite its North African location, Morocco is very much a part of the European surf trail. Located between 20° and 35° latitude with a NW-facing coastline, Morocco has all the key elements for an outstanding surf destination. The Taghazout area nestles behind a big cape, which funnels the predominant N winds offshore, and a string of righthand points peel forever down sand covered rocks. With balmy winter land temperatures, cheap living and a fascinating cultural diversity, Morocco is a must for the European surf traveller.

January

SANTA BARBARA & VENTURA CALIFORNIA

+ Iconic SoCal pointbreaks
+ Super-long righthanders
+ Longboard or shortboard
+ Winter NW offshores

− Crazy crowds
− Channel Island S swell filter
− Private access issues
− Traffic and localism

RINCON

DAVID PU

Although Santa Barbara is on a south-facing coastline, the swell window is blocked to the S-SW by the Channel Islands and narrowed to the NW by Point Conception. But what it lacks in quantity, it makes up for in quality with an unrivalled set of right pointbreaks, including the "Queen of the Coast", Rincon, which straddles the Santa Barbara/Ventura county line. This area is the best set-up in California whenever a medium to large swell arrives from the W-NW (especially from 270° to 285°), lighting up the leg burning points, which are never short of takers.

NORTH PIURA PERU

+ Summer NW swells
+ Great lefts with good winds
+ Warm water, plenty of sun
+ Close to S swell breaks

− Short swell season
− Fairly inconsistent
− Basic lodging and prices rising
− Long distance from Lima

CABO BLANCO

JAVIER FERNANDEZ

Most of the Peruvian coastline is chilled by the Humboldt Current and rocked by S swells, but the northwest corner enjoys different conditions. The north part of Piura province is warmed by the southern extremity of the Panama Current and it favours North Pacific swells. It's not as consistent as the rest of Peru and is only worth visiting in the middle of summer, when it gets quite busy with Lima surfers coming up for Cabo Blanco barrels. If it does go flat, then it's only a short distance to the beaches exposed to the more consistent S swells.

MALUKU PACIFIC INDONESIA

+ Regular N monsoon swell
+ Quality, mid-sized waves
+ Calm winds, small tides, no crowds
+ Super scenic and wild

− Short surf season
− Long distances between spots
− Lack of reliable local transport
− Few organised boat trips

SERENADE

DAN HAYLOCK

The original Spice Islands, the Maluku (Moluccas or Molluques) are part of the easternmost archipelago of Indonesia, and the only Indonesian island chain in the Pacific. Despite waves as good as the Philippines, these islands remain largely ignored by travelling surfers. Occasional forays into the region by boat have revealed an outstanding variety of breaks, most of which go unsurfed. Small numbers of feral surfers make the overland trek to stay in basic village accommodation and surf the ledgy lefts of Serenade during the Indo off-season.

NORTHWEST MAUI HAWAII

HONOLUA BAY

+ Thinner crowds than Oahu
+ World-class spots
+ Windsurfing mecca
+ Amazing volcanic scenery

− Swell shadows
− Strong trade winds
− Difficult access to some spots
− High prices

While Oahu's North Shore has dominated media coverage of Hawaiian surf, each island in the chain gets its share of awesome waves and Maui has some of the best. This beautiful island of contrasts sees both lush green valleys alongside barren lava landscapes, but more importantly is home to some legendary waves, including the flawless perfection of Honolua Bay, the incredible speed of Maalaea and the ultimate big wave challenge of Jaws. Also famed for extreme wind and kitesurfing, Maui is for strong surfers, looking for a hardcore Hawaiian experience.

CACIMBA DO PADRE
LAT. -3.848397° LONG. -32.437134°

FERNANDO DE NORONHA
BRAZIL

+ Powerful tubing reef & beachbreaks
+ Consistently offshore
+ Untouched, wild environment
+ Peaceful island vibe

− Short surf season
− Difficult access
− Isolated island location
− Very expensive living costs

Looking down from the *mirantes* (viewpoints), Cacimba do Padre appears as a picturesque tropical beach with perfect clean waves in crystal clear water, against the backdrop of the gnarled volcanic brothers known as the *Dois Irmãoes*. This is the most consistent spot on the island and the swell can be doubled in size here, reaching heights of up to 15ft (5m) offering huge, cavernous barrels, before shutting down hard on the fine-sand beach. With enough NW-N swell, it starts breaking on an outside shelf and rolls left through to the inside, getting meaner all the way. There are rights as well, but most of the action is concentrated on the longer, more makeable lefts. Smaller, peakier swells can see a high tide left, wedge off the base of the rocks, but no matter what the size, Cacimba is always hollow and powerful. Only gets crowded when the Jan pro contest is on.

This island cluster is the summit of a huge underwater volcano, rising 4.3km from the ocean floor. The surrounding depth allows the N swells to hit with unimpeded speed and power, jacking up wave heights in the process. The island's colourful history includes use as a battlefield, jail, air base and weather station, but has now become a tourist heaven for divers and surfers. The NW oriented coastline has perfect topography and offshore winds, where the steeply sloping beaches make for some fast barrels, perfectly suited to bodyboarders and tube junkies.

January

MALTA & GOZO MALTA

RIVIERA

+ NW and NE swells
+ No crowds
+ No tides
+ Architecture, history & scuba diving

− Winter only
− Lack of consistent spots
− Jellyfish & shallow rocks
− Urban sprawl & mad traffic

The southernmost limit of the European Community sits in the middle of the Mediterranean Sea, where it has withstood a pounding from millennia of Mistral or Grecale wind-driven waves. These two small dots in the Med suffer from poor water resources, sparse vegetation and no fauna apart from rabbits, yet it has got the second highest density of cars after the USA. Winter is the ideal time to go for the NW-NE swells and there are only a handful of occasional locals, so getting the exposed north coast breaks to yourself is almost guaranteed.

WEST CEARA BRAZIL

ICARAI POINT

+ Two sources of swell
+ Quality hollow waves
+ Punchy beachbreaks and right points.
+ Fortaleza facilities & superb beaches

− Often blown-out in summer
− Lack of size
− Crowds and pollution
− Big tidal variation

The powerful waves discovered in Fernando do Noronha, shows that Brazil also relies on a significant supply of North Atlantic winter swells, allowing a separate surf season on this north-facing coast. Long sand dunes and coconut palms create the regularity of the Ceara coast, only broken by some calm bays and narrow rivermouths. Fortaleza is known for having the wildest Monday nights in the world at Praia Iracema, plus some good reefbreaks, while Paracuru is a proper surf town with four right points that fire from Nov to Feb.

JAMAICA

MAKKA'S

+ Decent winter consistency
+ Warm water, friendly waves
+ Various left pointbreaks
+ Rastafari culture and music

− Frequent onshore conditions
− Poor roads on eastern side
− Sometimes small & gutless
− Difficult access, some private coast

Being the third largest island in the Caribbean, Jamaica stands out on the map, but it is relatively obscure in terms of Caribbean surf destinations. Famous for Bob Marley, reggae music and Rastafarian culture, its natural bounty includes 120 rivers, 240km of beaches and six mountain ranges, where the tallest peak reaches (2256m) in the Blue Mountains. Despite its size, only the eastern tip receives a decent amount of windswell worth exploring, with options for bigger NE swells on the north coast or more consistent, offshore conditions on the south coast.

ALMADIES PENINSULA SENEGAL

OUAKAM

PHILIPPE CHEVODIAN

+ Spot quality and quantity
+ Easy access
+ Budget trip
+ African lifestyle

− Urchins
− Onshore winds on exposed NW shore
− Local hustlers
− Quite inconsistent

Most surfers who visit Senegal head straight to the prime surf area on the Almadies Peninsula, just outside Dakar. This westernmost tip of Africa juts out into the ocean and the peninsula has one of the largest swell windows in the world. Swells can appear from the SE and all the way around to the N, which is about 260°! Another great thing about this zone is that most of the spots lie within easy walking distance of each other or else take a short boat ride out to the exposed left and right N'gor reefs of *Endless Summer* fame.

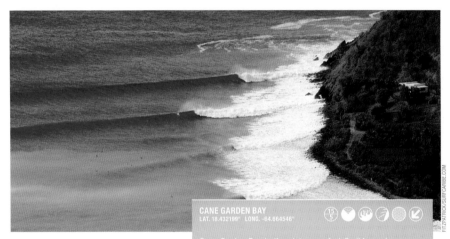

FITZPATRICK/SURFCARIBE.COM

CANE GARDEN BAY
LAT. 18.432199° LONG. -64.664546°

Cane Garden Bay is the picture-perfect Caribbean dream wave that peels alluringly into the sunset-facing bay which is usually a safe anchorage for expensive, ocean-going yachts. Appearances can be deceptive as the throaty barrels at the tip of the point hit the numerous coral heads, then race down the line to the inside bowl section, before shouldering off into deep water. There are no easy ones and since it only breaks maybe 20-30 days a year, the locals are as hungry as the Gillette coral. Any NE-E wind is offshore (SE messes it up) and tide isn't a problem, rather it's timing a NW-NE swell that is big enough to make the hairpin journey around the island to the bay. Due E swell has its power sapped by Anegada, but there are more exposed breaks on Tortola's north coast.

BRITISH VIRGIN ISLANDS

+ World-class Cane Garden Bay
+ Consistent beachbreaks
+ Safe tropical destination
+ Unspoilt Caribbean islands

− Short swell season
− Lack of consistent reefs
− Boat access only breaks
− Expensive

The Virgin Islands represent the beginning of the Leeward Islands and are the peaks of submerged mountains rising only a few hundred feet above sea level. The four large and 42 small islands consist mainly of rolling green hills and white sandy beaches, open to Atlantic swells. Shallower waters offshore means that waves can't reach the size of those on Puerto Rico, however big winter swells will awaken the famous line-up at Cane Garden Bay. On Tortola, there is a distinct lack of consistent spots, so utilising a boat will increase the likelihood of finding surf.

February

LIMON COSTA RICA

+ Consistent, seasonal swell
+ Powerful reefbreaks
+ Insignificant tidal range
+ Laid-back Caribbean style

− Flat between seasons
− Lack of good beachbreaks
− Extremely wet
− Petty crime

SALSA BRAVA

FITZPATRICK/SURF-CARIBE.COM

Costa Rica receives swell from two very different suppliers on its schizoid coastline. The Pacific Ocean delivers year-round, long-distance swells, while the Caribbean side receives fairly big and wild waves from short-lived, localised seasonal storms. It's amazing how much power is in the short fetch Caribbean swells, which break in the 2-12ft range. The Caribbean coastline is short (212km), the majority is within the Tortuguero National Park, a long sandy stretch backed by huge waterways with countless beachbreaks plus the dead coral reefs of Puertos Limon and Viejo.

NORTHWEST GREECE

+ Various winter swells
+ Quality waves for the Med
+ Best spot density in Greece
+ Temples, mythology, sightseeing

− Inconsistent
− Short-lived swells
− Winter conditions
− Long drive from Athens

KASTRO POINT

YANNICK LE TOQUIN

With slightly more than 1000 islands, the Greek coastline is split between 4,000km of mainland and 10,000km of islands. However, it's the coast of Epirus, right below Albania, that gets both S swells from the Ionian Sea as well as NW swells from the southern Adriatic Sea, which combined with the highest density of quality surf spots, make this region Greek surf central. Italian and French surfers are starting to make the trip there when winter storms coincide with cheap air tickets, joining the growing number of locals riding some decent quality lefts.

GUAYAS & MANABI ECUADOR

+ Two surf seasons
+ Clean warm-water waves
+ Calm winds
+ Trips to the Andes

− Lack of heavy waves
− Some crowds
− Rainy winter season
− Petty thefts in the cities

MONTAÑITA

GEOFF RAGATZ

Ecuador receives plenty of long distance swells from the N and the S that roll in with moderate power and break onto forgiving reefs and beaches. Whereas most of the Pacific coast of South America is influenced by the cold Humboldt Current, Ecuador's waters are warmed by the Panama Current. There are many potential spots to the north of Salinas that are better exposed to N swells, but most of them only get good when it reaches double overhead. Spots to the south of Salinas, towards Playas, only break on S-SW swells.

ELEUTHERA & ABACO BAHAMAS

+ Good, varied reefbreaks
+ Low crowd pressure
+ Incredibly clear water
+ Great weather

– Flat summers
– Unreliable hurricane swells
– Unpredictable winds
– Quite expensive

ELEUTHERA

ALEX WILLIAMS

Seen from the air, the Bahamas is a swirling mass of deep blue ocean, dotted with patches of turquoise water touching ribbons of white sand. Technically speaking, the archipelago is not a part of the Caribbean, but these 700 low-lying islands, along with over 2,400 islets called cays, are surface projections of two oceanic banks composed of coral with a limestone base. With 5% of the world's coral, an amount surpassing even Australia's Great Barrier Reef, there's plenty of good surf potential, especially on the eastern "out islands" of Abaco and Eleuthera.

BILL MORRIS

THE BOX
LAT. -33.971500° LONG. 114.979000°

Mutant Margaret River righthand slab that earns its name from the square-shaped pits, just across the bay from famous Surfers Point. Make the air-drop then negotiate the dry sucks, boils or stepped faces to claim serious shack time. The lip is so thick and loves nothing better than to hurl the pit-jockeys onto the shelf, with or without a few inches of water. W swell helps make-ability as does more water over the sharp, sharky reef. Insane wave, best left for the clinically insane, while average Joes can try their luck at The Point. Heart-stopping drops, lumpy bowls and cutback walls are all part of the ride and it can handle a healthy dose of onshore wind, maintaining shape for long, swooping turns. Getting caught inside is no fun and positively dangerous if taking on the rights. It's still a major ASP contest site and one of the most reliable waves in WA.

SOUTHWEST WA, AUSTRALIA

+ Massive swell exposure
+ World-class reefs
+ Lots of power
+ Dramatic coastline

– Cold and wet winters
– Isolated, dangerous reefs
– Windy
– Sharky

The Margaret River area of W.A. is perceived as Australia's most consistent and challenging big wave forum, where pretensions and pretenders are quickly washed away. Whilst the NW conceals Indo-like lefts, the area S of Cape Naturaliste is littered with rocky ledges and point breaks, that get battered by giant Roaring Forties swells. The scenic Caves Road skirts the coastline, meandering through forests, gentle hills and around vineyards that overlook the sea where a truly hardcore crew shreds dozens of world-class spots.

February

FUERTEVENTURA CANARY ISLANDS

●①●●●●●●●○●●●

+ Powerful lava reefbreaks
+ North track spot density
+ Great weather and water temps
+ Good restaurants and nightlife

– Sharp, shallow reefs
– Strong winds
– Dangerous roads
– Wavesailing crowds

LOS LOBOS
DAVID SERI

While Lanzarote is undoubtedly the best bet for world-class conditions, Fuerteventura conceals many short, sucky lava reefs as well as the long sandy beaches that attract so many kite and windsurfers. The island's name has become synonymous with strong wind, so every year in August, the world speed windsurfing championships are held, while the biggest surf contest was the 1998 longboard world championship. This young volcanic island is the second largest of the Canaries, the least developed island accessible by plane and offers the potential for less-crowded surf.

CARIBBEAN COLOMBIA

●⊛●●●●●●●●●●●

+ Very consistent
+ Uncrowded
+ Dry surf season
+ Exploration possibilities

– Poor quality, smaller waves
– Frequent onshores
– Street crime
– Heavy drug trade

LOS NARANJOS
STÉPHANE ROBIN

For the majority of travellers, Colombia brings to mind images of guerrillas, drug cartels, kidnapping and cocaine. In reality, this is an unfair and increasingly irrelevant portrayal of a region that is tipped to become a major tourist destination in the next few years as security improves. Colombia is a beautiful, sensuous country of unexplored jungles and sophisticated towns and cities. The Pacific breaks, many of them still unsurfed, work best from April to October. From November to March, the more developed and easier-going Caribbean coastline is the focus.

SOUTHWEST SRI LANKA

●⊛●●●●●●●○○●●

+ Quality mellow waves
+ Offshore NE monsoon
+ Warm and tropical
+ Cheap

– Conflicting wind and swell patterns
– Small waves
– No world-class spots
– Sewage and localism

HIKKADUWA
LAURENT NEVAREZ

Sri Lanka, a teardrop shaped island below India, is the highest latitude, reliable surf destination in the Indian Ocean. The south coast is open to the same regular, long-distance SW swells that pepper Indonesia, however onshore monsoonal wind patterns arrive during the prime May-Oct swell season. To score offshore conditions, venture here during the much quieter swell period of Dec-March, when waist to headhigh waves are common and the conditions are perfect for all abilities. The centre of the south coast surf scene focuses on the handful of fun reefs in the resort town of Hikkaduwa.

ST MARTIN & ST BARTHÉLEMY

+ Good reefs and pointbreaks
+ Multiple swell and wind combos
+ Small sized islands
+ Uncrowded & friendly locals

− Short groundswell season
− Wind sensitive breaks
− Fickle top spots
− Very expensive

TOINY

St Martin and St Barthélemy are the northernmost eastern Caribbean islands, with good exposure to northern swells and a mixture of sand, rock and coral breaks. St Martin's hilly interior is hemmed by 36 white sandy beaches and is the smallest island in the world to be shared by two governments (French and Dutch). St Barth's oozes class in shopping, yachts, hotels and restaurants, plus it is also blessed with some great waves for the fortunate few. Its coastline is irregular and has many coves and bays that are protected by coral reefs.

PONTA PRETA
LAT. 16.605813° LONG. -22.930408°

SAL CAPE VERDE

+ Generally uncrowded
+ Shapely reef waves
+ Further exploration possibilities
+ Windsurfing heaven

− Inconsistent, seasonal swells
− Windy
− Flat desert landscape
− Fairly expensive

Ponta Preta is the best wave, 30 mins walk from Santa Maria, which has long rights peeling for up to 300m over sharp, black boulders. Barrel sections, speed walls and wind whipped copings are shared out between the surf and wind crews. It's best with a decent NW swell, low tide and when the usual sideshore wind is light. The more E in the wind the better and early starts often avoid sharing the line-up with the kites and sails. There's also an awesome, even hollower left off the outside peak, but it's exposed to the wind and closes-out suddenly on the barely submerged rocks so experts only. This is a world-class wave so be sure your ability matches up. Not making a section will usually put you and your board on the rocks. Paddle from the beach, timing the shorebreak, or sprint from the point on small days.

The Cape Verde islands are the southernmost group in the boomerang shaped archipelago of Macaronesia. Sal is the flattest island and has become synonymous with wind and kitesurfing. Powered by the heat of the Sahara, the ever-present NE trades blow throughout the year and provide cross or offshore conditions on the west-facing lava reefs that benefit from the Atlantic winter NW swell train. Ponta Preta has emerged as a world-class wind, kite and surf spot, which is quite an achievement and sometimes sees large waves that tower above the average mast.

February

SANDAUN & EAST SEPIK PNG

+ Consistent monsoon swell
+ Fun-sized, uncrowded waves
+ Low tourist numbers
+ Cheap surf camp options

− No outstanding breaks
− Tricky access and transport
− Hot and sticky weather
− Street crime and diseases

LIDO'S RIGHT

MICHAEL KEW

Papua New Guinea is known as 'the land of the unexpected' and it is one of only three tropical areas in the world that also supports a glacier, on Mount Jaya's 5,000m (16,404ft) peak. The Bismarck Sea produces NW-N swell, affecting many different provinces including Kavieng, PNG's best-known surf area. Sandaun was formerly West Sepik province, an undeveloped region bordering Irian Jaya, with 260km of mostly grey-sand coastline. Logging industry expats based in Vanimo soon discovered good surf on this mountainous coast during the NW monsoon season.

GUANACASTE COSTA RICA

+ Consistent year-round
+ Fun-sized waves
+ Pointbreak heaven
+ Rich in wildlife

− Lack of size and lefts
− Oppressively hot weather
− Millions of insects
− Tourist price inflation

POTRERO GRANDE

CHRISTOPHE 'KIKI' COMMARIEU

Costa Rica's Pacific side gets pounded by medium-sized swells all-year-long from a 180° swell window. The northern province of Guanacaste is very consistent with long-distance Pacific swells arriving from the north and south. The area around Tamarindo is best during the winter dry season when clean, offshore conditions, sunshine and easy access make it a veritable tropical paradise, but crowds are a problem. May-Oct is the wet season, however this is a surf-rich time, when perfect, SW groundswell, provides bigger waves at quality rights like Potrero Grande, aka Ollie's Point.

NORTHERN ECUADOR

+ N & S swell exposure
+ Exploration potential
+ Lowest Ecuador crowds
+ Cheap lodging and transport

− Short, rainy N swell season
− Flat spells
− Hard to reach Mompiche
− Security issues

MOMPICHE

PAUL KENNEDY

Ecuador has long been popular with surfers looking for a warm water fix after enduring the cold Humboldt Current that pervades along the South American Pacific coast. Travelers concentrated on the Montañita area in the south but rumours of a perfect left set-up in Mompiche have attracted the more adventurous to the "green province" of Esmeraldas. The northernmost coastal province enjoys lush vegetation, from tropical rainforest to mangroves while estuaries cut the land into remote territories only accessible by boat.

TRINIDAD & TOBAGO

MOUNT IRVINE

BABY MARMOTTE

+ Magic Mount Irvine
+ Spot density on Tobago
+ Cheap, excellent food
+ Craziest Carnival

– Inconsistent larger swells
– Strong localism
– Long drives to Trinidad surf
– Thievery and police roadblocks

Trinidad is located at the very southern end of the Windward Island chain and only 7km from Venezuela on the South American continent. The main surfing areas are situated in the north and northeast of the island near Toco, but there is still a huge amount of coastline unexplored by surfers. Two thirds of Tobago is volcanic and mountainous and the southwest coast is where almost all the surf spots are located. The Buccoo Reef National Park is the main coastal feature, offering not only great surf but also fantastic snorkelling and diving.

KIRRA
LAT. -28.164474° LONG. 153.535268°

Kirra is probably the world's best righthand point that breaks over sand. Air drops into various tube sections, which seem to suck out below sea level, adding sand to the already ridiculously powerful and thick lips. Super long, slabby sections need breakneck speed to negotiate while praying the inevitable drop-in won't happen on the deepest tube of your life. Sand pumping and re-nourishment projects have destroyed or magically resurrected the tubes over decades and the changeable set-up usually breaks at half the size of the prevailing swell. Big, solid SE groundswell is the preferred element, while E and even NE cyclone swells can also produce epic barrels if the sand is right. Despite the advent of the Superbank, crowd pressure remains enormous. The sweep down the point is legendary, so many opt to run back up the point after every ride.

GOLD COAST QUEENSLAND

+ World-class right points
+ Near-perfect tropical climate
+ Flat day entertainment
+ Concentration of breaks

– Super-crowded surf arena
– Constant drop-ins
– Few lefts
– Generally small waves

Queensland's Gold Coast is one of the most intense surf zones in the world, combining 40km of legendary spots with a huge, hungry surf population. It's the most visited stretch of coastline in Australia, but don't be misled by the name "Surfer's Paradise", as this zone is dominated by skyscrapers not palm trees and the mass-tourism hordes rule out anything approaching deserted. Year-round warm temperatures, raging nightlife and endlessly long, right pointbreaks tempt southerners and foreigners alike, to try their luck in Australia's most competitive line-ups.

March

BOCAS DEL TORO PANAMA

● ● ⊛ ● ● ● ● ● ● ● ● ●

+ Seasonal consistent swell
+ Quality, non tide-dependant reefs
+ Cheap and safe area
+ Less crowded than Costa Rica

− Flat between seasons
− Lack of rights
− Wet and windy afternoons
− Time-consuming trips to spots

SILVERBACKS

Christopher Columbus landed in Bocas del Toro in October 1502, unaware that if he had arrived a few months later, his crew would have had to fight through some decent surf to get to terra firma. Located off Panama's northwest coast, these islands are only 32km south of the Costa Rican border. The wooden built city of Bocas del Toro has seen a tourism boom attracting many to the beautiful, virtually deserted beaches. Remarkable surf spots like the powerful Silverbacks define this zone, but the two windows of surf throughout the year are slender.

ANDAMAN ISLANDS INDIA

● ● ⊛ ● ● ● ● ● ● ● ● ●

+ Virgin coral reefbreaks
+ Epic Kumari Point
+ No regular boat operator
+ Untouched paradise with wild tribes

− Unfavourable winter season
− Short, expensive surf season
− Limited accommodation
− Oppressive humidity & sand flies

KUMARI POINT

Dubbed "The land of the head-hunters" by Marco Polo, this chain of 572 islands, islets and rocks is now referred to as the Andaman and Nicobar Islands. Geographic isolation, heavily restricted travel and a mysterious Stone Age culture characterise this zone. Geographically more 'Indo' than India, the Andaman's have been on many surfer's travel wish list, but the first surf trip took only took place in 1998, when photographer John Callahan discovered the perfect long lines of Kumari Point. Whilst foreigners are permitted to visit the Andaman Islands, the Nicobars are only accessible to Indians.

SUNSHINE COAST QUEENSLAND

● ● ⊛ ● ● ● ● ● ● ● ● ●

+ Ground and cyclone swells
+ Lots of right pointbreaks
+ Many easy access beaches
+ Beginners paradise in Noosa

− Intense crowds
− Fickle pointbreaks
− Lack of power and size
− Fairly expensive

TEA TREE

The Sunshine Coast is the northernmost stretch of reliable surf in Australia and home of the fabled right points of Noosa Heads. Noosa has become a ritzy resort village with beachfront boutiques, bars and restaurants, surrounded by lush, tropical vegetation and National Parks. Heading south down to Caloundra are a string of modern tourist towns and miles of golden sand beachbreak, broken only by a couple of headlands. In stark contrast, a trip north in a 4WD over 80km of low tide beach, arrives at Double Island Point and the totally wild landscape of Frasier Island.

SHEVENINGEN

NETHERLANDS

+ Mellow beachbreaks
+ Top beach facilities
+ Good transport links
+ Close to Amsterdam

– Lack of groundswells
– Flat, crowded summers
– Freezing winters
– Expensive

Nearly a quarter of The Netherlands sits below sea level, so the population, who rely on dykes to defend the country from the worst North Sea swells, may not consider waves a blessing. Much of the seabed is shallow, continental shelf, bordered by a predominantly soft coastline of sand dunes, saltmarsh and the world's largest stretch of uninterrupted mudflats at Waddensea. The surf favours the in-between seasons of autumn and spring when strong lows send NNW swells to endless flat beaches, where conditions improve in the vicinity of huge boulder jetties.

PUNTA DE LOBOS
LAT. -34.423878°   LONG. -72.049645°

Proclaimed "The best left pointbreak in Chile", Lobos is not just for the charging XXL crew in winter. There's a ripable, sand-bottomed section known as Diamante on the inside for the groms and the pilots and the El Mirador section has summer peelers rotating past the shoreline rock clusters, or muscle-bound walls linking from the rocks all the way to the beach sections in a lined-up SW-W swell. Too much S swell will ramp up the current, while W will shut down the outside barrels so SW from 235° should be perfect. Prefers lower tides, but will break right through. The paddle-out from the iconic island rocks (Los Morros) has achieved legendary status for sketchiness. Experts only when it gets above double-overhead. Punta Lobos is one of the most consistent spots in the southern hemisphere, let alone Chile so don't expect to get it to yourself.

PICHILEMU CHILE

+ Super consistent
+ Lots of long left pointbreaks
+ Big wave options
+ Great countryside, laid-back people

– Cold water year-round
– Rainy winters and windy
– Lack of night entertainment
– Hard access to some spots

Chile is twenty five times as long as it is wide, extending for 4,300km down to the tip of South America. South Pacific lows pushed along by the Humboldt Current generate the most consistent swells on the planet, aided by a deep-water trench, which allows SW swells to hit the coast with speed and power. Together with the dominant S winds, perfect set-ups abound in the north-facing bays and Pichilemu has more than its share of reeling offshore lefts, creating a goofy-footers heaven in what has become Chile's most famous surf town.

March

🌎 SÃO MIGUEL AZORES

+ Very consistent swells
+ Uncrowded quality waves
+ Good pointbreaks
+ Nearby islands for further exploration

– Constantly changing conditions
– Scary, heavy reefbreaks
– Cool, wet climate
– Hard access to many spots

RABO DE PEIXE

When compared to the Indian and Pacific Oceans, the Atlantic contains very few islands. The Mid-Atlantic ridge, an underwater volcanic mountain chain, runs the entire length of the Atlantic Ocean, but only breaks the surface in a few places. The nine islands of the Azores sit 1300km west of Lisbon, and the main island of Sao Miguel has waves on all sides, including some challenging, big wave spots.. This reputation for sizeable waves is attracting seasoned surf travellers to take on some of the powerful breaks on these steep, oceanic island shores.

🌎 ADELAIDE SOUTH AUSTRALIA

+ Southern Ocean swells
+ Wide variety of spots
+ Choice of coastlines
+ Rare crowd hassles

– Cold water, hot air temps
– Mainly for experienced surfers
– White pointers, snakes & flies
– Potholes and rough roads

CHINAMANS

Adelaide, South Australia's capital city, has crowded and inconsistent surf because of a very narrow swell window. Yorke Peninsula is a 4h drive west and this crooked finger of rock presents some incredibly good waves at its tip, which is part of the Innes National Park. A concentration of short and powerful reefbreaks below sheer cliffs, suit advanced surfers with no fear of air drops and Australia's dangerous wildlife like sharks and snakes. Kangaroo Island features many remote and spooky surf spots, exposed to the full force of the Great Southern Ocean swell.

🌎 COLIMA & MICHOACAN MEXICO

+ Big swell consistency
+ Calm wind patterns
+ Uncrowded, barrelling waves
+ Cheap and exotic

– Summer swell excess
– Wet summer climate
– Muddy road access
– Mosquitoes and banditos

PASCUALES

With 4,000kms of Pacific coastline facing directly into SW swells and a deep-water trench to funnel this swell energy, mainland Mexico is a classic surf destination. It receives ample swell from both the North and South Pacific, whilst the Inter-Tropical Convergence Zone produces the strongest hurricane swells on earth. These swells slam into the beaches, rocky headlands, rivermouths and points, providing the biggest surfable waves in Central America. Colima and Michoacan States have their fair share of waves, including great rivermouth set-ups and ultra-heavy beachbreaks.

KAMPAR RIVER INDONESIA

+ Longest rideable waves
+ Both fast & mellow waves
+ Reliable and predictable
+ Amazing, unusual experience

– Only one set of waves per day
– Mainly boat expeditions
– Long, bumpy zodiac rides
– Costly trip

SEVEN GHOSTS

BONOSURF.COM

Tidal bores are only found on 55 waterways and have never been truly understood, even though predicting a bore wave's arrival and size is fairly easy. Unlike ocean waves, the bore has two currents: one at the top pushing ahead and another one below from the downstream river flow. The Bono was discovered in 2010 and quickly became the world's best river wave with 10ft faces, barrels and a new Guinness Book of Records longest ride of 20.65km in 1 hour and 4 minutes.

LENNOX HEAD
LAT. -28.805620° LONG. 153.604570°

DON BALCH

Generally regarded as Australia's finest righthand point. Few waves compare for speed, barrel sections, length of ride and an ability to handle the biggest NE-S swells. While a NE swell meeting a SW wind is considered primo, Lennox will also bend a S to its will, hitting a number of launch sites along the half kilometre headland. During the boulder-skirting ride, expect full-throttle, ruler-edged walls to gusset multiple times and envelop those fast and canny enough to hold the right line. Holds proper size when the prospect of leaping off the rocks looks suicidal and the current running down the point is likely to challenge the strongest paddlers. Needless to say, this is an experts only wave and hard-core riders from the surrounding countryside keep a long pintail under the house for those all-too-rare big days when Lennox awakes from its regular slumber.

BYRON BAY NEW SOUTH WALES

+ Beautiful right pointbreaks
+ N-S swell window
+ Byron Bay backpacker heaven
+ Warm, clear water and dolphins

– Rarely any big swells
– Intense and constant crowds
– Pricey accommodation
– Sharky waters

Byron Bay is mainland Australia's eastern tip, where a veritable array of long golden beaches and rocky headlands has attracted surfers for almost half a century. While there are some epic set-ups, a lack of decent size swell dictates conditions are fairly inconsistent, relying on summer cyclone swells or big winter S to create waves worth remembering. Typically, shoulder-high waves snap across the sandbanks in clean, small size swells, while bigger days see the handful of pointbreaks rumble into life, when the locals descend from miles around.

March

🌐 GUATEMALA

+ Hardly ever flat
+ Dry season offshore winds
+ Completely uncrowded
+ Cheap lodging & food

– Beachbreaks only
– High crime rate
– Lack of tourism infrastructure
– Onshore & rainy summer

LA BARRA

It may not be the best surf in Central America, but warm water and uncrowded beachbreaks will always find takers. With over thirty volcanoes and many peaks rising above 4,000m (13,100ft), it's surprising not a single rock can be spotted along the 250km coastline, making for a continuous stretch of mostly black-sand beachbreaks, only interrupted by the occasional rivermouth. Considered a transit zone between Mexico and El Salvador, the lack of coast roads means long drives between breaks, but few crowds to share the punchy beach and rivermouth peaks with.

🌐 TARANAKI NEW ZEALAND

+ Variety of conditions
+ Consistent big swells
+ Many quality, uncrowded spots
+ Snowy volcanic scenery

– Cold and wet climate
– Windy conditions
– Cold water
– Lack of public transport

SECRET SPOT

New Zealand plunges far into the Southern Ocean and feels the full force of the Roaring Forties swells that march out of the SW. The most famous wave is the super-long, perfect left point of Raglan in the Waikato region south of Auckland, but another 5hr south is the reliable Taranaki area and the host of waves that fan around the base of Mt Egmont. This area gets the most swell and has the greatest concentration of quality spots on the North Island. The locals have their secret spots, but there is a lot of breaks on offer and plenty of scope for exploration.

🌐 TEXAS USA

+ Warm water
+ Some uncrowded breaks
+ Friendly locals
+ Nice climate

– Small, short-lived swells
– Rare offshore winds
– Difficult barrier island access
– Spring break crowds

BOB HALL PIER

The Texas coastline accounts for a good proportion of the USA's beaches on the massive Gulf of Mexico, referred to by surfers as the Third Coast. The state may not be first choice when planning a USA surf trip, but should not be overlooked altogether. Its 373mi of low-lying coastline are all beaches with a continuous string of barrier islands receiving regular windswell and occasional hurricane swell from the Gulf. There are numerous passes, inlets, piers and jetties, providing the focus for waves along the endless, featureless strands where a 4WD will help escape any crowds.

AMBER COAST DOMINICAN REPUBLIC

PLAYA GRANDE

OBDULIO LUNA

+ Indented coastline with good reefs
+ Great surf/wind/kite combo
+ All-inclusive, comfortable resorts
+ Cheap for the Caribbean

− Short swell season
− Unfavourable trade winds
− No real surf shops
− Shallow, urchin-infested reefs

DR is the second largest and most populous country in the Caribbean, occupying the eastern two-thirds of the island of Hispaniola. To the east is the Mona Passage, which separates it from the famous waves of Puerto Rico. Both the Atlantic Ocean to the north and the Caribbean Sea to the south, produce rideable surf on an ideally indented coastline. The mountainous interior fringed by golden sandy beaches attracts tourists to the hotels and resorts on the Amber Coast, which has become a cool destination for surfing in the morning and kiteboarding in the afternoon.

STEVE RYAN

BELLS BEACH
LAT. -38.371668° LONG. 144.283621°

Victoria's most famous surf spot is a classic and consistent right point that breaks on almost any tide, any wind and any decent swell from SE-SW. It's a long wave broken into three sections (which may just link up in huge swells), starting outside at Rincon, leading into Bell's Bowl and finishing in the beach shorebreak. Power is always associated with this wave and few escape the flogging of an outside set on the head and gruelling paddle outs as it grows beyond double overhead. When small, it's playful and ripable, offering endless carve and cutback corners along a lengthy platform reef that is prone to some long, unmakeable sections. Will be at its best in wrapping SW swell and NW winds, but will still have takers in ugly onshore conditions as well. Bells is a pilgrimage site so expect plenty of other worshippers.

 GREAT OCEAN ROAD VICTORIA

+ Consistent swell
+ Dominant offshore winds
+ Big-wave right pointbreaks
+ Spectacular scenery

− Unpredictable weather
− Cool water year-round
− Summer flat spells
− Crowded breaks

Victoria is hemmed in by the angry waters of Bass Strait and the Tasman Sea, but perfectly situated to receive the mountainous swells from the Southern Ocean. The Great Ocean Rd twists atop limestone cliffs overlooking an eroded coast of sea stacks and caves, where a plethora of beach, reef and pointbreaks unload in a pristine environment. Torquay and Bells Beach have become a surfing epicentre, home to leading surfwear manufacturers Quiksilver and Rip Curl, plus the site of the longest running contest and the first Surfing Recreation Reserve on the planet.

April

● KADAVU PASSAGE FIJI

+ Powerful and consistent swells
+ Quality tubular lefts
+ Resort crowd – no locals
+ Superb scuba diving

– Big and windy in winter
– Costly deals
– Heavy rain
– Outboard access only

FRIGATES

WWW.WAIDROKA.COM

The southern coast of Fiji's main island, Viti Levu has a fringing reef, closer to the white sand beaches of the resort-studded Coral Coast. Powerful waves come surging in from deep water, hitting shallow reef ledges that unfortunately, are very exposed to the strong afternoon trade winds that buffet this coast. Finding offshore conditions requires long journeys in boats out to the reliable left walls of Frigates Pass or else an expensive, island-hopper flight to Kadavu Island where the contorted reef offers a selection of waves for most wind directions.

● COSTA DEL BALSAMO EL SALVADOR

+ Perfect right pointbreaks
+ Mellow warm waves
+ Good wind patterns
+ Cheap living

– Rarely big
– S swells only
– Rainy swell season
– Thefts and robberies

PUNTA ROCA

FITZPATRICK/SURF-CARIBE.COM

El Salvador hides an insane array of long righthand pointbreaks making it a natural-footers dream destination. Whilst its reputation has been built on the waves of Punta Roca in La Libertad, El Salvador has more than just one wave. Considering its small size, El Salvador could easily claim the highest density of quality pointbreaks in Central America. With 6.3 million people in El Salvador crowds are still reasonable, except around the bigger centres. The area to the west of La Libertad is an excellent place to search for totally empty waves in the regular offshores.

● PHILLIP ISLAND VICTORIA

+ Consistent summer swell
+ Right pointbreaks
+ Easy access
+ Quality, powerful beachbreaks

– Cool/cold water
– Competitive crowds
– Rips and onshores
– Unpredictable weather

CORSAIR

STEVE RYAN

The Great Ocean Road draws most Melbourne surfers' attention as dominant SW winds are offshore, but what the East Coast lacks in quality, it gains in quantity with spots like Gunnamatta on the Mornington Peninsula or Woolamai on Phillip Island, rarely going flat. The indented coastline allows for a few offshore spots when the SW'ers are blowing, producing some quality rights in stormy winter conditions. Portsea is only 91km from Melbourne and in Dec '67, made national headline news when Prime Minister Harold Holt either drowned or got taken by a shark at Cheviot Beach.

PUNTA HERMOSA PERU

PICO ALTO

JAVIER FERNANDEZ

+ Consistent swells
+ Great density of spots
+ Big wave potential
+ Cheap and easy living

− Lack of perfect conditions
− Cold water
− Coastal fog
− Weekend crowds

Peru has one of the oldest surf cultures in the world with 'totora reed horses' being ridden for up to 3000 years. The capital, Lima, sits on the shores of the Pacific and has become Peru's surf city, but due to crowds and pollution most travellers head 1hr drive south to the Punta Hermosa area. The waves are typically big-shouldered rights along with some hollow lefts, plus a few offshore bomboras that handle serious size and power like the fabled Pico Alto. Consistently overhead and offshore in the morning, help make this region a safe winter bet.

CHRIS VAN LENNEP

CAVE ROCK
LAT. -29.932700° LONG. 31.014936°

When the swell gets overhead, Cave Rock comes to life, whipping up world-class, Hawaiian-style, righthand barrels that explode across the shallow reef. Made famous by Shaun Thomson and the Free Ride generation of the '70s, these gaping, spitting tubes are best when the S swell wraps in and the morning land breeze drifts down from the mountainous interior. The Pool section peels in front of the tidal sea pool while the gnarlier Rock rights are opposite the rock that gave the break its name. Paddling out at either is a real mission so time the lulls carefully. This wave is capable of snapping both boards and people who push the limits, since the reef is so unforgiving and shallow. Suitable for experienced cave hunters only and there is never any shortage of them in the line-up. Not the sharkiest of spots, but keep an eye out.

DURBAN SOUTH AFRICA

+ Consistent
+ Quality beachbreaks
+ Urban entertainment
+ Cheap

− Lots of onshore days
− Crowds
− Street violence
− Sharks at un-netted beaches

South Africa is one of the world's best surf destinations with 3,000km of coastline split between the Atlantic and Indian Oceans. Despite better waves elsewhere in South Africa, Durban has become the country's surf centre because of a high population density of surfers and a great year-round climate. South swells wrap around the Bluff Peninsula, and focus on the long piers and groynes that punctuate the coastline, resulting in powerful, hollow beachbreaks. There are a few reefs to consider, including the world-class tubes of Cave Rock.

April

ANTOFAGASTA CHILE

● ● ● ● (♦) ● ● ● ● ● ● ● ●

+ Great left pointbreaks
+ Consistent swell
+ Spot diversity
+ Never rains

− Few rights
− Cool water
− Desert area
− Lack of tourist interest

CÚPULA
ALFREDO ESCOBAR

Much like Chile itself, the city of Antofagasta is long and narrow, sandwiched between the Pacific Ocean and the Andes mountains. Lying just 10km south of the Tropic of Capricorn, it's off the beaten path for surfers, who tend to congregate at the northern cities of Arica and Iquique. With 20km of sandy beaches scattered among the wild, rugged coastline, this port town is increasingly turning into a beach resort and the variety of powerful set-ups includes close to shore reef slabs complimented by some rocky points and beachbreaks.

KAIKOURA NEW ZEALAND

● ● ● ● (♦) ● ● ● ● ● ● ● ●

+ Consistent swells
+ Quality right pointbreaks
+ Uncrowded, friendly atmosphere
+ Great surf and snowboard combo

− Cold water and strong windchill
− Poor Christchurch beachbreaks
− Frequent onshores
− Long flights

MANGAMAUNU
WARREN HAWKE

This zone is one of the lowest latitude, bona fide surf destinations in the Southern Hemisphere, so think cold. While much of the South Island relies on quality beachbreaks, here is a zone littered with right pointbreaks, helping hardcore surfers avoid ice-cream headache paddle-outs. The South Island, (aka Te Wai Pounamu meaning Jade Island), with 3,200km of coastline has a small population so crowds are usually low out of town and either side of winter should see good waves as the winds can blow a bit more offshore.

SEYCHELLES

● ● ● ● (♦) ● ● ● ● ● ● ● ●

+ Small fun waves
+ Few crowds
+ Warm water
+ Unreal island scenery

− Very inconsistent
− Bloody expensive
− Lots of windchop
− Flat summers

ANSE AUX POULLES BLEUES
MICHAEL KEW

The Seychelles were put on the '60s surfing map when hot-dogging small clean waves on heavy longboards was the go. Small, clean, relatively uncrowded surf does exist, but these islands suffer from shallow offshore waters and extremely inconsistent swells that struggle to produce more than a dozen good days a year. Poor SW swell exposure means major S-SE swells are required, or for consistent onshore winds to create surf on the few exposed beaches. It's rarely big enough to wrap around to the W coast, where offshore conditions can ignite a couple of decent reefs.

CAPE PENINSULA SOUTH AFRICA

OUTER KOM

PAUL KENNEDY

+ Consistent, multi-aspect spots
+ Wide swell window
+ Mountain and sea landscapes
+ Cheap urban entertainment

– Cold water year-round
– Unstable windy weather
– City environment & insecurity
– Kelp stress

The coastline of South Africa.is the oldest shoreline on earth, and aeons of erosion have created an underwater topography ideal for creating good waves. This has made South Africa home to some of the best mid-latitude surf you'll find anywhere in the world. The irregular shoreline of the Cape Peninsula, along with its 180° swell window, allows it to offer the best density of varied spots in the whole country, ranging from beginners beachbreak to fearsome big-wave venues like Outer Kom, Crayfish Factory and Dungeons.

PERUECOSURF.COM

CHICAMA PERU

+ Perfect, uncrowded, lefthand pointbreaks
+ Excellent wind patterns
+ Cheap living costs
+ Historical sites

– Strong, constant currents
– Chilly water and fog
– Petty thefts in the cities
– Difficult, tedious access

CHICAMA
LAT. -7.704944° LONG. -79.452749°

The distance between Chicama's furthest take-off point (El Cape) and the fishing jetty ending is 4km, although a single ride is impossible. Most people catch 3-5 different waves, surfing through four defined breaks and using the constant, north-sweeping current to drift down to the next take-off spot. El Cape is always the biggest, with long sections of slightly tapered, lip-feathering walls that demand a repetitive approach of drive, lip bash, float and snap until a temporary shoulder gives respite for a roundhouse or two. Keys can be a racy wall with barrel potential and wind protection leading to popular El Point where an ideal tempo peels like it was designed in a laboratory. The last El Hombre section in front of the beachfront hotels is the place to get barrelled. Walk back up the beach, or fork out for the surf camp zodiac taxi.

The region of La Libertad is home to the longest lefthand pointbreak on earth, but the utopian wave of Chicama is not the only drawcard. There's also Pacasmayo, which probably lines up a bit better and is possibly a bit longer in the makeable single ride category. Punta Huanchaco holds another 800m of sectiony lefts in the home of the totora reed Caballito riders and is a tourist party town. Cooler water, sea fog and strong currents are not enough to detract from one of the quintessential South American surf experiences, for all surfers past the early beginner stage.

April

 HUVADHOO ATOLL MALDIVES

●●●(♠)●●●●●●●●●

+ Atoll pass perfection
+ Choice of charter boats or resorts
+ Relatively low crowds
+ Awesome fishing and scenery

− Stormy winter seas
− SW monsoon onshore winds
− Long transfers
− Expensive charters and camps

BLUE BOWLS

TIM NUNN

The 26 pancake-flat atolls of the Maldives formed around the edges of volcanic peaks, which then subsided, leaving the characteristic ring shaped atolls to continue to grow around the original coastline. This pattern has created a surfing playground rife with reef passes amongst the 1,200 islands. Southern hemisphere swells cross the equator bringing lined-up, smaller swell to the shallow fringing reefs, and predictable monsoonal winds govern the seasons. South Huvadhoo has an exposed south-facing coast, boasting a dozen good passes in a 2hr cruising zone.

 MAHIA PENINSULA NEW ZEALAND

●●●(♦)●●●●●●●●

+ Variety of aspects
+ Dominant offshore winds
+ Consistent, quality spots
+ Beautiful wild area

− Cold and wet climate
− Windy
− Cold water
− Some localism

RAILWAYS

CORY SCOTT

The Mahia peninsula is located on the east coast of the North Island, between Gisborne and Napier. It has a flexible array of reefs, points and beaches, which between them catch any swell direction going. The predominant SW winds are perfect for many of the exposed spots plus somewhere will always be offshore, no matter what the wind direction. It attracts outdoor sports people from all over the country, yet there are no hotels, resorts or amusement parks and everything remains truly wild, which is just how the locals like it.

 ARICA CHILE

●●●(♦)●●●●●●●●

+ Very consistent
+ Big, powerful waves
+ Chilled, uncrowded atmosphere
+ Perfect climate

− Shallow reefs and urchins
− No mellow waves
− Long journeys
− Monotonous, sun-baked landscape

EL GRINGO

ALFREDO ESCOBAR

The extreme north of Chile showcases a string of gnarly reefbreaks, breaking close to the shore, on the wave-rich Alacran Peninsula. When the pro circus arrived in 2007, even the world's best struggled to tame the shallow, hard-breaking tubes like El Gringo, so this is definitely not a zone for beginners. Wave height can be deceptive and what looks like 4ft is actually 6-8ft! It is super-consistent for swell and light winds so autumn may be the ideal time to visit this city of eternal spring in the world's driest desert, the Atacama.

MAR DEL PLATA ARGENTINA

 ●●●●⓪●●●●●●●●

+ Spot concentration
+ Break diversity
+ Many wind and swell options
+ Wide range of accommodation

– Crowded urban spots
– Summer surfing bans
– Freezing winters
– Built-up coastline

PLAYA GRANDE

PEDRO SALINAS

Second largest country on the South American continent, Argentina counts around 300km of surfable beaches, most of them located in Buenos Aires Province. The east side of the country called Pampas, consists mainly of grassy plains while the country's western regions climb into the vertiginous Andes. Argentina recently celebrated 40 years of surfing at a variety of breaks ranging from natural pointbreaks to man-made jetties. Mar del Plata is the main summer getaway, with beaches bisected by dozens of piers and jetties, creating many surf spots.

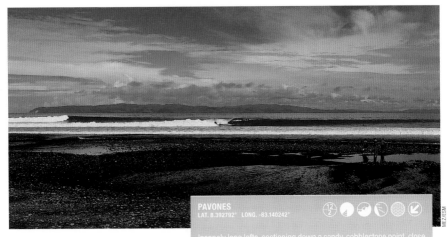

GOLFO DULCE COSTA RICA

●●●⓪●●●●●●●●●

+ Pavones long pointbreak
+ Good quality rights and lefts
+ Calm winds
+ Wild, exotic rainforest area

– Crowded & inconsistent
– Intense rainy season
– Lack of roads
– Tropical diseases and insects

PAVONES
LAT. 8.392792° LONG. -83.140242°

MEZ/ESM

Insanely long lefts, sectioning down a sandy, cobblestone point, close to shore. Being buried deep in a bay makes it incredibly inconsistent, as only big S-SW swells will penetrate the Golfo Dulce. Modern swell forecasting means plenty of surfers will be on hand when it does work and the expat crew are notorious for sewing up the best set waves and making it past the hollower low tide rivermouth section all the way down to the cantina where the breakneck speed lets up a bit. At high tide the La Esquina del Mar section starts breaking and occasionally the wave connects up, offering rides of up to a kilometre for those quick enough to beat the longer sections. Main problem is the crowd and jelly-legs, which get little respite on the long walk back up the point. Roads wash out readily in the wet season, which corresponds with the best swell season.

Costa Rica is known for the perfect small waves found around the Guanacaste area, but it was actually the Pavones area that made the country famous, thanks to photos of some of longest lefts in the world. Add in the wonderful tropical scenery and plenty of great waves to choose from, it's little wonder this is a popular surf trip for many Americans. The Golfo Dulce provides a watery divide between Pavones lefts and Matapalo rights, whilst the surrounding jungle hides many other spots on the Osa Peninsula and down towards the Panamanian border.

May

NW WESTERN AUSTRALIA

+ World-class lefts
+ Mostly uncrowded
+ Very high consistency
+ Unique wildlife & diving

− Challenging waves
− Strong wind factor
− Remote break accesses
− Far from Perth, no hospitals

THE BLUFF

DEAN DAMPNEY

Western Australia is the largest state, but it has the lowest population density of any state in Australia and maybe even the world. Travelling to the northwest-facing coast takes the word 'remote' to another level and accordingly most surf spots are uncrowded, with the exception of the world-class lefts at Gnaraloo. The natural habitat is rich and diverse along with the unique wildlife that surrounds it, especially along the 280km long Ningaloo Reef. Large numbers of fish, whales, turtles, dugongs and dolphins frequent the reef including plenty of big sharks.

SOUTHWEST PANAMA

+ World-class pointbreaks
+ Calm wind patterns
+ Close to the Caribbean coastline
+ Wild exotic area

− Crowded Santa Catalina
− Intense rainy season
− Lack of roads
− Tropical diseases

LA PUNTA

DAN HAYLOCK

Panama joins Central America to continental South America via a thin isthmus of land, severed by the amazing engineering feat that is the Panama Canal. Panama feels like a less crowded version of Costa Rica, plus there's the added bonus of offshore islands like Coiba to explore. It's slightly less exposed to the North Pacific swells, but does have a good window for W and S swells along with calm wind patterns. Santa Catalina has sprung up as the main surf town thanks to the ultra-reliable righthanders at the point plus a handful of fun options nearby.

WESTERN CAPE SOUTH AFRICA

+ Variety of left pointbreaks
+ Some easy mellow waves
+ Cheap and uncrowded
+ Scenery and wildlife

− Few consistent spots
− Cold water year-round
− Kelp and mussels
− Lack of tourism infrastructure

ELAND'S BAY

TOSTEE.COM

South Africa's time eroded coastline creates a tremendous proliferation of right pointbreaks on the East Coast, while the Atlantic West Coast north of Cape Town is more goofy-friendly. The shivering cold Benguela Current, which brings lower water temps in summer than winter, also acts as a highway for swells to arrive at several kelp-covered, north-facing, left pointbreaks tucked behind headlands. Discovered by John Whitmore in 1957, the piping lefts of Eland's Bay have become a popular spot for Cape Town waveriders, whenever there is some significant swell action.

GOLD COAST GHANA

● ● ● ● 🌐 ● ● ● ● ● ● ●

+ Mellow right pointbreaks
+ Consistently head-high
+ Relatively cheap and safe
+ Virgin, warm water surf

– Lack of powerful waves
– Flat dry season
– Beach pollution
– Hot, humid and malarial

BLACK MAMBAS
OLLIE FITZJONES

Most surfers would know little about surfing in Ghana, apart from the backwash waves that were surfed out to sea in *The Endless Summer*. Ghana was the first country in Africa (1957) to claim independence from Britain, is densely populated and despite its turbulent neighbours, has evolved democratically. West of Accra, a 250km stretch of sand and rocky patches is interspersed with numerous lagoons near the river estuaries. Few have taken advantage of the easy surf conditions, but local and expat surfers can be found around the main spots like Busua Beach.

SAINT-LEU
LAT. -21.165254° LONG. 55.283213°
JS CALLAHAN/SURFEXPLORE

WEST RÉUNION

● ● ● ● 🌐 ● ● ● ● ● ● ●

+ Consistent year-round
+ Spot diversity
+ Scenic countryside
+ Safe tourism

– Expensive
– Crowd pressure
– Huge shark threat
– Busy road traffic

The famous lefts of St-Leu provide a truly world-class wave when stronger SW swells hit, usually in winter. It starts with a quick drop and open face carvable wall, before bending sharply round the reef into a couple of bowly, hollow sections that throw out a shallow tube. Coral heads surface at low and the line-up breaks into sections when small, so it needs to be overhead to start linking up for the full 300m ride. Experienced surfers only, despite the easy paddle-out and be respectful of the local pecking order. A horrific spate of 12 shark attacks in two years with five fatalities has resulted in surfing being banned for a short time in 2013. 90 tiger and bull sharks are being culled inside the marine reserve, and surfers will be fined $50 for surfing outside the shallow lagoon. Needless to say, crowds are at an all time low!

French-governed Reunion Island is located on the perfect latitude to receive consistent swells and great tropical weather. Rain has shaped canyons that funnel water into the sea and then through coral passes, forming awesome waves like St-Leu. Most of the 32 reported spots on the W coast break on fragmented barrier reefs, quite a distance from the beach. There are also a few average black-sand beachbreaks and some rocky reefs, but they usually have murky water, attracting the omnipresent sharks that have been attacking surfers with increasing regularity.

May

SWAKOPMUND NAMIBIA

●●●●⊛●●●●●●●●

+ Uncrowded, consistent swells
+ Awesome left barrels
+ Amazing scenery and wildlife
+ Undiscovered possibilities

– Cold water & constant fog
– Extreme temps
– Onshore winds
– Difficult, expensive access

FACTORY POINT

ROD BRABY

Namibia is not your standard surf trip destination. A harsh environment, heavy waves and the cold Benguela current make it a place suitable only for the most hardcore of riders. It's an 1800km drive from Cape Town to Swakopmund and a lot further up to the long, peeling lefts of Cape Cross. With thousands of aggressive seals lining the beaches and great white sharks cruising through the constant sea fog looking for a meal, it's no wonder that crowds are never a problem, but there are some fine rewards for the brave.

RIO DE JANEIRO BRAZIL

●●●●⊛●●●●●●●●

+ Brazil's best beachbreaks
+ Consistent year-round
+ Drier winter months
+ Rio access and services

– Lack of points and reefs
– Ultra-crowded main spots
– High street-crime rate
– Rarely epic conditions

BARRA DE TIJUCA

JS CALLAHAN/SURFEXPLORE

Rio's physical features are dominated by the Sierra do Mar mountain range, which is cloaked by the Mata Atlantica forest. Mountains plunge into the sea, forests meet the beaches and cliff faces rise abruptly from the extended lowlands. It's one of the most densely populated places on earth, with seven million "Cariocas" indulging in dancing, drinking, beach-going and sunbathing. To the west of Rio, magnificent beaches extend along the coastal avenidas like Prainha, Barra da Tijuca and Arpoador, which are also the scene of many contests, including when the WCT is in town.

THAA & LAAMU MALDIVES

●●●●⊛●●●●●●●●

+ Consistent SW monsoon
+ Long, wrapping atoll reef waves
+ Waves for all abilities
+ Comfy safari boats, peaceful villages

– Lack of consistent lefts
– More cruising between spots
– Expensive domestic flight necessary
– No cheap beer

MIKADO

YEP

Laamu and Thaa atoll are newly discovered Central Atolls surf zones, presenting 150 islands to the wide E-W swell window. They enjoy an abundance of medium-sized, perfect reefbreaks, most of which are righthanders. Access to the majority of these waves is by charter boat, or by staying in one of the new guesthouses or resorts nearby, where the surf guides ensure crowds are spread among the numerous reef passes. With classy waves such as Mikado and Yin Yang known for their pristine barrels, under the right conditions the central atolls are tropical perfection.

GARDEN ROUTE SOUTH AFRICA

●●●●①●●●●●●●

+ High swell consistency
+ Variety of right pointbreaks
+ Cheap and uncrowded destination
+ Fabulous nature activities

− Virtually no lefts
− No major airport nearby
− Packed tourist season
− Great white sharks

MOSSEL BAY

MIKE KNOTT

Half way between Cape Town and J-Bay are clusters of right pointbreaks, condensed in a popular area known as the Garden Route. This 250km stretch of coastal towns with exposed beachbreaks or sheltered bays, usually produce fine pointbreak set-ups. Amongst the more obvious are Mossel Bay, Knysna and Plettenberg while the likes of Stillbay or Victoria Bay stay out of the limelight. The Southern Cape is rugged country, backed by mountains, providing habitat for many animals, while the water teems with life as whales and dolphins frequent the ocean off South Africa's tip.

G-LAND
LAT. -8.734644° LONG. 114.338334°

ALAN VAN GYSEN

GRAJAGAN BAY INDONESIA

●●●●①●●●●●●●

+ Awesome G-Land
+ Long, empty black sand beachbreak
+ Small swell, off-season option
+ Discovery potential

− G-land surf camp crowds
− South coast onshores
− Currents and close-outs
− Slow road network

Furthest out on the km-long reef is *Kongs*, a shifty, messy section that prefers small W swells and lighter winds. *Money Trees* attracts the bulk of the campers to what looks like perfect peeling barrels for 2-300m. The tubes can undulate from cavernous pits to tight, high envelopes and getting caught behind is guaranteed. *Launching Pad* only appears on moderate to heavy swells as wider rogue sets hit the patch of reef beyond the normal whitewash line and look like tapering into nothing, before jumping up and launching into the pedal-to-the-metal section – *Speed Reef*. Making the drop while drawing the right line and maintaining velocity are crucial as it doesn't let up or offer an easy escape for 200m of precision peeling. The reef whizzes by in clear menace, and is the sharpest, shallowest patch so surf it on the push from quarter tide.

This 600km south-facing stretch of Javanese shores represents the lightest surfed coastline in Indo's southern hemisphere wave zone, thanks to a year-round, side to onshore wind exposure, plunging volcanic cliffs, islets and skerries, separated by long, current scoured, black sand beaches. Dangerous, thumping close-outs drum the sand in the swell season, but the smaller, peaky, SE-SW swells can create piping beachbreaks in the shoulder and off season. Balancing out the account at the eastern tip of Java are the majestic, incomparable lefts of G-Land.

May

 ## SOUTHEAST MADAGASCAR

●●●●◉⊛●●●●●●●●

+ Uncrowded spots
+ Beach and reefbreaks
+ Consistent swells
+ Dirt cheap local costs

– Sharks
– Windy days
– Expensive flights and 4WD hire
– Poor roads

MONSEIGNEUR BAY

ALAN VAN GYSEN

Despite Madagascar being one of the most uncrowded, and potentially epic surf zones on the planet, it has been kept off the surfing map mainly because of a reputation for shark-infested waters. Fort Dauphin is the regional hub of the far southeast, located on a peninsular with the sea on three sides at the bottom of the eastern mountain range. It is a beautiful place to visit as well as being home to a wide range of wave types as the SW swell bends into bays and points that can be cross-offshore in NE winds.

 ## SAVU & ROTE INDONESIA

●●●●◉⊛●●●●●●●●

+ Mellow, accessible waves
+ Cheap losmen option
+ Few boat charter crowds
+ Perfect dry season weather

– Small swell window
– Strong trade winds after 10
– Lack of nightlife & beer
– Isolated spots with no land access

NEMBERALA

JS CALLAHAN/SURFEXPLORE

Wallace and Darwin noted the 550 islands of eastern Nusa Tenggara have more in common with Australia than Indonesia. West Timor has remained a bit of a frontier, with most surfers looking to escape the Bali crowds by heading to Nusa Tenggara's more accessible islands of Lombok and Sumbawa. Tucked in above Australia with only its southwest corner facing the Indian Ocean swells, Timor has a smaller swell window and higher wind exposure, but in typical Indo fashion, minor islands like Rote and Savu hide major surf breaks.

 ## SAVAI'I & UPOLU SAMOA

●●●●◉⊛●●●●●●●●

+ Powerful barrels
+ Year-round consistency
+ Warm and uncrowded
+ Samoan culture

– Many blown out-days
– Difficult reef access
– Wet climate
– No surfing on Sundays

BOULDERS

TOM CAREY/A FRAME

Amongst the largest of the South Pacific islands, Savai'i and Upolu are well situated to receive numerous swells from both the N and S. Upolu is the more developed, with the majority of the resorts and decent surf spots. Generally, the waves are very hollow and powerful, breaking over shallow barrier reefs within 500m of shore, unless big gaps allow the surf to break on lava reefs fringing the shore. South-facing coasts hold the best quality, shallow waves, more suited to expert surfers. The north coast has fewer spots and receives less swell, making it perfect for intermediates.

NORTHWEST LIBERIA

+ Fairly consistent SW swells
+ Virgin, warm-water surf
+ Best left pointbreaks in Africa
+ Not too challenging

– Inconsistent in summer
– Extremely wet during surf season
– Bugs, malaria, yellow fever
– Relatively high costs

COTTON TREES

JS CALLAHAN/SURFEXPLORE

The name Liberia comes from the word liberty and refers to the nation's origin as a colony of freed African American slaves returning to Africa in the early 19th century. Since 1989, two violent civil wars have plunged the country into chaos, leading to the deaths of up to 200,000 people. Liberia is now on the road to recovery, which is good news for surfers because it has the greatest concentration of quality lefthanders in just about all of Africa and combined with warm water, virgin line-ups and friendly locals, these empty barrels deserve more surfer's attention.

THE POINT - LAGUNDRI BAY
LAT. 0.568591° LONG. 97.733914°

JS CALLAHAN/SURF EXPLORE

It's been called many things including Nias, Lagundri, Sorake and most often just The Point, but whatever name is used, it always ends up in the world's top 10 waves. Here's why; the paddle out through the keyhole is dry hair simplicity, the take-off is predictable, the barrel is a flawless almond shape that peels with precision at the perfect speed for up to 10 seconds, the reef is well covered, even though the recent up-thrust has made it barrel harder from waist high up to double overhead and beyond, plus the light seaward current from the channel deposits you nicely back at the peak. It's all tides, all (light) winds, all year (with luck) and all too easy to stay encamped in one of the many cheap losmens or hotels that line Sorake Beach. Negatives include the crowd, some localism, flying boards, sealice, and the crowd.

NIAS & HINAKOS INDONESIA

+ World-class rights
+ Calm winds
+ Exploration possibilities
+ Inexpensive

– Long, hard access
– Malaria
– Crowds
– Suffocating heat and heavy rains

The perfect righthander at Lagundri Bay, Nias was the first world-class wave discovered in the Sumatra region. First surfed in 1975, by Aussie surf pioneers Troy, Lovett and Giesel, who put up with swarms of malarial mosquitoes and the most primitive of living conditions to ride absolute perfection in the remote jungle. These days, it's much easier to get to Nias and a slew of losmens fringe the deep bay, competing to accommodate the constant stream of surfers. Earthquakes have changed many reefs, improving Lagundri while damaging Bawa's bowly rights in the Hinako Islands.

June

VEZO REEFS  MADAGASCAR

● ● ● ● ● ● ⊛ ● ● ● ○ ● ●

+ World-class coral reefs
+ Consistent swells
+ Deserted spots
+ Dirt-cheap local costs

− Erratic trade winds
− Lack of beachbreaks
− Undeveloped infrastructure
− Expensive flights and transport

FLAME BOWLS
DAN HAYLOCK

The world's 4th largest island displays huge potential, especially along the southern coast between Fort-Dauphin and Morombe. This stretch has a 270° swell window, facing directly into the SW swells with mainly offshore conditions. Thanks to the harbour at Tulear, charter boats can access the 700km of varied coral including two barrier reefs, two coral banks, three lagoon reefs and a fringing reef. Powerful, challenging waves like Flame Bowls work in the winter months, plus there are easier waves a short boat ride from the basic village accommodations.

RIVAS PROVINCE  NICARAGUA

● ● ● ● ● ● ⊛ ● ● ● ● ● ●

+ Long swell season
+ Always offshore
+ Lots of wave choice
+ Quickly developing country

− Boat access to some surf spots
− No standout righthanders
− Slow land access
− Rapidly rising prices

MANZANILLO
DAN HAYLOCK

The bulk of Nicaragua's coastline makes up the Mosquito Coast on the Caribbean side, where an extensive, shallow shelf drains the meagre swells of power. The best surf spots are concentrated in the developed SW corner around San Juan Del Sur, where a narrow stretch of coastline separates Lake Nicaragua from the Pacific. This huge body of water creates the perfect atmospheric conditions, causing winds to blow offshore all day, for most of the year. The country's wealth of excellent beachbreaks and left points are best accessed by boat to escape the growing surf camp crowds.

WEST JAVA   INDONESIA

● ● ● ● ● ● ⊛ ● ● ● ● ● ●

+ Good consistency
+ World-class Panaitan Island
+ Variety of waves
+ Cheap

− Crowded Cimaja
− Sea urchins and sharp coral
− Hard access to some spots
− Pollution, disease and malaria

ONE PALM POINT
ANDREW SHIELD

West Java is the most densely populated region in Indonesia with around 42m inhabitants. Despite the huge population, this SW tip of Java is a wild, unspoilt land in places, blessed with a handful of world-class breaks, plus beachbreaks and rivermouths with something to suit everyone's style and ability. One Palm Point is legendary for long, scarily-shallow barrels, pinwheeling down the coral crusted lava of Panaitan Island, which forms a part of the Ujong Kulon National Park, while the mainland left Ombak Tujuh challenges for Indonesia's heavyweight, big wave crown.

ORIENTE SALVAJE EL SALVADOR

+ World-class right pointbreaks
+ Variety of unspoiled beaches
+ Warm water & friendly winds
+ Cheap living

– South swells only
– Rain through best swell season
– Gets crowded during season
– Petty theft & high crime rate

PUNTA MANGO

DAN HAYLOCK

Since the first surf explorers in the '60s discovered the great pointbreak potential of El Salvador the country has gone through a tumultuous time. A brutal army-led civil war killed nearly 100,000 people between 1979 and 1991, followed by economic devastation and violent social unrest. Things have improved dramatically and surfers have returned to both the western La Libertad area and the Oriente Salvaje (Savage East), where a handful of surf camps have sprung up close to some epic right points with only a few local surfers, plus a great range of waves suiting all standards.

CLOUDBREAK
LAT. -17.886336°   LONG. 177.186099°

JOLI

MAMANUCAS FIJI

+ Super-consistent
+ Variety of world-class waves.
+ Open access to Cloudbreak
+ Fantastically friendly Fiji

– Strong currents
– Dangerous reefs
– Very expensive
– Boat access only to many reefs

While the perfect pictures of Cloudbreak suggest flawless left barrels for one and all, this is a tricky wave with multiple sections and a malevolent side that keeps even the best surfers on their toes. The outside section at the top "Point" of the reef holds plenty of size and the vertiginous roll-ins lead into a flying wall section where speed carves are possible. Middles is where turns are less useful and the barrel starts to wind up, covering a lot of distance in a short time. Insides, or Shish-kabobs, is where the reef gets extremely shallow and the tubes get extremely...extreme! The three sections rarely link up, but when they do, usually on a long period, SSW swell of epic proportions, it is one of the seven wonders of the surf world. Advanced to expert surfers should be able to deal with the heavy waves, currents and bump-inducing frisky trades.

The 322 islands of Fiji form the epitome of the surf travel dream. A magical archipelago of white sand beaches and tropical vegetation ringed by shallow coral reefs, which get bombed by heavy, hollow lefthanders that set the standard for wave quality around the world. Most of the waves break on barrier reefs in the Mamanuca group of islands to the west of Fiji's main island, Viti Levu. Surf camps and boat access only to the waves around the Mamanucas make Fiji, or more to the point, Tavarua, an expensive, but essential surf experience.

June

 SOUTH BAHIA BRAZIL

●●●●●◉●●●●●●

+ Consistent windswells
+ Easy beaches, beginner's heaven
+ Boca da Barra long rides
+ Less crowded hiking spots

– Rarely epic
– Crowded main breaks
– Rainy autumn/winter
– Distant airports

JERIBUCACU
EASYDROP.COM

The overwhelming image of Brazil is Carnival and Salvador de Bahia undoubtedly hosts the most intense one. Surfers in the mid '70's searching the coast from Salvador found out about Itacaré, lying 300km south. It's the Bahia State capital, set amidst the Atlantic rainforest and home to an abundance of juicy, warm-water beachbreaks, reefbreaks and an amazingly long rivermouth right. Early travellers would have come across the surfing godfather "Old Joaquim", who befriended every surfer and told many tales under moonlight, before Itacaré became a renowned backpacker town.

 SYDNEY NORTHERN BEACHES NSW

●●●●●◉●●●●●●

+ Wide swell window
+ Variety of beach and reef waves
+ Urban entertainment
+ Easy access

– Rarely classic
– Thick city crowds
– Rather expensive
– Summer slop and jellyfish

DEE WHY POINT
SEAN DAVEY

Since Duke Kahanamoku arrived and gave a surfing demonstration at Freshwater Beach in 1915, surfing has grown intensely in popularity right around Australia. Sydney hosted the World Championships in 1964 and has subsequently produced a string of talented surfers, unequalled by any other city in the surf world. This large urban population takes pride in its beach culture, and has in many ways ruled the Aussie surf scene, centred around iconic breaks like North Narrabeen, Dee Why Point and Manly.

 PHUKET THAILAND

●●●●●◉●●●●●●

+ Uncrowded, mellow waves
+ Occasional pointbreaks
+ Cheap, party destination
+ Easy, safe tourism

– Short swell season
– Mushy, onshore conditions
– Inconsistent and rainy
– Mass tourism

KATA BEACH
CHRIS BURKARD

Thailand is rarely thought of as a country to take a surfboard to, yet it now houses the largest surfboard manufacturer in the world. Thailand's western shoreline has enough decent waves to attract surfers looking for cheap local costs and the famously warm Thai smile and hospitality. Phuket now holds annual surf contests and supports a growing and enthusiastic surfing fraternity. The "Land Of Smiles" should not be rated as a mainstream surfing destination, but a fun surf in uncrowded and friendly conditions is on the cards for those passing through.

● RAPA NUI

+ Year-round swells
+ Powerful lava reefbreaks
+ Uncrowded south shore
+ Good weather with clear water

– Big, wild waves
– No quality beachbreaks
– Tricky exit/entry points
– Expensive and remote

MATA VERI

PAUL KENNEDY

Known as Rapa Nui by its inhabitants, Easter Island is the most remote, inhabited place on earth. Its world-famous statues, the Moais, are 3-21m tall, made of volcanic basaltic rock, weighing up to 300 tonnes and amazingly, were moved as much as 18km without mechanical help. Geologically, the coastline is young, formed by a single volcanic eruption and consists of rugged lava cliffs, making entry/exit points scarce. Most spots are heavy reefs dotted along the west and south coasts, plus two average quality beachbreaks with remarkable scenery on the north coast.

TAMARIN BAY
LAT. -20.326852° LONG. 57.372085°

DAMIEN POULLENOT

A moderate to big SW swell has to wrap heavily to break along the famous reef at Tamarin Bay. Hypnotic, cultured barrels tour the NW-facing reef when a moderate to large SW swell tacks in and long tube time is logged by the mix of locals and lucky holidaymakers. This long, perfectly-formed, barrelling left becomes ultra-shallow at low tide, so higher tides are safer. Tuck-ins and speed slashes are the order of the day so lesser surfers should stick to the inside reform or beachbreak. The blind aggression has gone, but behave and avoid eye-contact with the humourless crowds, foot-contact with the legion of urchins, face-contact with the coral crusted limestone and any contact with the ever-present sharks. Tamarin has been forgotten to an extent, since Indonesian consistency and price have deflected the hordes, but it is still a beauty to behold.

● MAURITIUS

+ Tamarin world-class left
+ Quality reefbreaks
+ Exotic conditions
+ Moderate prices

– Localism
– Lack of SW swell exposure
– High population density
– Expensive flights

Mauritius has gained an exotic image in the heart of surfers thanks to the 1974 surf film, *Forgotten Island of Santosha*. It focused on Tamarin Bay, a perfect, almond-eyed left that became a symbol of escapism. The epic 8-10ft swell featured in the film, captured the attention of the surfing world, but it turned out to be inconsistent, leaving many travelling surfers disappointed. Localism flared in the '90s, with incidents of violence from the now notorious "White Shorts" enforcers, but when it fires, Tamarin is a true slice of surfing paradise.

June

SOUTH PROVINCE NEW CALEDONIA

●●●●●●①●●●●●○○●

+ Virgin spots
+ Variety of barrier reef breaks
+ Exotic yacht trip
+ Low crowd factor

− Most spots only accessible by boat
− Easily blown out
− Very expensive
− Not super-consistent

TENIA

ANDREW SHIELD

Nouméa sits on the edge of the largest lagoon in the world making it a big kite and windsurfing destination. The outer reefs conceal waves that are the equal of anywhere else in the South Pacific, but the problem is they break on reef passes between 5-20km offshore, which is too far for even the most hardcore of paddlers! Stretched along a 700km fringing barrier reef riddled with passes and bends, only an expensive charter yacht or spending a couple of hours commuting each day will make it possible to explore this potentially great region.

YEMEN

●●●●●○①●●●●○●●

+ SW monsoon guaranteed surf
+ Powerful, virgin beachbreaks
+ Very warm water
+ Unique desert environment

− Messy windswell surf
− Lack of points and reefs
− Remote, difficult access
− Visas, permits and high costs

SHEBA'S

STUART BUTLER

Yemen has an ill-founded reputation for feisty tribes, intent on war, kidnapping and terrorism in this fundamental Islamic nation. Instead, the adventurous will discover a warm-hearted and friendly people for whom pride, hospitality and honour are the pillars of life. Only a handful of people have ridden the waves breaking along Yemen's long south-facing Indian Ocean coastline. A 2003 trip led by US expat Jay Quinn found surf before British journalist Stuart Butler unveiled 6-8ft beefy wedging lefts and a Surfing US team shot some A-grade barrels on the remote island of Socotra.

GISBORNE NEW ZEALAND

●●●●●●①●●○●●○●

+ Many right pointbreaks
+ Clean mid-season swells
+ Hollow, powerful beachbreaks
+ Untouched coastline

− Small and crappy summers
− Semi-crowded main spots
− Chilly winter temps
− Some difficult access

MAKARORI

CORY SCOTT

With nearly 3,500km of coastline, there are plenty of areas to check on the North Island. Many of New Zealand's best competitive surfers come from the Gisborne area, because it is generally consistent, cleaner and just as powerful as the surf on the west coast, although it's usually a bit smaller. A wide swell window means more choice for wind/swell combos, firing up some great reefs and points. These quality spots, conveniently hidden amidst the sunniest and most untouched part of New Zealand, gives rise to Gisborne's reputation as the surf capital.

WILD COAST SOUTH AFRICA

●●●●●●(↑)●●●●●●●

+ Top-class right pointbreaks
+ Crowd free
+ Warm water
+ Cheap living costs

– Sharks
– Poor road network
– Lack of facilities
– Poverty and petty crime

NTYLONYANE

GARTH ROBINSON

The Wild Coast is a 280km stretch of cliff faces, perfect beaches and rich tidal estuaries, between East London and KwaZulu-Natal Province. Long distances between towns, bad roads, a lack of facilities and some strenuous access to breaks, this region suits the more experienced searcher with some pioneering spirit. There is an even mix of exposed, quality beachbreaks and protected right pointbreaks, plus many bays have both! The imbalance comes with the inordinately high population of large, dangerous sharks including the ubiquitous great whites.

KERAMAS
LAT. -8.598839°   LONG. 115.339514°   (12/2) ●●●●●↘

JEREMY WILMOTTE

BALI INDONESIA

●●●●●●(↑)●●●●●●

+ Concentrated world-class spots
+ Wet and dry season waves
+ Beginner and expert spots
+ Wild nightlife

– Very crowded waves
– Dangerous roads and traffic jams
– Pollution
– Touts and hustlers

Jet-set plaything and new pro contest hangout as its reputation for barrels and high-octane performance ramps grows. Picks up plenty of east coast swell and focuses it on a jagged lava reef that opens up straight from the drop then just asks to be bashed before the wave closes-out on the inside. Sometimes can barrel all the way or else leaves an open canvas for progressive moves and large punts on the steeper shut-down end section. Keramas is tidally sensitive, preferring higher, incoming tides and light morning land breezes. Conditions are always quite changeable on the east coast, but if the onshores are light, it still can be rideable and surprisingly consistent. Gets increasingly crowded for the dawn glass sessions and some bad vibes from over-zealous ex-pats and local surf guides. Watch out for the current when it gets bigger.

Blessed by the gods, Bali is a tropical surf paradise with one of the highest concentrations of quality waves on the planet. While 40 years of booming tourism development has drastically transformed the landscape and the line-ups, Bali remains an essential surfing experience. SW swells wrap consistent lines around the Bukit Peninsula into straight offshore trade winds, creating a list of world-class lefts including Uluwatu, Padang Padang, Bingin and Kuta Reef, plus there's the early morning, wet season, east coast rights of Nusa Dua, Sanur and comp site Keramas.

July

WEST SUMBAWA INDONESIA

+ Consistent swells
+ World-class waves
+ Semi-crowded
+ Cheap living costs

− SE trade wind restricts choice
− Slow overland access
− Lack of alternative activities
− No direct flights

SCAR REEF

ANDREW SHIELD

West Sumbawa has been surfed for decades, but due to lack of good transport links, it has remained a boat itinerary for most. Scar, Supers and Yoyo's are firm favourites, all situated on the west-facing coast and offshore in the strong SE trades from April to October. Fast, hollow lefts are the norm, plus a few bonus rights keep everyone happy in this tidally sensitive zone that can churn out some quality barrels. A wave wilderness opens up along the south coast for 180km, but a dearth of safe anchorages mean few spots are regularly surfed.

INHAMBANE MOZAMBIQUE

+ Fast, hollow waves
+ Warm water
+ No crowds
+ Cheap

− Frequent onshores
− Lack of spot density
− Inconsistent
− Malaria and AIDS

PIEGE A SABLE

GARTH ROBINSON

With a tragic history of war, floods and disease, Mozambique probably doesn't rate on most surfers' wish lists, despite being a surf explorer's paradise. There's roughly 2,500 km of coastline, most of which receives ample, seasonal swell and almost no crowds. Famous breaks include Ponta D'Ouro, a fabulous right point nestled up against the South African border, or Ilha de Inhaca, an island right near the capital Maputo. Travelling surfers searching for quality and consistency have found the best area to focus on is probably Inhambane Province a 6hr drive from Maputo.

GOLFO DE NICOYA COSTA RICA

+ Great left pointbreaks
+ Consistent powerful beaches
+ Both south and north swells
+ Exotic, warm and friendly

− Best swells in rainy season
− Beaches close-out easily
− Crowded breaks, busy resorts
− Some bad roads and petty crime

BOCA BARRANCA

JS CALLAHAN/SURFEXPLORE

Costa Rica has an incredible number of surfing expats and travellers, representing 10% of all tourists. Areas such as Guanacaste, became crowded, so new waves were sought around the Nicoya Gulf, opening up places like Mal Pais. Despite the shocking access roads requiring 4WD in the wet season, this wild area has become a surf-school haven, trading on idyllic tropical scenery, incredible national park wildlife and mellow beachbreaks. On a major swell, Boca Barranca sees endless peeling lefts and Playa Hermosa barrels have made Jaco 'Surf City CR'.

ANDHRA PRADESH INDIA

+ Set of virgin right pointbreaks
+ Perfect longboard waves
+ SW monsoon consistency
+ Cheap beach hotels

− Small waves
− Sideshore trades
− Appalling poverty & crazy traffic
− People shitting on beach

LAWSON BAY

JS CALLAHAN/SURFEXPLORE

Visakhapatnam boasts 3M residents and its large harbour is the focus for naval operations, steel production and other heavy industry. Lawson Bay is the most obvious spot producing the longest and the biggest waves within walking distance from the Beach Road hotels. A huge fleet of 2,000 fishing pirogues punch out through the surf every day and then surf the boat on some long waves when they return. Only the kids are allowed to play in the surf and lots of them do on the inside, but these are the only locals to contend with in the long, empty line-ups.

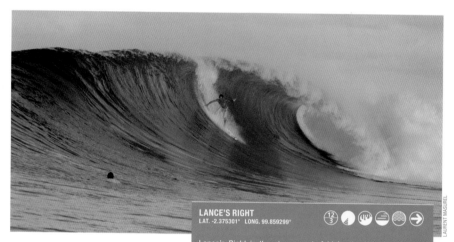

LAURENT MASUREL

LANCE'S RIGHT
LAT. -2.375301°   LONG. 99.859299°

Lance's Right is the pin-up centrefold for the Mentawai islands, bringing a new machine-like level to wave perfection. At the top of the coral platform, The Office section breathes in sharply, scooping up the next lucky expert who is hoping to be there when it exhales deeply, then launches through the Main Peak and into the inside where the shallowness of the Surgeons Table awaits. Size determines whether these three link and if any turns can be attempted. Perfection arrives with 6-8ft of S-SW swell, light W or no wind and at least 2hrs of tide. It's surprisingly consistent and the afternoon land breezes can clean it up quickly. Dangers are coral heads appearing, trying to duck dive when caught inside and being pushed too deep by the entrenched crowd. Answers are don't fall, go in over reef to deep paddling channel and surf somewhere else!

MENTAWAI INDONESIA

+ Top swell consistency
+ Variety of world-class spots
+ Warm, clear water
+ Exotic islands, unique culture

− Very expensive charters/resorts
− Crowded line-ups
− Malaria infested
− Dangerous navigation

This wild and remote chain of islands lying 90km off the Sumatran mainland attract increasing numbers of yacht charters into this fragile environment to ride "the best waves in the world". The secret is a concentration of truly world-class breaks and an unmatched flexibility when it comes to handling different swell and wind combinations. Picking one from an honour roll including Bankvaults, No Kandui, Rifles, Telescopes, Lances Left, Lances Right, Macaronis, Greenbush, Thunders and The Hole is impossible and pointless since they all can be perfect on any given day.

July

🌎 NAYARIT MEXICO

●●●●●●◉●●●●●●

+ Surfable year-round
+ Top longboard spots
+ Surf schools, camps and boats
+ Resorts option

− Lack of "Mexican Juice"
− Restricted access spots
− Bugs from hell in San Blas
− Rainy peak surf season

LAS ISLITAS

The Mexican State of Nayarit is an extremely scenic area, with lush tropical jungles, mangroves and deciduous forests lining the coast. To the east and south lie high volcanic mountains and rivers cut the landscape into valleys and deep gorges. Since the late '60s, hardcore surfers have been scoring epic sessions at Matanchen Bay, San Blas, known as the longest right in the world. The local biting sand flies and mosquitoes (jejenes) are legion along with 500,000 tourists who visit Puerto Vallarta each year, a once a tiny fishing village in the neighbouring state of Jalisco.

🌏 WEST MAKRAN PAKISTAN

●●●●●●◉●●●●●●

+ Constant monsoon swell
+ Mellow right pointbreaks
+ Discovery potential
+ No disease or bugs

− Short surf season
− Onshore winds
− Tough, hot, dusty access
− Military restrictions

MIRAGES

The Makran Coast's deserted sandy beaches stretch 700km along the Arabian Sea, but the main problem for surfers is it's too shallow! The white-clay cliffs erode into the sea, building huge, shallow banks, especially around reefs and capes, dissipating rather than focusing the swell power. The best bet for finding surf is on the hammer-shaped headlands that once were islands, but became joined to the mainland by a thin sandbar (tombolo), like Ormara or Gwadar. Around Karachi there are several spots surfed by expats and travellers fresh off the plane.

🌍 IVORY COAST

●●●●●●◉●●●●●●

+ Empty line-ups
+ Light wind patterns
+ Cool beachbreaks, easy points
+ Jungle scenery and animals

− Inconsistent swell
− Lack of big waves
− Fairly expensive
− Malaria and hygiene threats

GRAND DREWIN

Located on the Gulf of Guinea, the Ivory Coast contains 515km of exposed southerly facing shoreline. This equatorial country picks up the South Atlantic swells, which break on a variety of beaches and reefs, backed by swaying coconut trees and endless lagoons. Close to the Ghanaian border, Assinie is the most popular surf destination in the country with fast, hollow beachbreak conditions and a French run surf camp. When the swell picks up then there's reef and pointbreak action to the west and more mellow waves ideal for longboarders and beginners.

LAMPUNG INDONESIA

+ Consistent sizable surf
+ Uncrowded for Indo
+ Exploration potential
+ Cheap surf camps

− Cross-shore winds
− Few services, no nightlife
− Tedious access
− Isolated

UJUNG BOCUR

ALEX WILLIAMS

Sumatra's mainland has remained off the radar of most travelling surfers. Despite an ideal orientation to Indian Ocean swell hitting the contoured coastline of the fifth biggest island in the world, Sumatra remains a quiet surfing backwater. Lampung is scarcely populated, takes hours to get to by road and is rarely visited by tourists, but the fishing town of Krui has a growing reputation as the spot to hang out at a number of surf camps for the accessible lefts of Ujung Bocor (aka Karang Nyimbor or Flying Coral) and the heaving barrels of Way Jambu.

CHRIS VAN LENNEP

J-BAY
LAT. -34.032934° LONG. 24.934619°

The longest, most perfect righthand pointbreak on the planet, consists of 10 different sections; Kitchen Windows, Magnatubes, Boneyards, Supertubes, Impossibles, Salad Bowls, Coins, Tubes, The Point and finally Albatross. Fingers of basalt hold the sand uniformly, creating the perfect bathymetry for 1km long rides between Boneyards and The Point when the swell is just the right size and perfectly lined up. Supertubes is the stellar section, where the pro competitions are held and the crew are most combative, while Point and Albatross are slower, more manageable walls. Maintaining speed and a high line is critical for threading the multiple tube sections and cutting back is rarely a good idea. SW-W is offshore for most of the sections, while NW-NE Berg (or Devil) winds blow into the barrels and create a nasty chop that is too hard to handle on a wave where speed is king.

ST FRANCIS BAY SOUTH AFRICA

+ J-Bay's world-class rights
+ Consistent swells
+ Frequent offshore winds
+ Cheap

− Cool water and wind chill
− Sharp mussel covered rocks
− Sharks
− Packed J-Bay line-up

Halfway between Durban and Cape Town is South Africa's best and most consistent surf zone. The frequent winter SW swells and the occasional E swells that hit this SE-facing coastline, turn on dozens of classic pointbreaks that are hidden away inside crescent shaped coves. Jeffreys Bay (J-Bay) is obviously the most renowned wave and is considered one of, if not 'The best righthander in the world'. St Francis Bay is blessed with other quality waves, including the fickle Bruce's Beauties, which featured in the seminal '60s surf film *The Endless Summer.*

July

RAROTONGA COOK ISLANDS

+ North and south swells
+ Uncrowded reef passes
+ Easy paddles from shore
+ Outer island potential

− Limited reef pass set-ups
− Shallow high tide reefs
− Tropical downpours
− Expensive local costs

RUTAKI PASSAGE
JEREMY WILMOTTE

Considering these 15 islands sit in between world-class locations like Fiji, Tonga, Samoa and Tahiti, plus bear the name of the ultimate surf discoverer, James Cook, good surf should be guaranteed. The capital Rarotonga is volcanic with a rugged, eroded centre of peaks and ridges, surrounded by flat lowlands. Most of the reef passes are too narrow and explains why there are only a handful of surf spots in the Cook Islands. The waves break over shallow reef, so it's usually safest to surf at high tide by paddling out one of the passages or directly over the reef.

LOS CABOS MEXICO

+ Warm water and weather
+ Right points
+ Good swell and wind patterns
+ Plenty of sunshine

− Lack of power
− Jellyfish and desert bugs
− Crowds around Cabo
− Some bad roads

CABOS POINT
BAJASURFADVENTURES.COM

Cabo is a complete contradiction to Baja's wilderness and one of Mexico's most developed ports, offering a distinctly civilised version of Baja. Boardshort warm seas offer a 200° swell window from the SE around to the NNW, roads are surfaced and the seaside resorts offer all mod cons to the holiday hordes. This area favours S swells, but the W coast also receives plenty of NW swells. The Gulf of California breaks continue the natural footer's playground by wrapping in when a heavy S or local hurricane (*chubasco*) forms, but crowds and boardies make it an alien Baja experience.

SOUTHEAST SRI LANKA

+ Consistently clean and rideable
+ Various right sand pointbreaks
+ Laid-back friendly vibe
+ Amazing sightseeing and wildlife

− Consistently small and mellow
− Crowded Arugam Bay
− Long access, slow driving
− Intense heat and insects

ARUGAM BAY
EMILIANO MAZZONI

Sri Lanka has been shaped by two modern catastrophic events: the civil war, raging since 1983 (64,000 deaths) and the 2004 tsunami (3,000 deaths). First surfed in 1964, Arugam Bay was almost erased off the surfing map by the three waves, estimated to be 45ft (13m) high, flattening the fishing villages, hotels and restaurants and destroying 80% of Sri Lanka's entire fishing fleet. Despite this disaster, the waves are still breaking, with consistently small, perfect, right peelers that make Arugam Bay and the many other sandy points along this coast an intermediates heaven.

TONGATAPU TONGA

+ Uncrowded spots
+ Perfect reefs
+ Great climate
+ Laid-back vibe

− Short rides
− Live coral reef dangers
− Cooler winter waters
− Expensive location

MOTELS

The Tonga archipelago includes 170 islands divided into four separate groups. Tongatapu is the main island which is made up of a raised coral platform. Constant wave action has cut a shelf into the cliff-bound south coast, unlike the north that's dotted with low-lying reefs and offshore islets. Most surf spots are all squeezed onto a remarkable reef bend on the W side of the island, where trade winds blow straight offshore. SW swells create grinding lefts through the S hemisphere winter (April-Oct), whilst less consistent N swells favour the shorter, shallow rights from Nov-March.

SULTAN'S
LAT. 4.313543°   LONG. 73.586281°

NORTH MALÉ MALDIVES

+ World class rights and lefts
+ Calm winds
+ Atoll perfection
+ Luxury resorts and boats

− Consistently small
− Consistently crowded
− Boat access restrictions
− No budget land trips

Impressive, point-style, righthand reefbreak that forms half of the Thamburudhoo Island double act along with Honky's. Sultan's regularly delivers the biggest, longest waves in North Male and is one of only three righthanders that will work when the SW monsoon blows throughout the middle months of the year. It starts with a swift, steep, yet manageable drop into a carving wall that throws some nice hooks on the faster inside reef, a full 300m down the line on big SE swells. Handles as much size as this corner of the Indian Ocean can muster, when waiting for a tip to tail bomb will be extremely worth it. Sultan's is North Malé atoll's most surfed spot with at least 100 surfers a day, because it is accessible to improvers, intermediates and out of shape mid-lifers thanks to its user-friendly nature. Under threat from a US-backed, private island resort development.

Maldives has gained a solid reputation for clean, almost beginner-friendly waves that break on the most exposed parts of the atoll reefs. Surfing in the Maldives has remained focused on North Malé, which claims the best density of lefts and rights within a 2hr cruise. Combined with an appealing proximity to the airport, it's a convenient, fun-wave playground for time-restricted, wealthy travellers. The four passes gathering the bulk of the swell are often crowded with all types and abilities of recreational surfers from the resorts, guest-houses or charter boats, but the vibe is usually friendly.

August

EAST OAXACA MEXICO

●●●●●●●●⊛●●●●

+ Consistent summer swells
+ Little or no crowds
+ Many classic breaks
+ No mass tourism

– Strong trade winds
– Mainly righthanders
– Sketchy access to some breaks
– Rainy surf season

SALINA CRUZ
WESLEY ALLISON

Mexico still has plenty of surf potential to be uncovered and those looking for warm water, peeling pointbreaks, powerful beachbreaks, offshore winds and no one else out, should seriously think about the eastern part of Oaxaca. The state is one of the last frontiers in mainland Mexico, despite also being home to Puerto Escondido. Huatulco to Salina Cruz is almost untouched by development and the difficult to access coastline conceals a plethora of breaks that are peppered by powerful swells from April to October.

SIMEULUE & BANYAKS INDONESIA

●●●●●●●●⊛●●●●

+ Reef quality
+ Consistent swells
+ Light crowds
+ Untouched scenery

– No budget options
– Lack of information
– Dangerous navigation
– Malaria infested

TREASURE ISLAND
SURFBANYAK.COM

Simeulue and Banyak still maintain a frontier status, avoiding the charter boat congestion of the Mentawais through a combination of lower consistency and spot density, treating smaller groups to some lively waves, including one of Indo's best rights. Not surprisingly, these "Many" islands have kept off the radar and some spots remain nameless, or have multiple names from the different boat operators that ply these waters. There are a wide choice of lefts and rights, ranging from shallow barrels to deeper, long, cruisey waves as well as some good off-season beachbreaks.

BALUCHESTAN IRAN

●●●●●●●⊛●●●●

+ Totally empty waves
+ Break diversity
+ Consistent monsoon surf
+ Exotic culture

– Short swell season
– Painful heat
– Mild onshores
– Language barrier

KABAB
OLIVIER SERVAIRE

Tucked between Iraq, Afghanistan and Pakistan, the political and geographical landscape of Iran isn't exactly perfect for a trouble-free surf trip. Yet Iran has coasts on three seas, and while the Caspian and the Persian Gulf are too enclosed to produce much surf, it's not the case for the Gulf of Oman, which connects with the Indian Ocean. The region of Baluchestan and its Makran coast continues into Pakistan, offering endless opportunities to discover new waves in the bays and on the headlands of this sparsely inhabited seaboard that picks up monsoon swell from June to August.

KENYA

● ● ● ● ● ◉ ● ● ⊛ ● ● ● ●

+ Semi-consistent during surf season
+ Warm water
+ Virgin reefs & beachbreaks
+ Fascinating wildlife

− Lots of onshore mush
− Mombassa sharks
− Remote reefs with tidal flats
− Robberies and muggings

MALINDI

MICHAEL KEW

Kenya and Tanzania have recently unveiled a few surfing secrets along their considerable Indian Ocean coastlines. A small expat surfing community has been tapping the surf here for decades, but Kenya is now starting to attract inquisitive surfers to the fringing reefs that break consistently during the southern hemisphere winter. Mombasa Island makes sense as a base for surf exploration, with waves right on its doorstep. South of Mombasa check Diani Beach, while the coastal area to the north features Arab and Portuguese forts and some of the finest beach hotels in Africa.

REPOSAR/A-FRAME

DESERT POINT
LAT. -8.749826° LONG. 115.824170°   (15/5) 🏄 ⊛ ▨ ◎ ↖

Desert Point is one of the longest, makeable lefthand barrels on the planet with over 20secs tubes possible. The take-off area can shift around a bit, but generally rewards a deep attack. High speed is the key as it quickly winds up and starts peeling mercilessly across the shallow reef. The caverns get larger and faster as the inside section commits the tube rider to a lock-in that usually ends on dry reef. Only surfers good enough to deal with the tricky exit, the shallow reef, evil out-going currents and plenty of wave-starved rippers should apply. Desert's has a reputation for inconsistency, with only the biggest groundswells igniting it and high tides making it disappear as fast as it came. Surf charters keep flocking from Bali and dedicated hardcore surfers wait for weeks in basic beach shacks, forming a frenzied, barrel-hungry pack on those rare classic days.

LOMBOK INDONESIA

+ Voted world's best wave
+ Consistent year-round surf
+ No mass tourism
+ Cheap lodging and food

− Overcrowded Desert Point
− Only one outstanding break
− Hard access to eastern spots
− Lack of accommodation outside Kuta

Lombok sits only 18km east of Bali, yet major physical, cultural, linguistic and religious differences exist. The deep strait separating these islands links the Indian and Pacific oceans and is part of the "Wallace Line", an established physical division between Asia and Australia. Most surf breaks are truly breathtaking, but are generally regarded as of lower quality or intensity than Bali's, with the notable exception of Desert Point, elected "Best Wave in the World" by Tracks magazine's readers. More than any other island in Indo, Lombok is a year-round surfing destination.

August

NOVA SCOTIA CANADA

+ Great hurricane swells
+ Break quality and diversity
+ Minimum crowds
+ Unspoilt coastline

– Icy water temps
– Harsh weather
– Inconsistent summer
– Thick wetsuits

MINUTES

DAVID PU'U

Nova Scotia belongs to the Maritime Provinces of Canada, where it is impossible to be more than 56km away from the sea. While most towns are located along the coast, the province's interior is pitted with thousands of lakes scattered among forests and rocky hills. A narrow isthmus connects Nova Scotia to mainland Canada and the Atlantic coastline ranges from bays, inlets and cliffs to gravel or sand beaches. This rugged shoreline provides a wealth of pointbreaks, offshore reefs and plenty of beachbreaks, with a huge variety of wind and swell combinations.

SÃO TOMÉ

+ Quality, empty pointbreaks
+ Consistent summer swells
+ No rain during surf season
+ Untouched equatorial island

– Mostly small waves
– No access to west coast
– Expensive flights & local prices
– Malaria

RADIATION POINT

JS CALLAHAN/SURFEXPLORE

The archipelago of São Tomé and Príncipe is composed of three islands: São Tomé is the largest, followed by Príncipe which is 30min away by plane, and finally the tiny islet of Rolas (3km²). São Tomé and Príncipe is a developing country where oil and tourism have taken over from an economy based on coffee and cocoa, hence the nickname of the "Chocolate Islands". Australian and American surfers visited as early as the '70s, but travelling surfers remain rare. There are many promising set-ups along the east coast plus the equator straddling Point Zero Left.

SOUTH PIURA PERU

+ World-class lefts
+ Completely uncrowded
+ Always offshore
+ Pristine natural area

– 4WD access only
– Heavy line-ups and rips
– Zero facilities
– "El Nino" risk

PUNTA TUR

GONZALO BARANDIARAN

Heading towards remote Bayovar seems crazy when the ultra-long rides of Chicama or the deep tubes of Cabo Blanco are just a few hours south or north. However, rumours of 10ft barrels reeling forever are enough to lure the intrepid to this vast desert region of sand dunes and granite cliffs. Conditions are extremely harsh in this inhospitable land (no hotels) so be prepared for camping and desert survival in your 4x4 or take a surf tour. The rewards are the long, hardcore caverns at Nonura and Punta Tur, suited to rippers with rippling muscles to fight the serious currents.

 OMAN

●●●●●●●●⊕●●●●

+ Constant seasonal windswell
+ Hollow right pointbreaks
+ Trouble-free environment
+ Natural island idyll on Masirah

– Monsoon season only
– Onshore wind exposed spots
– No facilities, no entertainment
– Lack of quality conditions

AL ASHKARAH

JEFF DIVINE

The Middle East is not exactly a renowned surfing zone and is undoubtedly the least surfed area of the Indian Ocean. Recent expeditions awakened the surfing world to the area's possibilities, yet it's highly likely that expats from Dubai and Muscat have been riding some spots for years. Oman is 82% desert and overlooks three seas - the Arabian Gulf, Gulf of Oman and the Arabian Sea. Although the surfers of Dubai get some surf in the Gulfs, headhigh, clean surf is more likely to be found in the Arabian Sea, especially on the island of Masirah.

TEAHUPOO
LAT. -17.867243° LONG. -149.253582°

JASON FEAST

 TAHITI & MOOREA
FRENCH POLYNESIA

●●●●●●●●⊕●●●●

+ Powerful, consistent waves
+ Year-round barrels
+ Beautiful landscapes
+ Chilled-out island lifestyle

– Very expensive
– Difficult access
– Localism at some spots
– Dangerous coral reefs

Teahupoo has roared out of the deep blue and redefined what is possible, snatching the crown for the 'World's Heaviest Wave'. What sets Teahupoo aside is its sheer power and ferocity, containing a lip a few feet thick and a shape more rectangular than almond. More S in the swell will calm the beast slightly, but it's the straight on SW'ers that slam the reef and open up the caverns along the short 75-100m run for your life line-up. It's all about the drop and those able to set an early rail into the gasping tubes will do better. Mistakes are swiftly punished as the highly visible reef quickly runs dry, pushing the unlucky ones into the lagoon and the coral is famed for infecting cuts. Teahupoo consistently pulls in more swell than anywhere on Tahiti, but getting the ideal NE wind is less common, especially in the high season.

Tahiti sits at the centre of French Polynesia and thanks to the blanket media coverage of the scary reef-pass wave at Teahupoo, it sits firmly at the centre of the surfing universe. Comprising of about 118 small islands spread out over five archipelagos, (Société Islands, Marquesas, Tuamotu, Gambier, Tubuai) and covering an area of ocean the size of Europe, the scope for perfect waves is unlimited. Tahiti and Moorea hide a variety of exceptional quality spots and more often than not, away from the famous spots, many classic waves go unridden.

August

LOFOTEN NORWAY

+ Long, empty pointbreaks
+ Midnight sun
+ Unrivalled arctic scenery
+ Friendly vibe

– Cold summer conditions
– Short surfing season
– Difficult coastal access
– Super-expensive

UNSTAD LEFT

Until recently, Norway's surf potential has been mostly ignored, leaving it to a small core crew to enjoy the waves around Stavanger, in the south. However, way up north, above the Arctic Circle, the spotlight fell on Lofoten as a primo surfing destination, highlighted by many media projects. The Lofoten are a cluster of mountainous islands 100km off the north Norwegian coastline, stretching for more than 160km around the 68th degree parallel. Tall, ancient peaks plunge down into the wide-open ocean, where the bouldered fringe holds some superb lefts and rights at Unstad.

TOGO & BENIN

+ Consistent, long-range swell
+ No crowds
+ Exploration possibilities
+ Voodoo culture

– No epic spots
– Light onshores
– Rain in swell season
– Malaria

LOMÉ - RIVAGE

Benin and Togo are largely off the map for both surfers and travellers. The two tiny nations, home to voodoo and friendly beachbreaks, offer a tropical climate and consistent, uncrowded surf potential. A combined trip to neighbouring Ghana will increase wave quantity and quality, yet Benin and Togo offer an escape into a unique and magical culture. The coast is made up of a series of steeply shelving beaches, almost entirely backed by lagoons and the best waves like Anécho appear where a natural or manmade feature creates sandbanks, breaking up the endless shore-pound.

JEJU DO SOUTH KOREA

+ Strong typhoon waves
+ Beaches & lava reefbreaks
+ Uncrowded surf
+ World Heritage island

– Inconsistent, unpredictable typhoons
– Short surf season
– Expensive local costs
– Over-protective lifeguards

SQUID POINT

Lying off the southwest coast of the Republic of Korea, volcanic Jeju Island (Jeju Do) is a UNESCO listed World Natural Heritage site. The island's warm, sunny climate and myriad leisure facilities mean that it is one of the country's most popular tourist and honeymoon destinations. In August 2004, an international crew of surfers stumbled into 8-10ft surf and constant swell during the whole trip, thanks to two super-typhoons. Koreans rarely swim in the sea, even when it's flat, so most lifeguards don't want anyone near the water, let alone play in the surf when there is typhoon swell.

OUTER BANKS NORTH CAROLINA, USA

+ Wide swell window
+ Powerful beachbreaks
+ Uncrowded areas
+ Wild scenic area

– Windy conditions
– Beachbreaks only
– Cold winters
– Costly accommodation

CAPE HATTERAS

DOUG WATERS

The Outer Banks are a bow shaped string of barrier islands sitting in offshore isolation from the North Carolina coast. These low-lying strips of sand appeared less than a 1000 years ago, a result of the merger of the cold Labrador Current from the north and the warm Gulf Stream from the south. The Outer Banks are well exposed to all types of East Coast swell and the dozens of piers provide some protection from wind and cross-shore drift. When it's happening, there are full on, beachbreak barrels to be had, which are not short of power.

FITPATRICK/SURF-CARIBE.COM

PUERTO ESCONDIDO
LAT. 15.843107° LONG. -97.053091°

Peerless beachbreak where spectacular, cavernous barrels unload close to shore. Swells hit the Puerto Escondido sandbars at Zicatela Beach in such a way that the waves jack-up in size, which is often emphasised by a backwash. Magazine photos of this place are misleading; guillotine lips make the paddle-outs punishing and there's always plenty of board-snapping close-outs, so wave choice is critical. Requires high skill level when it gets overhead, when the thick crowds start to thin out. Locals, pros and travellers fight for the 1 in 3 that hopefully won't shut down, so committed surfers only need apply. Usually the rights break best and will often be blown out by 11am. There's large numbers of skilled surfers in the water hoping for the bomb that stays open long enough to escape. Despite all this, it's still a year-round Mecca for big barrel hunters!

WEST OAXACA MEXICO

+ World-class beachbreak
+ Consistent year-round
+ Fairly cheap
+ Good nightlife

– Lots of close-outs
– Crowds
– Crime
– Insects

Oaxaca is famous as the home of Puerto Escondido, where huge and spectacular barrels hurl themselves at the sands of Playa Zicatela. The offshore deep-water trench focuses the swell from the Southern Hemisphere and frequent tropical storms and hurricanes that pass by this coast in the summer time (April-Oct). Fortunately, Oaxaca (pronounced wah-hah-kah) is not only about huge death-defying barrels and there are a few user-friendly points, reefs and rivermouths for the average Joe, like the super right pointbreak Chacahua or the quiet beaches of Huatulco.

September

SHIKOKU

CHRIS VAN LENNUP

KAIFU RIVER

● ● ● ● ● ● ● ● ● ◉ ● ● ● ●

+ World-class rivermouth waves
+ Warm water in the surf season
+ Laid-back ambience
+ Amazing cultural experience

− Inconsistent rivermouth swells
− Flat winters
− Relatively wet climate
− Very high living costs

For those who have enough money and time to handle the flat spells, then Japan can be a rewarding surf destination. Shikoku, the country's fourth largest island, is quintessential Japan, full of temples, traditional fishing harbours, and water gardens. The exposed SE-facing coastline crosses the Kochi and Tokushima provinces, where the abundant rainfall feeds numerous rivers. When these rivers spill into the sea, they help to form decent sandbanks for the typhoon generated swells to break on, resulting in some grinding righthand rivermouth breaks.

LUANDA & BENGO

JS CALLAHAN/SURF EXPLORE

CABO LEDO

● ● ◉ ◉ ◉ ● ● ● ● ◉ ● ● ●

+ Easy, long left pointbreaks
+ Consistent swells
+ Warmish water
+ Undiscovered

− Windy, exposed spots
− Costly flights and visas
− War zone, land mines
− Sharks and crocs

Since independence in 1975, 30 years of civil war and western-backed resource war for oil and diamonds have wreaked havoc all over the country. Angola probably rates as the worst mine affected country in the world, with 31 land mines per square mile, totalling 15 million. Fortunately, the surfing areas in Luanda and Bengo, are free of significant mine contamination and Angola is thought to be an African Peru, with a long coastline of unknown surf spots. Very few waveriders have had the privilege of enjoying these long peeling left pointbreaks like Cabo Ledo.

CATANDUANES PHILIPPINES

JS CALLAHAN/SURF EXPLORE

MAJESTICS

● ● ● ● ● ◉ ● ● ● ◉ ● ● ●

+ World-class righthander
+ Empty waves
+ Exotic, tropical paradise
+ Cheap and mellow trip

− Long flat spells
− Lack of quality spots
− Unsuitable for beginners
− Difficult access

Catanduanes juts out into the Pacific and appears to be an ideal swell magnet for the NE typhoon swells. Intrepid travellers discovered a barrelling righthander dubbed Majestics, however, the pictures were deceiving, not showing how quickly the wave peeled or how shallow the reef was and most notably, how inconsistent the wave appeared to be. Many surfers have been drawn here by the pictures and ended up spending weeks waiting around for Majestics to do its thing, but those that score it good, rate it as the Philippine's best barrel.

VANCOUVER ISLAND CANADA

● ● ● ● ● ● ● ● ● (↑) ● ● ● ●

+ Consistent swells
+ Mix of beaches, reefs and points
+ Waves for all abilities
+ Wildlife

– Messy stormy swells
– Beaches often onshore and rainy
– Expensive local costs
– Rare, localised pointbreaks

SECRET SPOT

Canada has the world's longest coastline and with 52,455 islands, it should also host the largest number of surf spots. However, being located so far north (45°- 80° lat), frozen water and regular swell supply are the issues. Surfers have been exploring the southern corners of this vast country, finding Vancouver Island to be well-endowed with some quality reefs, points and beaches. Tofino is the closest thing to a surf town and dozens of spots exist along the remote nooks and crannies of the island, but access is challenging without a boat or seaplane.

THURSO EAST
LAT. 58.602648° LONG. -3.509707°

Thurso East is Scotland's premier righthand reefbreak and a world-class barrel on its day. In NW swells at mid tide a relatively simple drop leads into one of the longest, hollowest rides in Europe. Even the biggest W swells won't get in without a touch of N; WNW swells are hollowest and the more N in the swell the mellower the wave. SW winds blow into the barrel and bump it up but it can still be fun in an onshore. Thurso has been a contest site for all levels of amateur and pro surfers, but as crowds increase, locals are less tolerant of groups and those that don't wait their turn. Park responsibly in the farmyard in front of the break, as there's not much room with the new barn. Alternatively, park by the harbour in town and paddle out in the peat-stained river that brings seriously cold water to the line-up in winter.

CAITHNESS SCOTLAND

● ● ● ● ● ● ● ● ● (↑) ● ● ●

+ Quality reefs
+ Thurso East
+ Uncrowded waves
+ Fantastic scenery

– Cold water
– Wet and unstable weather
– Windy conditions
– Hard access

Scotland is better known for whiskey and bagpipes than for waves, but there's no doubt that all three of Scotland's coasts receive excellent surf. With the improvements in wetsuit technology, more and more surfers are braving the cold to seek out Scotland's thick, heavy barrels, in uncrowded line-ups. Thurso East is one of Europe's finest, albeit fickle waves, while super-consistent Brimms Ness will hoover up any swell going. The flat slab reefbreaks of Caithness have a wide swell window from the W round to SE, are often offshore and usually firing in autumn.

September

DONEGAL BAY IRELAND

●●●●●●●●●●⊕●●●

+ Concentration of reefbreaks
+ Powerful swells
+ Predominant offshores
+ Cool people

– Rainy climate and cold water
– Windy conditions
– Big tidal ranges
– Fairly pricey

THE PEAK

ROGER SHARP

NW Ireland is one of the most consistent surf destinations in Europe. Regular storms provide the region with regular swells, which hit a contorted coastline, offering numerous, quality surf options. Positioned so close to the most turbulent corner of the North Atlantic, NW Ireland is also prone to some vile weather and short-period windy swells. Travelling surfers will have to endure a few less-than-perfect days, but the awesome landscape and warm welcome mean that an Irish surf trip is always something more than just a frenzied hunt for waves.

SANTA CRUZ CALIFORNIA, USA

●●●●●●●●●●⊕●●●

+ Wide swell window
+ Spot variety
+ Dominant offshores
+ Laid back Santa Cruz

– Cold water year-round
– Competitive crowds
– Chilly winters and fog
– Great white sharks

STEAMER LANE

DAN HAVLOCK

Santa Cruz exudes a unique, laid-back style that adds credence to the town's claim as Surf City USA. Surf-wise, Santa Cruz is just about the most diverse county in California with its right pointbreaks, coves, rivermouths and beachbreaks. It's got the consistent, quirky reefs to the north, or the user-friendly, ultra-clean and crowded points in 'Town', including the pro contest site of Steamer Lane. To top it off, Monterey Bay and its beautiful underwater canyon focuses swell into the powerful, uncrowded and often merciless beachbreaks of south county.

SUMBA INDONESIA

●●●●●●●●●⊕●●●

+ Consistent groundswells
+ Many empty top-class spots
+ Tribal culture
+ Cheap living costs

– Wild & windy sometimes
– Isolated, unpredictable spots
– Lack of beach lodging choices
– Expensive Nihiwatu and travel costs

MILLER'S RIGHTS

PAUL KENNEDY

Nusa Tenggara is geographically and culturally different from the rest of Indonesia. Deep offshore trenches allow plenty of swell to hit the southwest-facing coast of Sumba, where waves of consequence get thrown onto the reefs of dead coral, volcanic rock and boulders. Sumba is not for everyone; the food and accommodation are basic and the mixed ethnic population speak three different languages. Huge megalithic tombs and thatched, peaked huts dot the landscape, while in the line-up, intrepid travellers are now sampling the oceanic power of this ancient island.

CHIBA PREFECTURE JAPAN

●●●●●●●●●●(🕴)●●●●

+ Great rivermouth breaks
+ Warm summer conditions
+ Typhoon swells
+ Unique cultural destination

– Inconsistent
– Frequently small and mushy
– Crowds and pollution
– Very expensive

TORAMI BEACH

JS CALLAHAN/SURF EXPLORE

Japan comprises of four major islands - Hokkaido, Honshu, Shikoku and Kyushu. Although the main island of Honshu gets occasional surf from NW windswells coming off the Sea of Japan, most of the more consistent spots are those exposed to the late summer typhoon swells, or short-lived NE groundswells. Surfing is now a well-established sport that has been growing in popularity since WW II. Kanagawa, Ibaraki and Shizuoka areas all have some good spots, but the most popular surf zone for Tokyo-based surfers is the Chiba peninsula, 30min drive from the city.

TRESTLES
LAT. 33.384399° LONG. -117.595007°

JEFF DIVINE

SAN DIEGO COUNTY
CALIFORNIA, USA

●●●●●●●●●●(🕴)●●●

+ Variety of spots
+ Lots of clean waves
+ Great weather
+ Flat day entertainment

– Constant competitive crowds
– Relatively cool water
– Pollution
– Urban atmosphere

Trestles consists of two separate cobblestone breaks known as Uppers and Lowers, which between them create one of the world's most famous wave-riding locations, right in the middle of the SoCal surf media scene. An often-stellar cobblestone peak, Lowers provides occasional hollow, zippering lefts, but is more known for its long, fast, bowling rights. Best with SW swells up to double-overhead. Can be good at any tide. Years of magazine exposure means it's as jam packed as an LA freeway and it's also a pro tour venue known for being conducive to high-performance aerial manoeuvres. Uppers is a cobblestone mini-point featuring quality rights, often hollow and fast. Lower tides best with W swells up to double-overhead. As the sun rises there will already be 50 bodies in the line-up, despite the long walk/cycle path in.

You can find almost any type of wave in San Diego County and every inch of this coastline has been thoroughly scoured by generations of surfers. Its ultra-crowded line-ups have featured in countless magazine spreads and dozens of webcams spy on the waves. San Diego surf is not exactly world-class, although like everywhere, it can be. The exposure to N swells is good, but not California's best, whilst the S swell exposure is not always ideal. There are at least 80 major spots, including some of California's most famous names like Trestles, San Onofre, Swamis, Blacks and Windansea.

September

GALICIA SPAIN

●●●●○○○○○○ (👤) ●●● ○

+ 180° swell window
+ Multiple swell/wind options
+ Campervan friendly
+ Beautiful countryside

– No world-class breaks
– Cool water all-year-round
– Long drives and hard access
– Unstable climate and lack of sunshine

PANTIN

WILLY URIBE

Galicia's landscape of steep forested hills hidden behind clouds of misty drizzle earned it the "end of the world" nickname from the Romans. Since then, the Celtic inhabitants have been left alone in this un-Spanish corner of Iberia. Plunging valleys cut across the landscape, leading to large inlets and estuaries called "rias". Similar to fjords, these flooded valleys punctuate the coastline and effectively filter the consistent NW swells. Galicia has mainland Europe's largest swell window and the jagged coastline means somewhere will always be offshore.

HOBART TASMANIA, AUSTRALIA

●●○○●○●○○ (👤) ●●● ●

+ Roaring Forties exposure
+ Variety of beach and points
+ Peninsulas and indented coast
+ Uncrowded and mountainous

– Windy and chilly winter surf
– Occasionally flat SE coast
– Slow access
– Expensive to get there

SHIPSTERN BLUFF

SEAN DAVEY

Australia's 6th state, a 300km long triangular island was, until around 10,000 years ago, joined to the mainland, but is now about 240km away across the shallow Bass Strait. Tassie was put on the map when a horrendous right ledge on the Tasman Peninsula was exposed to the world. It is a Teahupoo-like right, without the contest and tropical allure, but with awesome triple lips and huge screaming barrels. The majority of surfers will be seeking less life-threatening spots and Hobart makes a good base to explore from.

SITKA ALASKA, USA

●●○●●○○○○ (👤) ●●○ ●

+ Variety of quality spots
+ Empty, wilderness line-ups
+ Reasonable autumn water temps
+ Great salmon & halibut fishing

– Cold, inconsistent surf
– Heavy rain and changeable winds
– Remote, difficult access
– Very expensive

SHOAL'S REEF

KEVIN GRIFFIN

SE Alaska holds the best potential for surf along a fjord-pocked coastline with hundreds of islands, rivermouths and headlands, where the Alaska Range often plunges directly into the Pacific Ocean. Roads are virtually non-existent and huge mountains barricade the coastal fringe in the north and east. Travel to the SE region is via plane or boat and it's expensive. Alaska's largest surfing community is in Yakutat on the Gulf of Alaska, but historic Sitka also has some good beachbreaks, plus a few quality reefs and points on nearby Cruzof Island.

TAIWAN

● ● ● ● ● ● ● ● ● ⊕ ● ● ●

+ SE typhoon & NE monsoon swells
+ Powerful beachbreaks & left points
+ Cheap, easy access from Asia
+ Beautiful east coast

− No world-class breaks
− Suffocating summer heat
− Densely populated Taipei
− Risk of destructive typhoons

NANWAN BAY

ANDREW SHIELD

Taiwan is only 160km from the mainland where the People's Republic of China (PRC) have ruled since winning the civil war against the Republic of China (ROC), who still maintain some sovereignty over Taiwan. Surfing in Taiwan has a long history, despite government bans and surf arrives from a generous 225° swell window hitting all sides of the island. The seasonal monsoons bring consistent waist to headhigh waves and a pair of boardshorts will do for all but the depths of winter, making Taiwan an alluring, yet unusual tropical destination.

LA GRAVIÈRE
LAT. 43.666284° LONG. -1.443671°

DAMIEN POULLENOT

Sited on an old gravel pit, La Gravière is the legendary Hossegor tube spot and is the preferred location to host the Quiksilver Pro competition every September. A big swell usually white-caps outside then reforms, standing up over the shallow inside bars. Heavy, thick-lipped beasts, break perilously close to shore and often close-out, snapping more boards than just about anywhere. Tidal range radically affects the window for ideal conditions, as does swell period, which decides if it is messy and inconsistent or lined-up and bombing through. The rip speed usually rises in direct proportion with the swell height and on big days, only the tow crew will be able to get into the sets before being swept south in the current. Humbling for all, but the barrel experts and the pros. Use the slatted access paths through the fragile dunes. All facilities down the beach at Hossegor's Front de Mer.

LANDES FRANCE

● ● ● ● ● ● ● ● ● ⊕ ● ●

+ Top-quality beachbreaks
+ Hollow consistent waves
+ Empty beaches
+ Waves for all abilities

− No sheltered spots
− Frequent onshores
− Beachbreaks only
− Cold water in winter

Europe's longest uninterrupted stretch of sandy beach is also blessed by a swell-focusing, deep-water canyon, just off the coast at Hossegor, creating one of the best beachbreaks on the planet. Up to 3m, Hossegor's beaches deliver exceptionally powerful, hollow, perfect peaks, often very close to shore and spitting barrels can be spied far into the distance in either direction, spreading groups of surfers away from the main access points. Big currents, tidal ranges and wind exposure do little to deter the ever-growing crowds of surfers that call Hossegor home.

October

OREGON USA

●●●●●●●●●●◉⟨↟⟩●●

+ Powerful consistent swells
+ Seaside Point
+ Spot variety
+ Beautiful scenery

− Swells often too big
− Stormy climate
− Cold water
− Localism and sharks

CAPE LOOKOUT

BOB LEDBETTER

Oregon is a rugged land with a decent variety of surf spots, each requiring specific conditions to turn on. Lack of swell is never a problem, but the cross-onshore wind can be, so it's essential to search out one of the protruding points, capes and headlands to provide some protection. Some spots are crowded and well known, while others are empty and rarely spoken of. The city of Seaside, Oregon's first coastal resort, is home to the famous Seaside Point, reputed to be the best wave in the Pacific Northwest and the best lefthand pointbreak in North America.

REYKJANES PENINSULA ICELAND

●●●●●●●●●●◉⟨↟⟩●●

+ Lava righthand points
+ Empty line-ups
+ Discovery potential
+ Unique, volcanic environment

− Inconsistent summers
− Lack of winter daylight
− Zero equipment available
− Expensive destination

THORLI

GEORG HILMARSSON

With 4970kms of coastline to explore, Iceland presents a rare opportunity to surf virgin waves in an incredible landscape, yet most Icelandic surfers only ride around the Reykjanes peninsula, close to Reykjavik in the SW. Most of the waves break over volcanic reef or basalt rocks like Thorli, a popular choice with a defined paddling channel that works in the colder N winds. Many locals learn to surf at lower latitudes in higher temperatures, then bring back boards and thick wetsuits for Icelandic conditions, which are usually best in autumn.

GREAT LAKES USA/CANADA

●●●●●●●●●●◉⟨↟⟩●●

+ Unique freshwater experience
+ Rare crowds
+ Quality surf possible
+ Great local camaraderie

− Inconsistent
− Ice and thick rubber
− Long drives required
− Private access to some breaks

STONEY POINT

SETH TYLER

The five Great Lakes make up the biggest lake system on Earth, containing six quadrillion gallons, or one fifth of the world's freshwater. Their total shoreline extends for some 10,900 miles (17,549km), more than the US West and East coasts combined! The sheer size and concomitant fetch of these lakes explain the presence of surprisingly large, surfable waves with the right weather conditions. Despite poor consistency (about 10 surfable days per month in season) and often inhospitable conditions, there are more freshwater surfers joining the line-ups each year.

ERICEIRA PORTUGAL

●●●●●■●●●●●●①●●

+ **Super-consistent**
+ **Concentration of spots**
+ **World-class reefs and points**
+ **Relatively cheap Euro destination**

– **Few sheltered breaks**
– **Limited wind options**
– **Cool water year-round**
– **Crowded Coxos**

COXOS

RICARDO BRAVO

Ericeira has no shortage of Atlantic swell to play with. Numerous classic reef set-ups, rocky headlands and small rivermouth bays shape the swells into world-class waves such as Coxos, Ribeira d'Ilhas and Pedra Branca. Ericeira can be considered the centre of Portuguese surfing with its concentration of awesome breaks a mere 30km from Lisbon. It doesn't quite have the wind protection of Peniche and big, stormy swells tend to favour the south-facing coast of Lisbon, but for consistent quality and challenging waves, Ericeira rules.

CLOUD 9
LAT. 9.813958° LONG. 126.167131°

JS CALLAHAN/SURFEXPLORE

Cloud Nine is a perfect, top to bottom, barrelling peak that's short but sweet when the conditions align. Ideal swell direction is NE, as too much E tends to by-pass Cloud 9 a bit and focus on the adjacent reef of Quicksilver, while too much N can slam it shut. Higher tides also improve makeability as the coral lurks challengingly close to the open air. W wind holds up the coveted rights nicely and although the lefts are shorter, they are just as hollow off the peak, before quickly shutting down. Sucks in the swell and can handle pretty large faces before maxing out. Confident, nimble, experienced surfers will love it, while intermediates may struggle. The annual pro contest is a big event for Siargao, when it is a good time to visit for the party and pageantry, but not for getting shacked at Crowd 9! Lots of new accommodation has been built, including cheap or fancy resort options.

  # SIARGAO PHILIPPINES

●●●●●■●●●●●①●●

+ **World-class reefs**
+ **Plenty of uncrowded spots**
+ **Cheap living costs**
+ **Tropical conditions**

– **Generally small surf**
– **Long flat spells**
– **Long transfer journey**
– **Political instability**

Perfectly positioned as close to the plummeting depths of the Philippine Trench as possible, Siargao represents the highest concentration of good surf to be found in the 7,107 islands of the archipelago. There are a number of world-class reefs on the 27km of coastline exposed to swell, where many of the spots are outside reefs and islets that can only be accessed by boat, while others break closer to the beach on a fringing reef. General Luna is a good place to be based during the SW monsoon and Pilar is better during the NE trades.

October

ASTURIAS SPAIN

+ Epic left rivermouth
+ Consistent year-round swells
+ Many exposed beachbreaks
+ Lower crowds away from Rodiles

− Wet and windy
− Cold winter water
− Steep, slow access roads
− Crowded summers

RODILES

WILLY URIBE

In Asturias, the mountains run close to the coast, which means a much more rugged coastline than both Cantabria and the Basque Country. It has steep cliffs and very difficult access. However, there are also some excellent beachbreaks, many of which face west and are unaffected by the NE sea breezes that blow during summer. A few spots only come into their own during the larger swells of winter, including the regional classic Rodiles. Asturias is less consistent than those areas further west and a good place to visit during autumn.

KERALA & TAMIL NADU

+ Consistent swells
+ Countless virgin spots
+ Warm, tropical water
+ Laid back and cheap

− Small, onshore, closed-out beachbreaks
− Filthy, shitty water & beaches
− Long distances between spots
− Monsoon rains & appalling poverty

LIGHTHOUSE BEACH

JELLE RIGOLE

Western India presents one of the most significant, unexplored coastlines touched by the Indian Ocean. Swells are surprisingly consistent, although wave quality suffers because there's so much shallow nearshore water, endless shifting sands and frequent onshores during the SW monsoon, which coincides with the swell season. There is undoubtedly potential for year-round, decent size beachbreaks and some smaller, playful pointbreaks with no crowds except at the popular breaks and artificial reef at Kovalam.

RHODE ISLAND USA

+ Consistent winter swells
+ Fall hurricane surf
+ Spot diversity
+ Scenic New England

− Cold water
− Windy
− Summer flat spells
− Some crowds

RUGGLES

MEZ/ESM

Rhode Island may well be the smallest state in the USA, but with over 640km of coastline and 100+ beaches have earned it the nickname "the Ocean State". Narragansett Bay, a 48km long arm of the Atlantic Ocean splits the state in two parts. To the west are sand spits, barrier beaches, lagoons and salt ponds, while low rounded hills compose the landscape to the east. There's a good concentration of surf spots with cobblestone reefs helping to groom the lines of swell into nice defined peaks, plus the awesome Ruggles rights.

CÔTE BASQUE FRANCE

PARLEMENTIA

LAUREN MASUREL

+ Good variety of consistent waves
+ Stunning mountain backdrop
+ Beginner or big-wave zone
+ Cultural interests

− Wet climate year-round
− Pollution and crowds in summer
− Cold water in winter
− Expensive

The Côte Basque shares many characteristics with the north-facing Spanish coast and is blessed with some decent submarine geology. Slabs of reef dot the coast, focusing some of the most organised and unadulterated swell trains into scary, big-wave arenas at tow-in spots like Belharra and Avalanche. There are also coves, headlands and the Anglet jetties, offering wind protection unseen on the beaches to the north. Famous reefs like Guéthary and Lafitenia can turn on any time of year, attracting crowds from far and wide, especially when the beaches are maxed-out.

SEBASTIAN INLET
LAT. 27.862136° LONG. -80.445734°

MES/ESM

CENTRAL FLORIDA USA

+ Endless miles of beaches
+ Easy waves
+ Classic hurricane swells
+ Tourism heaven

− Small windchop waves
− Major spots crowded
− Pay to park
− High shark bite factor

Florida's most famous wave is undoubtedly one of its best and most reliable. It is situated on the northern side of the long jetty that protects the man-made entrance to the estuary waters of the Indian River. There are three main breaks: *First Peak* is a righthander that uses the rock-and-timber jetty formation to peel down the line. Side wash off the jetty can make it wedge, jack up, and barrel down towards the *Second Peak*, which can offer a left, depending on swell direction. *Third Peak*, further north of the jetty, provides fast, hollow lefts when the swell has some N. Best tide is low to mid incoming, but it will break through to high, unless it's small, in which case the backwash takes over. Hazards include sharks, man-o-war, rocks near the jetty, aggressive fishermen on the jetty and a zillion talented surfers alongside the jetty who, like local champ Kelly, are extremely competitive.

Florida is often the focus of the surf scene on the US East Coast thanks to a semi-tropical, year-round climate and a culture dedicated to leisure. The lack of swell, poor sandbanks and generally mushy conditions that occur most of the time are quickly forgotten when a hurricane brings powerful lines of swell to form classic waves at a few spots. The centrally located 'Space Coast' cradles such famous locations as Sebastian Inlet and Cocoa Beach, notorious for small waves, big surf shops and being the home of the greatest surfer ever – Kelly Slater!

October

DA NANG VIETNAM

● ● ● ● ● ● ● ● ● ● (❄) ● ●

+ Reliable seasonal windswell
+ Soft, empty beachbreaks
+ Discovery potential
+ Exotic, warm and friendly

– Small disorganised waves
– No known reefbreaks
– Short surf season
– Heavy rain and humidity

NON NUOC BEACH

JS CALLAHAN/SURF EXPLORE

Anyone who's seen the movie Apocalypse Now will already know that there is surf in Vietnam. Although the surfing scenes were shot in the Philippines, the reality is that US soldiers have surfed China Beach probably since the '60s. China Beach hosted Vietnam's first International Surfing Competition in 1992, when kids were taught to surf and 15 boards were left behind to create the Da Nang surf club. South China Sea surf only breaks four months of the year and when it does, beginners and longboarders will make the most of the small, glassy reforms.

BRITTANY FRANCE

● ● ● ● ● ● ● ● ● ● (↑) ● ●

+ Wide swell window
+ Multi-aspect coastline
+ Unspoiled Crozon peninsula
+ Rugged, scenic beauty

– Windswept region
– Cold and rainy
– Summer crowds
– Extreme tidal ranges

POINTE DE DINAN

KRISTEN PELOU

With 1500km of coastline, Brittany juts out to sea and provides variety in its coastal structure. The south-facing Atlantic shoreline has large bays, long peninsulas and low-lying land, while the north shore is characterised by high cliffs and deep, narrow, indented estuaries. Finistère combines all these features, while the dramatic tidal range, fierce storms and strict coastal development laws, leave long stretches of untouched coast. Accessible spots will be crowded in small and clean conditions, but there remains ample space for the growing surf population.

SANTA CATARINA BRAZIL

● ● ● ● ● ● ● ● ● ● (↑) ● ●

+ Great consistency
+ Wide range of spots
+ Tropical scenery
+ Safe and developed area

– Relatively crowded
– Local drop ins
– Cool water
– Wet climate

SILVEIRA

FLAVIO VIDIGAL

It is the deep south of Brazil that offers the best surf in the country, with bigger swells and more coastal variations than the N. While Parana and Rio Grande do Sul States have good potential, Santa Catarina Island, facing ESE, is definitely the best option. This island destination is commonly referred to as Florianopolis, which is actually the capital city of Santa Catarina State. It is a great destination, with a concentration of 20 breaks covering a 225° swell window, plus further south are the quality spots around Guarda, Garopaba and Imbituba.

CORNWALL ENGLAND

+ North wind protection
+ Handles large swells
+ Good reefbreaks
+ Easy access

– Cold water
– Cool and wet climate
– Crowds
– Pollution

PORTHLEVEN

For travelling English speaking surfers, a European surfari will usually begin in England. No language barriers and the international transport links that London provides, are the main reasons, but what many surfers fail to realise is England receives waves on all its coasts. Cornwall is the most consistent surfing area in the far southwest where year-round swells batter a mixture of small, rocky bays and long, sandy beaches. A system of coastal paths runs the entire length of the Cornish coast, offering extensive views of the beaches reefs, and points.

SUPERTUBOS
LAT. 39.345503° LONG. -9.365033°

The name speaks for itself! World-class spot and undoubtedly the best beachbreak in Portugal, Supertubos has become a favourite stop on the world pro tour and a perfect warm-up for Pipeline. Long, heavy, gas-filled tubes are guaranteed as well as a few close-outs, such is the speed of this technically difficult, board-snapping wave. The lefts are usually better, but plenty of shorter rights peel off the main peak, especially in NW conditions. It's at its best with NE winds, a decent SW swell and mid-tide, but these conditions don't come around everyday. There can be a few lesser peaks further along the beach to help dilute the concentration of bodyboarders and local tube-seekers, but there's no escaping the mega crowds or the foul smell from the nearby fish factory. Easy parking in front of the break, but theft from vehicles is commonplace.

PENICHE PORTUGAL

+ Wide swell window
+ Flexible wind and swell combos
+ Quality beach and reefbreaks
+ Relatively cheap Euro destination

– Summer onshores
– Increasingly crowded
– Cool water year-round
– Sardine factory stink!

The major fishing town of Peniche is not the prettiest spot on the Portuguese coast, but it's probably the most renowned surfing area in the country. Originally an island, Peniche became one with the mainland and now contains an obscene amount of wave variety that can provide the goods in almost any conditions. Most famous is Supertubos, regarded by many as one of Europe's best beachbreaks and annual pro contest venue. Peniche is a year-round destination with plenty of small swell exposure on the north side of town and shelter on the south.

November

WESTERN SAHARA

●●●●●●●●●●○ (↑) ●

+ Consistent winter conditions
+ Epic, empty right pointbreaks
+ Kitesurf and fishing hotspot
+ Desert beauty and wildlife

− Mostly windy conditions
− Remote surf spots
− Chilly desert conditions
− 4WD rental necessary

SECRET SPOT

JS CALLAHAN/SURF EXPLORE

When Spain pulled out in 1976, Western Sahara was occupied by troops from Morocco, who have controlled the region since then, treating it as a de facto southern province. The displaced Republic Sahrawi leadership (Polisario), remain in exile in Algeria, pending a UN referendum on future independence. Security conditions in the country are currently quiet and the coast is open to adventurous, well-equipped, foreign tourists who will find endless beachbreaks on the corniche of Laâyoune and a myriad of right points around the dusty desert towns of Dakhla and Nouadhibou.

HUAHINE & RAIATEA FRENCH POLYNESIA

●●●●●●●●●●● (⊙) ●

+ Year-round swell
+ Powerful reef passes
+ Postcard scenery
+ All types of accommodation

− Fierce localism
− Reef pass dangers
− Difficult access
− Very expensive trip

FARÉ RIGHT

JOLI

Raiatea is considered the traditional center of French Polynesia's religion and culture, where many voyages of Pacific discovery started. The surf spots are more remote and quality is highly dependent on swell direction and wind exposure. Huahine is smaller, but boasts a number of quality reef passes including the matching pair of Fare Left and Fare Right, the region's most surfed waves. They work on a wide swell window, all tides, E trades and it's possible to paddle from land, plus there are some fun reforms on the beach for the kids and beginners.

GOWER PENINSULA WALES

●●●●●●●●●●● (↑) ●

+ Diversity of reefs and beaches
+ Multiple wind options
+ Many easy waves
+ Scenic and culturally rich area

− Cold water and air
− Tight swell window
− Many inconsistent spots
− Windy and crowded

LANGLAND BAY

PHIL HOLDEN

Gower was the first area in the UK to be officially recognised an "area of outstanding natural beauty". This small peninsula projecting into the Bristol Channel has over 20 bays and sheltered coves along its rugged coastline. From long, expansive strands to tiny inlets, this stretch of coast provides a wide variety of breaks, combining endless wind options with good swell exposure. Surfing started in Wales in the early 1960s and took-off at spots such as Langland and Llangennith, which remain the focal points of Welsh surf today.

COSTA VERDE PERU

+ Highly consistent swell
+ Great spot density
+ Easy access and cheap
+ Lima entertainment

− Not Peru's best surf
− Cold water
− Coastal winter fog
− City crowds and pollution

LA HERRADURA

GONZALO BARANDIARAN

Peru's surf culture goes way back to the 'Totora reed horses' ridden since 1000BC and more recently, Felipe Pomar's world title victory in 1965. A true surf city, Lima was first surfed in the mid 1920's, as a dedicated group of riders formed the Waikiki Club in Miraflores, one of the first three surf clubs in the world. Peru's capital is constantly outgrowing its boundaries, so crowds, noise and pollution are serious issues. Miraflores is perfect for beginners, longboarders and SUP while La Herradura is a more challenging South American left pointbreak.

MUNDAKA
LAT. 43.408915° LONG. -2.695038°

PATRICE TOUHAR

Mundaka is a dream lefthand barrel and possibly the best rivermouth wave in the world. A long triangular sandbank catches the stronger NW swells, creating a long flawless tube with rides of up to 150-200 meters possible. From the peak, the wave sucks up hard, making for steep challenging take-offs straight into a sick barrel section. The ensuing long, fast wall, allows a few turns if you are going close to warp speed. The final two sections of the wave can vary in quality depending on the sandbar, but frequently they offer hollow cylinders with less crowd pressure. Perfect autumn conditions include strong S-SW winds and the tide must be low incoming, otherwise the outgoing rip is horrendous. Good conditions at Mundaka rarely last for more than two days, as the large swells fade, so this classy wave is only rideable about 50 days a year.

PAIS VASCO SPAIN

+ Magical Mundaka
+ Heavy tubing waves
+ Easy access
+ Fabulous scenery

− Lack of wave choice
− Inconsistent
− Windy
− Large tidal range

The Basque Country is the most popular surfing area in Spain and contains a variety of reefs, plenty of good-quality beachbreaks, some big-wave spots and a world-class rivermouth called Mundaka. This area has the most spots that can handle big waves, including one or two still rideable at 20ft. There are also a host of spots surfable in stormy conditions and sheltered from strong W or SW winds. Pais Vasco probably suffers the most from seasonal variability, with larger differences between summer and winter surf. In general, autumn is the best time to visit.

November

OKINAWA JAPAN

+ Epic typhoon swells
+ Subtropical reefbreaks
+ Secret spots and islands
+ Low crime rates

– Flat spring, mostly windswell
– Shallow reefs, no beachbreak
– Mainly high tide spots
– Crowded premier spots

KUDAKA

JS CALLAHAN/SURF EXPLORE

Okinawa is smack dab in the middle of Typhoon Alley, sandwiched between the Pacific Ocean and the East China Sea. This allows for a wealth of spots facing in all directions to pick up virtually any swell going. They break over very shallow shelves of coral reef or basaltic rock, which is why 90% of the spots are mid-to-high tide breaks. Most spots are covered by 2-5ft of water at high tide and there are only two sandy beachbreaks. Crowds are heavy at the main spots, but finding solitude is easy as most of the outer reefs and islands are still uncharted.

IQUIQUE CHILE

+ Very consistent, all year
+ Big, powerful waves
+ Chilled uncrowded atmosphere
+ Perfect climate

– Shallow reefs and urchins
– No mellow waves
– Long journeys
– Monotonous landscape

COLEGIO

GEOFF RAGATZ

Iquique holds a very concentrated stretch of challenging reefbreaks. Most of the waves along this coastline break close to the shore as cylindrical barrels slamming down hard onto shallow reefs full of urchins. It's often big and gnarly and many of the spots are more suitable for bodyboarders or the most skilled of surfers. Fortunately, there are channels, which enable safe paddle outs to most line-ups. When looking at the waves from the shore it's easy to be deceived by the size, what appears to be 4ft (1.5m) is actually 6-8ft (2-2.5m)!

TERCEIRA AZORES

+ 360° swell window
+ Epic Santa Catarina
+ Empty big wave spots
+ Beautiful landscapes

– Short-lived, disorganised swells
– E-facing spots need big swells
– Rapidly changing conditions
– Heavy waves, rocks and boulders

SANTA CATARINA

DAN HAYLOCK

Only the very tallest undersea mountains manage to break the surface of the empty Atlantic Ocean. The nine volcanic peaks of the Azores are all alone, almost equidistant from North America and Europe, with a full 360° swell window, right in the centre lane of the trans-Atlantic swell highway. Terceira means "3rd island", is circular in shape and a lot of the coast is inhospitable cliffs plunging into deep water, but when the big winter swells wrap down the east coast reefs, world-class waves appear for a small, dedicated and undoubtedly brave surfing community.

EASTERN SAMAR PHILIPPINES

+ Typhoons and windswells
+ Undiscovered quality breaks
+ Warm and tropical
+ Cheap and lively

– Erratic swell supply
– Heavy rains
– No tourist infrastructure
– Time consuming travel

PHILIPPINE DREAM

Of the 7,107 islands of the Philippines, Samar is the 3rd largest and divided into three provinces. Northern and Eastern Samar boast some undiscovered surf potential in a province of rough, hilly terrain covered by lush tropical vegetation. Borongan, the provincial capital, sits some 550km east of Manila and travelling in this region is always a long, slow process, especially if it rains. Local Borongan surfers reckon "we haven't even explored 30% of Samar waves" while boat expeditions from Siargao have made discoveries like the Philippine Dream.

MAVERICKS
LAT. 37.492362° LONG. -122.501421°

Pillar Point was a remote, derelict headland just a few years ago, but now, whenever the big swells come barrelling in from the N and W, Mavericks springs to life with armadas of jetskis, boats, helicopters, tripods, cameras, photographers, galleries of spectators and the world's best big-wave surfers. Primarily a right, but the lefts have been ridden by a few brave men. An incredibly hollow, jacking take-off in front of a series of house-sized boulders known as "The Boneyard", leads into a long, mountainous wall ending in a deep channel. Starts to work at 12ft and never closes-out. One of the biggest, scariest waves in the world with heavy currents and lethal rocks on the inside if a set cleans you up. Mavericks has already claimed the lives of big-wave surfer Mark Foo and a kayaker, plus there's been two non-fatal shark attacks. It's a 40min paddle from the harbour to the line-up.

SAN FRANCISCO & SAN MATEO COUNTIES USA

+ High swell consistency
+ Big wave spots
+ Great city attractions
+ Entertainment & nightlife

– Cold water
– Urban crowds
– Shark factor
– Fog and lack of sun

Despite being one of the world's best-loved tourist destinations, San Francisco is often overlooked by travelling surfers, who focus on the warmer water of Southern California or the numerous pointbreaks of Santa Cruz. The surfing media regularly ignores the city breaks, although this is definitely not the case with Mavericks, North America's prime big wave arena. Every winter, paddle-in or tow-in acts of bravado remind us that one of the heaviest breaks on the planet lies less than 48km away from the famous Golden Gate Bridge.

November

BLACK SEA TURKEY

+ Two different swell directions
+ No tides
+ Totally virgin
+ Istanbul, culture and snow resorts

– Inconsistent, short-lived swells
– Gutless small waves
– Cold and wet winter climate
– Lack of tourist infrastructure

KALESI REEF

There's a huge contrast between bustling Istanbul and rural Turkey, where most families own just a tractor and the roads are clear. Turkey is one of the few places where you actually surf in semi-fresh water, which greatly reduces buoyancy. Saltwater comes from the Mediterranean via the Bosphorus and the Sea of Marmara, whilst freshwater pours in from the bordering countries. Like bore-riders and lake surfers the world over, adjust your board accordingly. The winding coastal road from Erikli to Sinop reveals vast potential for untouched, empty waves.

MARTINIQUE

+ Good righthand reef set-ups
+ Consistent Tartane breaks
+ Summer bodyboard action
+ Safe tourist haven

– Seasonal North swells
– Onshore trade winds
– Some crowded spots
– Poisonous manchineel trees

PLAGE DES SURFEURS

Martinique lies in the heart of the Caribbean and its southern shores are highly regarded by tourists seeking picture perfect beaches, leaving surfers to focus on the northern and eastern coastline, ideally exposed to winter's North Atlantic swell. Volcanic and coral reefs pepper the island plus the southern beaches provide a summer swell bodyboard option. The waves are concentrated on the unusually protruding Caravelle Peninsula, allowing for offshores on a windblown east coast that is freckled with near-shore islets, cays and reefs.

NORTHERN BAJA MEXICO

+ Quality right pointbreaks
+ Consistent winter swells
+ Year-round destination
+ Cheap tacos, Mexican beer & tequila

– Lack of lefthanders
– Surprisingly cold water
– USA style crowds
– Basic accommodation

SECRET SPOT

Baja constitutes the major getaway for Californian waveriders, who jump in the 4X4 and drive the Mex1 Highway south, looking for countless, quality, righthand pointbreaks and cheaper, simpler living. There is no need to drive too far, since Baja Norte has all the prerequisites to satisfy the intermediate to expert surfers. The highway hugs the coast down to Ensenada, helping Northern Baja resemble a hybrid of line-ups north of the border, sharing the same crowds, cool water and south-facing coves that wrap the winter NW swells onto cobble and reef.

EASTERN PENINSULAR MALAYSIA

CHERATING

+ Frequent NE monsoon swells
+ Plenty of mellow beachbreaks
+ Small and friendly local surf population
+ Cheap and safe country

− Short, rainy swell season
− Mainly messy windswell
− Lack of reefbreaks
− Murky monsoon waters

Peninsular Malaysia abuts the South China Sea on the east and fringes the Straits of Malacca on the west coast. The east coast comprises of mainly sandy beaches (91%) exposed to South China swells from the N and E. These exposed beachbreaks seemingly work best in the early monsoon season, when the sand bars have built up during flat summers. The weirdest fact about Malaysian locals is that most of them have learned to surf at Sunway Lagoon, a wave pool in a major water-park west of Kuala Lumpur.

MALIBU
LAT. 34.032090° LONG. -118.678089°

One of the world's most famous and most crowded righthand pointbreaks. Mainly a summertime spot best on S swells. Three separate take-off zones: Third Point: at medium tide, fast, hollow rides off the northernmost point. Big swells will connect up with Second Point: long, hollow, workable wall at medium tide, unmakeable at low. First Point: the most consistent and therefore the most surfed of the Malibu waves. Can show perfect shape, excellent for any type of surf craft. Works through the full tidal range, getting hollower as the tide drops. Mega crowds is putting it mildly. Regular beach closures due to bacterial pollution from outdated, ill-located septic tanks that leak directly into the Malibu Lagoon after heavy rainfall, before flooding the line-up, leaving surfers with eye and ear infections, respiratory illnesses and rashes.

LOS ANGELES USA

+ Legendary Malibu
+ Consistent, diverse surf spots
+ Entertainment LA style
+ Great weather

− Mainly beachbreaks
− Uber crowds
− Bacterial pollution
− Hell-A traffic

A sprawling metropolis with a population of approximately 10 million people, Los Angeles is home to movie stars, extravagant homes, 12-lane freeways and nearly 96km of Pacific Coast beaches. Among the surf spots of California's largest city, none can claim to be as famous as Malibu and its long righthanders breaking beside the coastal Highway 1. Tom Blake pioneered the break in 1926, but Malibu's fame really took off in the late '50s and early '60s when a movie based on a Malibu surfer girl, Gidget, was presenting surfing to the mainstream.

December

KAUAI HAWAII

+ Year-round swells
+ Hawaiian power
+ Variety of coastline
+ Hawaiian surf culture

− Protective locals
− High local prices
− Rainy and windy
− Sharks

HANALEI BAY

SYLVAIN CAZENAVE

Known as the "The Garden Island", Kauai is an ancient and deeply eroded extinct volcano, rising 5000m (15,250ft) above the sea floor. There are more sandy beaches than many other islands and nearly 45% of its coastline is virtually deserted. Despite having over 300 surf spots, underwater topography is, allegedly, not as ideal as Oahu. High volcanic cliffs line the North Shore, reducing options, plus the inaccessibility of the Na Pali coast makes it very dangerous to find and ride the few spots that face the brunt of the winter swells.

SARDINIA ITALY

+ Fairly consistent surf
+ Spots facing a variety of directions
+ Mellow crowds
+ Historical and cultural sites

− Windy conditions
− Short-lived swells
− Cold winter conditions
− Tough access

SA MESA

GECKO

Italy is hardly the most popular of surf destinations, yet the dominant NW Mistral wind blows with such regularity and power that Sardinia really does get good waves. Sardinia is able to pick up swells from a full 360° swell window and host the largest, most challenging and consistent waves in the tideless Med. Sardinia is blessed with some great reefs and points on the west coast where the NW winds blow hard, but don't necessarily destroy the southwest-facing spots. Winter is guaranteed some regular action while autumn and spring can also be good.

PUERTO RICO

+ Consistently offshore
+ Quality pointbreaks
+ Warm, powerful waves
+ Easy access

− Windy
− Heavy crowds and locals
− Lots of tourists and traffic
− Pollution/sewage problems

TRES PALMAS

FITZPATRICK/SURFCARIBE.COM

Puerto Rico is to Florida what Hawaii is to California. It gets big, it's exotic, and it has fierce locals. Located in what is regarded as the best corner of the Caribbean for surf, Puerto Rico's premier surf spots are found on the northwest corner of the island. A deep-water trench offshore (the second deepest in the world) means N-NE swells hit the north shore with little loss in size and power, however it's often onshore and right next to the capital, San Juan. Most spots break on flat reefs of coral and lava.

HAINAN CHINA

+ China's best surf
+ Quality left pointbreaks
+ Consistent during NE monsoon
+ Very warm water and tropical

– Pollution
– Average beachbreaks
– Rare typhoon swells
– Difficult travel without guide

MAIN LEFT, RIYUE BAY

Hainan's eastern coastline is exposed to consistent NE monsoon swells and seasonal typhoon swells from within the South China Sea basin. The surf potential is still relatively unexplored, with hundreds of beaches and consistent left points. Long stretches of sand are divided by occasional headlands, with a backdrop of volcanic mountains. The pointbreaks have been ridden by visiting foreign surfers for decades and recently a small, but growing mix of Chinese and expat local surfers. The waves have been deemed good enough to hold top-level ASP contests at Riyue Bay.

P-PASS
LAT. 6.981970° LONG. 158.128000°

POHNPEI MICRONESIA

+ North Pacific & typhoon swells
+ Warm, crystal clear water
+ P-Pass perfection
+ Safe, politically stable and clean

– Inconsistent N swells
– Occasional crowds & rips
– Extremely rainy
– Very expensive trip

Late take-offs, fast down-the-line rides, and hollow barrels are what most surfed spots offer and the best of them is P-Pass (Palikir Pass). This wave has become the star of the Western Pacific by occasionally churning out impossibly perfect righthand pits, attracting pros and chargers to this remote island when the forecast looks right. It takes any swell from W-NE, with straight N being the best direction to avoid close-outs from the NW or missing the reef from the NE. P-Pass works with no winds or with light NE-E trades, which blow dead offshore as the swell lines wrap around the reef. These rights can be surfed at any tide, but it does get very shallow on a full low tide. Intermediates will enjoy the fun, consistent, headhigh, high tide sessions while pros will tackle the scary, rare, double-overhead, super-sucky days. It's a 20min boat ride from Kolonia, which is a long flight from anywhere.

Pohnpei is often confused with the ancient Italian city of Pompei, rather than a speck in the Pacific, forming part of the Federated States of Micronesia. The entire island is the tip of an extinct shield volcano made up of black basalt rock, surrounded by a deep lagoon up to 8km wide, circled by many linear, patch and pinnacle reefs. Pohnpei sits in the middle of the "Pool", the warmest ocean temperatures in the world and the media have frenzied over photos depicting the smoking barrels of P-Pass, generally considered as the best wave in Micronesia.

December

MADEIRA

●●●●●●●●●●●●● (🏄)

+ Big-wave spots
+ Spectacular mountain scenery
+ No crowds
+ Idyllic climate

− Inconsistent
− Few beaches and surf spots
− Dangerous entry and exit to the surf
− Relatively pricey

JARDIM DO MAR
ROGER SHARP

Sitting all alone in the Atlantic, around 550km west of the Moroccan city of Casablanca, Madeira stands defiantly in the way of any swell coming out of the Nth Atlantic. It is an extremely picturesque island, rising sheer out of the ocean and most of the coastline is made up of plunging cliffs, lava rocks and boulders. If the swell is less than 4-6ft then there is nowhere to surf, but once the surf picks up, it will hold as big as the Atlantic can throw at the bouldered right and left points.

GRANDE TERRE GUADELOUPE

●●●●●●●●●●●●● (🏄)

+ Consistent windswells
+ Long west coast rights
+ Small easy waves
+ Laid back Caribbean atmosphere

− Sloppy onshore waves
− School crowds
− Tourist development
− Pricey

ANSE SALABOUELLE
PIERRE DE CHAMPS

Guadeloupe is one of the east Caribbean's most consistent surf destinations. As well as regular trade wind swell it also receives N swell produced by cold fronts moving off the US East Coast in winter. Like Barbados the waves are often windy and rarely get bigger than 8ft (2.5m). French-governed Guadeloupe consists of two main islands, Grande Terre and Basse Terre, joined in the middle, which viewed from above, reveals a butterfly shape. Grande Terre has the majority of the surf spots while Basse Terre only gets surf from S and W hurricane swells.

GALAPAGOS ISLANDS

●●●●●●●●●●●●● (🏄)

+ Powerful reefbreaks
+ Waves year-round
+ Uncrowded
+ Wildlife mecca

− Inconsistent
− Cool water
− Few easy access spots
− Expensive

TONGO REEF
PAUL KENNEDY

These 17 isolated, oceanic oases have been declared a national park and only five of the Galapagos Islands are inhabited. The coastal fringe is made up of lava reefs and boulders, because the water is too cold for coral formation. Some islands don't have that many good spots thanks to steep and broken up lava outcrops, while other islands like San Cristobal have a concentration of top quality waves in a small area. Waves jack up suddenly out of deep water and have plenty of power, drawing the odd comparison with Hawaii.

CENTRAL ITALY

+ Santa Marinella quality reefs
+ Mediterranean climate
+ Great food and wines
+ Breathtaking cultural attractions

− Mostly inconsistent spots
− Potential crowds when good
− Often onshore / very windy
− Pollution and urchins

BANZAI

EMILIANO CATALDI

Few surfers would have guessed it, but Italy actually receives regular waves, sometimes as high as double overhead. Winter low pressure systems, cross the Iberian Peninsula from the Atlantic or form up in the western Med and tuned-in surfers then track the storm, hoping for strong onshore winds to blow hard and long enough to bring swell to the Italian coastline. The Lazio coast receives these swells from a full 180° window, anytime from autumn through winter to spring, with the closest spots sitting a mere 30min from Rome.

BERNARD TESTEMALE

PIPELINE/BACKDOOR
LAT. 21.664939° LONG. -158.053075°

The most famous peak on the planet explodes onto an uneven, lava-slab reef a scant 80m offshore, forming the benchmark by which all other waves are measured. The left at Pipe is best awakened by W swells that filter and reform over the outer reefs, focusing energy and extra height on the peak, before abruptly releasing a lip that guillotines mercilessly along the first section, until the explosion of spit heralds the shoulder. When the swell direction heads beyond NW, Backdoor swings open and welcomes the best tube-jockeys to an expansive room, but the door often slams shut on this ultra-shallow, incongruous reef. Air drops are the only way in if you want the inside at Backdoor and ideal conditions include mid tide, ESE wind and headhigh to double-overhead faces. The legion of hazards is eclipsed by one defining factor - the crowd.

OAHU NORTH SHORE HAWAII

+ The proving ground
+ 7 Mile Miracle
+ Mythical surf culture
+ Great spectator arena

− Dangerous surfing conditions
− Amazing crowd pressures
− Not suitable for beginners
− Expensive

There is no denying that the North Shore of Oahu is surfing's Mecca. Its undisputed attractions challenge every surfer on the planet to find out if they have got what it takes. Conquering the fear of dropping into a bomb at Pipe, or paddling over the edge of a Waimea cliff represent the zenith of the surfing experience. Thousands make the pilgrimage every year to the Hawaiian Islands, including all the professional surfers for the Dec Pipeline Masters, when it becomes a major achievement to snag a wave off the hungry pack.

December

TEL AVIV ISRAEL

+ Good jetty sandbanks
+ Historical sites
+ Top quality hotels
+ Unusual place to surf

– Inconsistent mushy waves
– Crowded line-ups
– Parking hassles
– Fairly expensive

HILTON
BEN RAK

The Middle East is the only part of the mid-latitudes where surfing has never taken off. Israel, on the eastern Mediterranean coast, may seem an odd place to surf, having never been known for its consistency or quality. It's not the place you'd go for a hard-core surf trip, where rideable swell is by no means guaranteed, so a blend of patience and luck is a must. However, in this land where western civilisation began, there is no shortage of cultural diversions to while away the time during flat spells.

KAVIENG PAPUA NEW GUINEA

+ Consistent, seasonal swells
+ Clean, tropical waves
+ Uncrowded, perfect surf
+ Short idyllic boat rides

– Lack of power and size
– Very rainy surf season
– Difficult and expensive access
– High malaria risks

NEW IRELAND
ANDREW SHIELD

Papua New Guinea may rank as the world's 2nd largest island, but some of the best waves in the country break on tiny coral specks scattered throughout the Bismarck Archipelago. Decidedly Melanesian in flavour, it is these islands, bearing unlikely European names such as New Britain, New Ireland and New Hanover that hold the best potential for maximizing the power of any available WNW to ENE swells. Kavieng is the main town and jump off point for the islands that nestle not too far offshore, where idyllic tropical settings frame some pretty Pacific peelers.

NW LUZON PHILIPPINES

+ Consistent NE monsoon swell
+ Occasional SW typhoon swell
+ Many uncrowded breaks
+ Cheap living costs

– Small size waves
– Some Manilla crowds
– Natural and social disasters
– Sex tourism

CAR-RILLE POINT
JS CALLAHAN/SURF EXPLORE

Northwest Luzon is outlined by a beautiful coastline, airbrushed by constant offshores and lucky enough to pick up the wrapping NE swells on the South China Sea side of the archipelago. US airmen have been surfing Mona Liza Point in La Union since the early '70s, paving the way for surf resorts like Badoc to set up on a few of the offshore islands. If long, cruisey pointbreaks are your thing, then Urbitzondo, Mona Liza and Car-rille are sure to impress, cementing this coast's reputation as a longboarder's favourite.

ALGARVE PORTUGAL

●●●●●●●●●●● (👤)

+ Large choice of breaks
+ Reefs and beaches
+ Wide swell window
+ Warmest European climate

– No world-class spots
– Growing crowds and surf schools
– West coast onshores
– Cool water

CORDOAMA

The Algarve is an intoxicating mix of Atlantic and Mediterranean influences, where a gently undulating mesh of forests and fields, borders an undeveloped coastline of high cliffs and long empty beaches scattered with rocks. It might lack some of the wave quality of Peniche and Ericeira, yet attracts ever-increasing numbers of foreign surfers escaping from the icy winters of northern Europe. Sagres has the widest swell window in the country receiving both big, wrapping, winter NW plus occasional SE windswells, fanned by regular offshores on the south coast.

SOUP BOWL
LAT. 13.215318° LONG. -59.521318°

Famous east coast right, full of power and intensity, combining vertical drops, thick barrels and big shut down sections that continue to work in the regular onshore trade winds. Kelly Slater puts Soup Bowl in his "top three waves in the world" thanks to its "really good curve that allows all sorts of manoeuvres and airs". Winter N swells bring the heavy "Bowls", while a hurricane S direction may provide the fun "Soup" part of the name, yet still holding excellent shape. No matter what direction, this is a wave of consequence as it shifts up the size scale. Some days you do need to be Slater to get a set off the dialled-in local crew, but there's rarely a flat day and average midweek crowds will often be mellow. Another unavoidable constant is the army of urchins nestling among the rocks on the inside reef shelf, along with the omnipresent NE-E trade winds.

BARBADOS

●●●●●●●●●●● (👤)

+ Consistent swells
+ Fun, punchy waves
+ Variety of spots
+ Perfect climate

– Constant trade winds
– Rarity of big swells
– Crowded town breaks
– Relatively expensive

Barbados belongs to the Windward Islands, sitting far to the east of the main Caribbean chain. It has the Caribbean's most consistent surf, since strong, constant trade winds make for reliable, year-round swell on the east coast, while in winter, not so regular N swells light up the north and west coasts. Barbados offers some heavy waves, but it is best suited to the surfer who enjoys chilling-out on the beach and riding fun waves with an idyllic tropical backdrop. Most of the spots break onto flat coral reefs or on beautiful sandy beaches.

BLUE TOMATO
A SHOPPING
PARADISE

Trip Log Map

Where	When	Page no		Where	When	Page no

Where	When	Page no		Where	When	Page no

PARRY ISLANDS

EAST SIBERIAN SEA

BEAUFORT SEA

BAFFIN BAY

GREENLAND

WRANGEL I.

CHUKCHI SEA

VICTORIA ISLAND

BAFFIN ISLAND

ALASKA

BERING SEA

GULF OF ALASKA

Great Bear Lake

Great Slave Lake

HUDSON BAY

LABRADOR SEA

Aleutian Islands (US)

BRITISH COLUMBIA

CANADA

NEWFOUNDLAND & LABRADOR

WASHINGTON

Great Lakes

MAINE

NOVA SCOTIA

OREGON

UNITED

MICHIGAN

NEW YORK

N.H.

MASSACHUSETTS

STATES OF

AMERICA

MD.

DE.

NORTH

PACIFIC

OCEAN

CALIFORNIA

VIRGINIA

NORTH CAROLINA

SOUTH CAROLINA

NORTH

ATLANTIC

OCEAN

MISSISSIPPI

ALABAMA

GEORGIA

TEXAS

LOUISIANA

HAWAII (US)

MEXICO

FLORIDA

GULF OF MEXICO

THE BAHAMAS

PUERTO RICO

VIRGIN ISLANDS (US)

BRITISH VIRGIN ISLANDS (UK)

ANGUILLA

ST KITTS & NEVIS

ANTIGUA & BARBUDA

GUADELOUPE

DOMINICA

MARTINIQUE

ST LUCIA

BARBADOS

GRENADA

CUBA

DOM. REP.

JAMAICA

HAITI

MARSHALL ISLANDS

CARIBBEAN SEA

GUATEMALA

EL SALVADOR

NICARAGUA

ST VINCENT & THE GRENADINES

COSTA RICA

TRINIDAD & TOBAGO

PANAMA

VENEZUELA

GUYANA

SURINAME

FRENCH GUIANA

NAURU

KIRIBATI

COLOMBIA

SOLOMON ISLANDS

TUVALU

Galápagos Islands (Ecuador)

ECUADOR

VANUATU

SAMOA

WALLIS & FUTUNA

AMERICAN SAMOA (US)

TONGA

COOK ISLANDS (NZ)

NIUE

PERU

BRAZIL

ALEDONIA

FIJI

FRENCH POLYNESIA (FR)

PITCAIRN ISLANDS (UK)

Rapa Nui (Chile)

SOUTH

PACIFIC

OCEAN

MAN SEA

NEW ZEALAND

CHILE

URUGUAY

ARGENTINA

FALKLAND ISLANDS (UK)

SOUTH GEORGIA ISLAND (UK)

Trip Log

Where

When

Who

How

Rating

Notes

Gear

Quiver

Where

When

Who

How

Rating

Notes

Gear

Quiver

Where

When

Who

How

Rating

Notes

Gear

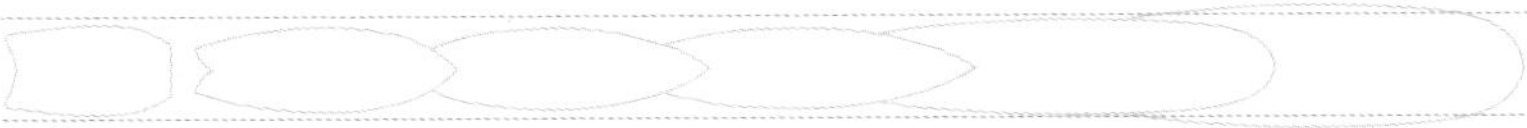

Quiver

Where

When

Who

How

Rating

Notes

Gear

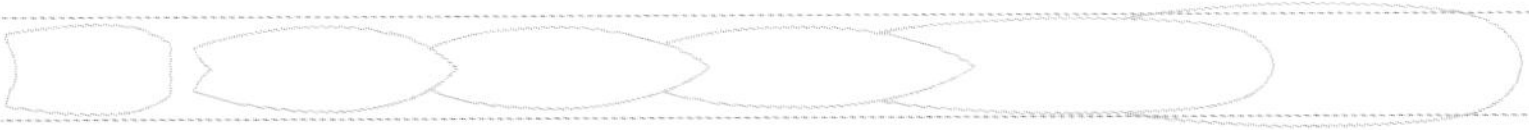

Quiver

Trip Log

Where ....

When ....

Who ....

How ....

Rating ....

Notes ....

....

....

....

....

Gear ....

Quiver

Where ....

When ....

Who ....

How ....

Rating ....

Notes ....

....

....

....

....

Gear ....

Quiver

Where

When

Who

How

Rating

Notes

Gear

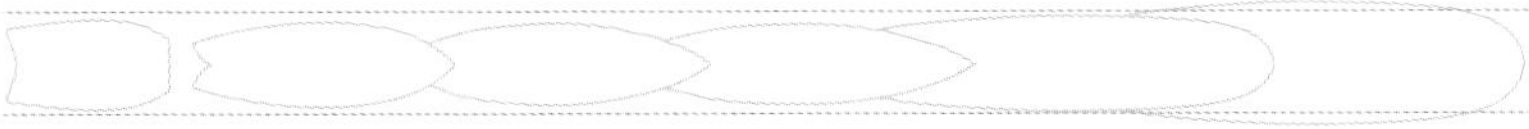

Quiver

Where

When

Who

How

Rating

Notes

Gear

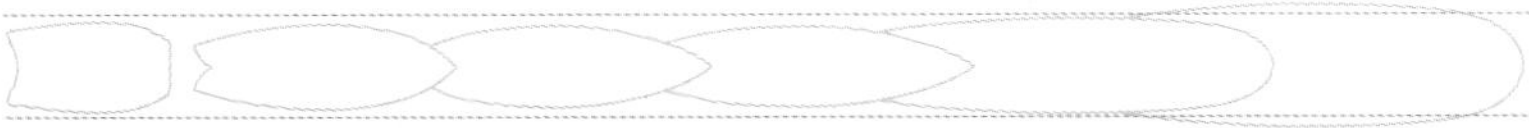

Quiver

Trip Log

Where .... ☆

When .... ☆

Who .... ☆

How .... ☆

Rating .... ☆

Notes .... ☆

.... ☆

.... ☆

....

....

....

Gear

Quiver

Where .... ☆

When .... ☆

Who .... ☆

How .... ☆

Rating .... ☆

Notes .... ☆

.... ☆

.... ☆

....

....

....

Gear

Quiver

Where

When

Who

How

Rating

Notes

Gear

Quiver

Where

When

Who

How

Rating

Notes

Gear

Quiver

Trip Log

Where

When

Who

How

Rating

Notes

Gear

Quiver

Where

When

Who

How

Rating

Notes

Gear

Quiver

☆
☆
☆
☆
☆
☆
☆
☆
☆

Where

When

Who

How

Rating

Notes

Gear

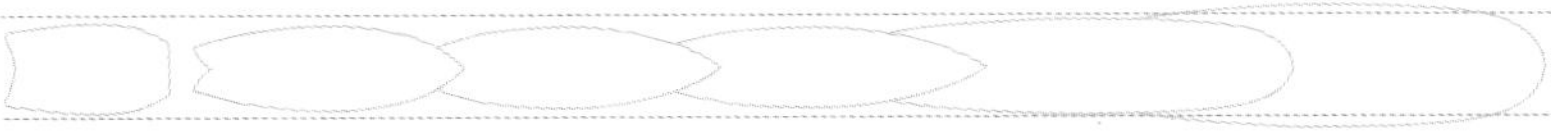

Quiver

☆
☆
☆
☆
☆
☆
☆
☆
☆

Where

When

Who

How

Rating

Notes

Gear

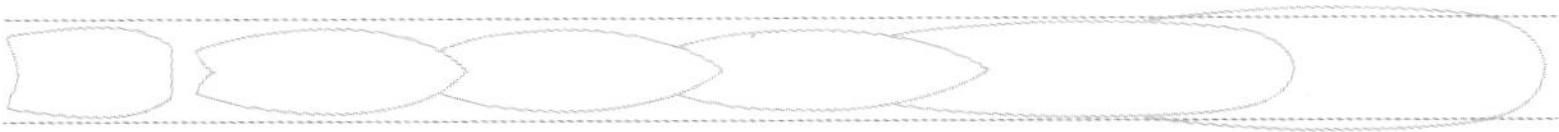

Quiver

Trip Log

Where

When

Who

How

Rating

Notes

Gear

Quiver

Where

When

Who

How

Rating

Notes

Gear

Quiver

Where

When

Who

How

Rating

Notes

Gear

Quiver

Where

When

Who

How

Rating

Notes

Gear

Quiver

Trip Log

Where .... ☆

When .... ☆

Who .... ☆

How .... ☆

Rating .... ☆

Notes .... ☆

.... ☆

.... ☆

....

....

....

Gear ....

Quiver

....

Where .... ☆

When .... ☆

Who .... ☆

How .... ☆

Rating .... ☆

Notes .... ☆

.... ☆

.... ☆

....

....

....

Gear ....

Quiver

Where

When

Who

How

Rating

Notes

Gear

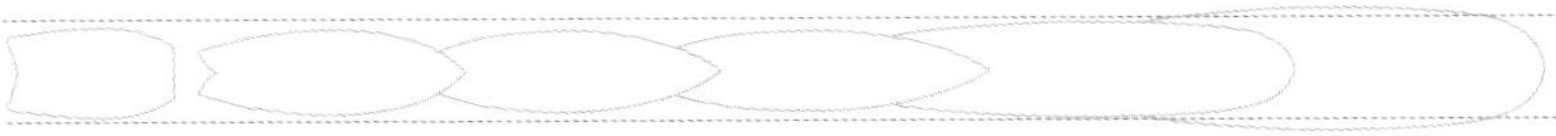

Quiver

Where

When

Who

How

Rating

Notes

Gear

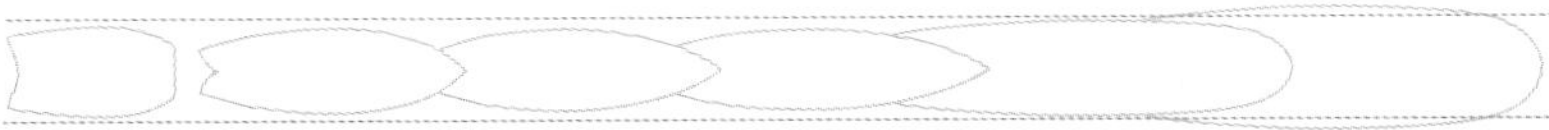

Quiver

Trip Log

Where

When

Who

How

Rating

Notes

Gear

Quiver

Where

When

Who

How

Rating

Notes

Gear

Quiver

☆
☆
☆
☆
☆
☆
☆
☆
☆
☆

Where

When

Who

How

Rating

Notes

Gear

Quiver

☆
☆
☆
☆
☆
☆
☆
☆
☆
☆

Where

When

Who

How

Rating

Notes

Gear

Quiver

Wave Log

/ /20

time

size

swell

wind

tide

crowd

waves

gear

/ /20

time

size

swell

wind

tide

crowd

waves

gear

/ /20

time

size

swell

wind

tide

crowd

waves

gear

/ /20

time

size

swell

wind

tide

crowd

waves

gear

/ /20

time

size

swell

wind

tide

crowd

waves

gear

/ /20

time

size

swell

wind

tide

crowd

waves

gear

Wave Log

/   /20

- time
- size
- swell
- wind
- tide
- crowd
- waves
- gear

/   /20

- time
- size
- swell
- wind
- tide
- crowd
- waves
- gear

/   /20

- time
- size
- swell
- wind
- tide
- crowd
- waves
- gear

WAVE LOG

/ /20

time
size
swell
wind
tide
crowd
waves
gear

/ /20

time
size
swell
wind
tide
crowd
waves
gear

/ /20

time
size
swell
wind
tide
crowd
waves
gear

Wave Log

/ /20

⊕ time ....

◯ size ....

⊕ swell ....

⊕ wind ....

◯ tide ....

◯ crowd ....

◯ waves ....

◯ gear ....

/ /20

⊕ time ....

◯ size ....

⊕ swell ....

⊕ wind ....

◯ tide ....

◯ crowd ....

◯ waves ....

◯ gear ....

/ /20

⊕ time ....

◯ size ....

⊕ swell ....

⊕ wind ....

◯ tide ....

◯ crowd ....

◯ waves ....

◯ gear ....

/   /20

☆
☆   time ⊛
☆
☆   size ◯
☆
☆   swell ⊕
☆
☆   wind ⊕
☆
☆   tide ◯
☆
☆   crowd ◯

                                                     waves ◯

                                                     gear ◯

/   /20

☆
☆   time ⊛
☆
☆   size ◯
☆
☆   swell ⊕
☆
☆   wind ⊕
☆
☆   tide ◯
☆
☆   crowd ◯

                                                     waves ◯

                                                     gear ◯

/   /20

☆
☆   time ⊛
☆
☆   size ◯
☆
☆   swell ⊕
☆
☆   wind ⊕
☆
☆   tide ◯
☆
☆   crowd ◯

                                                     waves ◯

                                                     gear ◯

Wave Log

/ /20

time

size

swell

wind

tide

crowd

waves

gear

/ /20

time

size

swell

wind

tide

crowd

waves

gear

/ /20

time

size

swell

wind

tide

crowd

waves

gear

☆
☆
☆   /   /20
☆   time
☆
☆   size
☆
☆   swell
☆
☆   wind
☆
                                     tide

                                     crowd

                                     waves

                                     gear

☆
☆   /   /20
☆   time
☆
☆   size
☆
☆   swell
☆
☆   wind
☆
☆   tide

                                     crowd

                                     waves

                                     gear

☆
☆   /   /20
☆   time
☆
☆   size
☆
☆   swell
☆
☆   wind
☆
☆   tide

                                     crowd

                                     waves

                                     gear

Wave Log

/ /20

time

size

swell

wind

tide

crowd

waves

gear

/ /20

time

size

swell

wind

tide

crowd

waves

gear

/ /20

time

size

swell

wind

tide

crowd

waves

gear

☆
☆
☆
☆
☆
☆
☆
☆
☆
☆

/ /20

time

size

swell

wind

tide

crowd

waves

gear

☆
☆
☆
☆
☆
☆
☆
☆
☆
☆

/ /20

time

size

swell

wind

tide

crowd

waves

gear

☆
☆
☆
☆
☆
☆
☆
☆
☆
☆

/ /20

time

size

swell

wind

tide

crowd

waves

gear

Wave Log

/ /20

- time
- size
- swell
- wind
- tide
- crowd
- waves
- gear

/ /20

- time
- size
- swell
- wind
- tide
- crowd
- waves
- gear

/ /20

- time
- size
- swell
- wind
- tide
- crowd
- waves
- gear

☆
☆
☆
☆
☆
☆
☆
☆
☆
☆

/ /20

time ⊕

size ◯

swell ⊕

wind ⊕

tide ◯

crowd ◯

waves ◯

gear ◯

☆
☆
☆
☆
☆
☆
☆
☆
☆
☆

/ /20

time ⊕

size ◯

swell ⊕

wind ⊕

tide ◯

crowd ◯

waves ◯

gear ◯

☆
☆
☆
☆
☆
☆
☆
☆
☆

/ /20

time ⊕

size ◯

swell ⊕

wind ⊕

tide ◯

crowd ◯

waves ◯

gear ◯

Wave Log

/ /20

- time
- size
- swell
- wind
- tide
- crowd
- waves
- gear

/ /20

- time
- size
- swell
- wind
- tide
- crowd
- waves
- gear

/ /20

- time
- size
- swell
- wind
- tide
- crowd
- waves
- gear

/ /20

time

size

swell

wind

tide

crowd

waves

gear

/ /20

time

size

swell

wind

tide

crowd

waves

gear

/ /20

time

size

swell

wind

tide

crowd

waves

gear

Wave Log

/ /20

- time
- size
- swell
- wind
- tide
- crowd
- waves
- gear

/ /20

- time
- size
- swell
- wind
- tide
- crowd
- waves
- gear

/ /20

- time
- size
- swell
- wind
- tide
- crowd
- waves
- gear

☆ ──────────────────────────────── / /20
☆
☆ ──────────────────────────────── time
☆
☆ ──────────────────────────────── size
☆
☆ ──────────────────────────────── swell
☆
☆ ──────────────────────────────── wind
☆
☆ ──────────────────────────────── tide
☆
crowd

waves

gear

☆ ──────────────────────────────── / /20
☆
☆ ──────────────────────────────── time
☆
☆ ──────────────────────────────── size
☆
☆ ──────────────────────────────── swell
☆
☆ ──────────────────────────────── wind
☆
☆ ──────────────────────────────── tide
☆
crowd

waves

gear

☆ ──────────────────────────────── / /20
☆
☆ ──────────────────────────────── time
☆
☆ ──────────────────────────────── size
☆
☆ ──────────────────────────────── swell
☆
☆ ──────────────────────────────── wind
☆
☆ ──────────────────────────────── tide
☆
crowd

waves

gear

Wave Log

/ /20

time

size

swell

wind

tide

crowd

waves

gear

/ /20

time

size

swell

wind

tide

crowd

waves

gear

/ /20

time

size

swell

wind

tide

crowd

waves

gear

☆
☆
☆
☆
☆
☆
☆
☆
☆
☆

/ /20

time ⊛

size

swell ⊕

wind ⊕

tide ⊖

crowd ◯

waves ◯

gear ◿

☆
☆
☆
☆
☆
☆
☆
☆
☆
☆

/ /20

time ⊛

size

swell ⊕

wind ⊕

tide ⊖

crowd ◯

waves ◯

gear ◿

☆
☆
☆
☆
☆
☆
☆
☆
☆
☆

/ /20

time ⊛

size

swell ⊕

wind ⊕

tide ⊖

crowd ◯

waves ◯

gear ◿

Wave Log

/   /20

- time
- size
- swell
- wind
- tide
- crowd
- waves
- gear

/   /20

- time
- size
- swell
- wind
- tide
- crowd
- waves
- gear

/   /20

- time
- size
- swell
- wind
- tide
- crowd
- waves
- gear

☆
☆
☆
☆
☆
☆
☆
☆
☆
☆

/ /20

time
size
swell
wind
tide
crowd
waves
gear

☆
☆
☆
☆
☆
☆
☆
☆
☆
☆

/ /20

time
size
swell
wind
tide
crowd
waves
gear

☆
☆
☆
☆
☆
☆
☆
☆
☆
☆

/ /20

time
size
swell
wind
tide
crowd
waves
gear

Wave Log

/ ___ /20

- ⊛ time ___
- ◯ size ___
- ⊕ swell ___
- ⊕ wind ___
- ◯ tide ___
- ◯ crowd ___
- ◯ waves ___
- ◑ gear ___

/ ___ /20

- ⊛ time ___
- ◯ size ___
- ⊕ swell ___
- ⊕ wind ___
- ◯ tide ___
- ◯ crowd ___
- ◯ waves ___
- ◑ gear ___

/ ___ /20

- ⊛ time ___
- ◯ size ___
- ⊕ swell ___
- ⊕ wind ___
- ◯ tide ___
- ◯ crowd ___
- ◯ waves ___
- ◑ gear ___

☆
☆
☆
☆
☆
☆
☆
☆
☆
☆

/ /20

time

size

swell

wind

tide

crowd

waves

gear

☆
☆
☆
☆
☆
☆
☆
☆
☆
☆

/ /20

time

size

swell

wind

tide

crowd

waves

gear

☆
☆
☆
☆
☆
☆
☆
☆
☆

/ /20

time

size

swell

wind

tide

crowd

waves

gear

Wave Log

/ /20

- time
- size
- swell
- wind
- tide
- crowd
- waves
- gear

/ /20

- time
- size
- swell
- wind
- tide
- crowd
- waves
- gear

/ /20

- time
- size
- swell
- wind
- tide
- crowd
- waves
- gear

☆
☆
☆
☆
☆
☆
☆
☆
☆
☆

/ /20

time

size

swell

wind

tide

crowd

waves

gear

☆
☆
☆
☆
☆
☆
☆
☆
☆
☆

/ /20

time

size

swell

wind

tide

crowd

waves

gear

☆
☆
☆
☆
☆
☆
☆
☆
☆

/ /20

time

size

swell

wind

tide

crowd

waves

gear

Wave Log

/ /20

- time
- size
- swell
- wind
- tide
- crowd
- waves
- gear

/ /20

- time
- size
- swell
- wind
- tide
- crowd
- waves
- gear

/ /20

- time
- size
- swell
- wind
- tide
- crowd
- waves
- gear

☆
☆
☆
☆
☆
☆
☆
☆
☆
☆

/ /20

time

size

swell

wind

tide

crowd

waves

gear

☆
☆
☆
☆
☆
☆
☆
☆
☆
☆

/ /20

time

size

swell

wind

tide

crowd

waves

gear

☆
☆
☆
☆
☆
☆
☆
☆
☆
☆

/ /20

time

size

swell

wind

tide

crowd

waves

gear

Wave Log

/ /20

- time
- size
- swell
- wind
- tide
- crowd
- waves
- gear

/ /20

- time
- size
- swell
- wind
- tide
- crowd
- waves
- gear

/ /20

- time
- size
- swell
- wind
- tide
- crowd
- waves
- gear

☆
☆
☆
☆
☆
☆
☆
☆
☆
☆

/ /20

time

size

swell

wind

tide

crowd

waves

gear

☆
☆
☆
☆
☆
☆
☆
☆
☆
☆

/ /20

time

size

swell

wind

tide

crowd

waves

gear

☆
☆
☆
☆
☆
☆
☆
☆
☆

/ /20

time

size

swell

wind

tide

crowd

waves

gear

Wave Log

/ /20

⊛ time

○ size

⊕ swell

⊕ wind

⊖ tide

○ crowd

○ waves

◔ gear

/ /20

⊛ time

○ size

⊕ swell

⊕ wind

⊖ tide

○ crowd

○ waves

◔ gear

/ /20

⊛ time

○ size

⊕ swell

⊕ wind

⊖ tide

○ crowd

○ waves

◔ gear

☆
☆
☆
☆   /   /20
☆   time
☆
☆   size
☆
☆   swell
☆
☆   wind

                                                     tide

                                                     crowd

                                                     waves

                                                     gear

☆
☆
☆   /   /20
☆   time
☆
☆   size
☆
☆   swell
☆
☆   wind

                                                     tide

                                                     crowd

                                                     waves

                                                     gear

☆
☆
☆   /   /20
☆   time
☆
☆   size
☆
☆   swell
☆
☆   wind

                                                     tide

                                                     crowd

                                                     waves

                                                     gear

Wave Log

/ /20

time

size

swell

wind

tide

crowd

waves

gear

/ /20

time

size

swell

wind

tide

crowd

waves

gear

/ /20

time

size

swell

wind

tide

crowd

waves

gear

☆
☆
☆
☆
☆
☆
☆
☆
☆
☆

/ /20

time
size
swell
wind
tide
crowd
waves
gear

☆
☆
☆
☆
☆
☆
☆
☆
☆
☆

/ /20

time
size
swell
wind
tide
crowd
waves
gear

☆
☆
☆
☆
☆
☆
☆
☆
☆

/ /20

time
size
swell
wind
tide
crowd
waves
gear

Wave Log

/ /20

○ time
○ size
○ swell
○ wind
○ tide
○ crowd
○ waves
○ gear

/ /20

○ time
○ size
○ swell
○ wind
○ tide
○ crowd
○ waves
○ gear

/ /20

○ time
○ size
○ swell
○ wind
○ tide
○ crowd
○ waves
○ gear

☆
☆
☆
☆
☆
☆
☆
☆
☆
☆

/ /20

time
size
swell
wind
tide
crowd
waves
gear

☆
☆
☆
☆
☆
☆
☆
☆
☆
☆

/ /20

time
size
swell
wind
tide
crowd
waves
gear

☆
☆
☆
☆
☆
☆
☆
☆
☆
☆

/ /20

time
size
swell
wind
tide
crowd
waves
gear

Wave Log

/ /20

⊛ time
○ size
⊕ swell
⊕ wind
⊖ tide
○ crowd
○ waves
⊘ gear

☆ ☆ ☆ ☆ ☆ ☆ ☆ ☆ ☆

/ /20

⊛ time
○ size
⊕ swell
⊕ wind
⊖ tide
○ crowd
○ waves
⊘ gear

☆ ☆ ☆ ☆ ☆ ☆ ☆ ☆ ☆

/ /20

⊛ time
○ size
⊕ swell
⊕ wind
⊖ tide
○ crowd
○ waves
⊘ gear

☆ ☆ ☆ ☆ ☆ ☆ ☆ ☆ ☆

☆
☆
☆
☆
☆
☆
☆
☆
☆
☆

/ /20

time
size
swell
wind
tide
crowd
waves
gear

☆
☆
☆
☆
☆
☆
☆
☆
☆
☆

/ /20

time
size
swell
wind
tide
crowd
waves
gear

☆
☆
☆
☆
☆
☆
☆
☆
☆
☆

/ /20

time
size
swell
wind
tide
crowd
waves
gear

Wave Log

/   /20

- time
- size
- swell
- wind
- tide
- crowd
- waves
- gear

/   /20

- time
- size
- swell
- wind
- tide
- crowd
- waves
- gear

/   /20

- time
- size
- swell
- wind
- tide
- crowd
- waves
- gear

/ /20

time

size

swell

wind

tide

crowd

waves

gear

/ /20

time

size

swell

wind

tide

crowd

waves

gear

/ /20

time

size

swell

wind

tide

crowd

waves

gear

Wave Log

/ /20

time

size

swell

wind

tide

crowd

waves

gear

/ /20

time

size

swell

wind

tide

crowd

waves

gear

/ /20

time

size

swell

wind

tide

crowd

waves

gear

☆
☆
☆
☆
☆
☆
☆
☆
☆
☆

/ /20

time ⊛

size ⊖

swell ⊕

wind ⊕

tide ⊖

crowd ◯

waves ◯

gear ◔

☆
☆
☆
☆
☆
☆
☆
☆
☆
☆

/ /20

time ⊛

size ⊖

swell ⊕

wind ⊕

tide ⊖

crowd ◯

waves ◯

gear ◔

☆
☆
☆
☆
☆
☆
☆
☆
☆
☆

/ /20

time ⊛

size ⊖

swell ⊕

wind ⊕

tide ⊖

crowd ◯

waves ◯

gear ◔

Wave Log

/ /20

○ time
○ size
○ swell
○ wind
○ tide
○ crowd
○ waves
○ gear

/ /20

○ time
○ size
○ swell
○ wind
○ tide
○ crowd
○ waves
○ gear

/ /20

○ time
○ size
○ swell
○ wind
○ tide
○ crowd
○ waves
○ gear

☆
☆
☆
☆
☆
☆
☆
☆
☆
☆

/ /20

time ⊛

size

swell

wind

tide

crowd

waves

gear

☆
☆
☆
☆
☆
☆
☆
☆
☆
☆

/ /20

time ⊛

size

swell

wind

tide

crowd

waves

gear

☆
☆
☆
☆
☆
☆
☆
☆
☆
☆

/ /20

time ⊛

size

swell

wind

tide

crowd

waves

gear

Wave Log

/ ___ /20

- ⊕ time
- ○ size
- ⊖ swell
- ⊕ wind
- ⊖ tide
- ○ crowd
- ○ waves
- ◌ gear

☆☆☆☆☆☆☆☆

/ ___ /20

- ⊕ time
- ○ size
- ⊕ swell
- ⊕ wind
- ○ tide
- ○ crowd
- ○ waves
- ◌ gear

☆☆☆☆☆☆☆☆

/ ___ /20

- ⊕ time
- ○ size
- ⊕ swell
- ⊕ wind
- ⊖ tide
- ○ crowd
- ○ waves
- ◌ gear

☆☆☆☆☆☆☆☆

☆
☆
☆
☆
☆
☆
☆
☆
☆
☆

/   /20

time

size

swell

wind

tide

crowd

waves

gear

☆
☆
☆
☆
☆
☆
☆
☆
☆
☆

/   /20

time

size

swell

wind

tide

crowd

waves

gear

☆
☆
☆
☆
☆
☆
☆
☆
☆
☆

/   /20

time

size

swell

wind

tide

crowd

waves

gear

APPENDIX

Responsible Travel

Travelling responsibly means conserving natural resources, supporting local cultures, and minimizing our environmental impact as we travel.

BEFORE TRAVELLING

- Research your destination as much as possible. Look into history, culture, natural environment, customs, legends, advisory notices and more. Avoid high season if possible.
- Learn a few words in the local language. People appreciate any effort to speak the local language and simple words like "Hello, Please" and "Thank you" can go a long way.
- Pack light and remove any new packaging items (cardboard, plastic, etc) that consume luggage space and create excess trash for foreign countries lacking recycling services. Take environmentally friendly clothing and travel gear made from recycled, reused, organic, and sustainable natural materials such as cotton, hemp, and bamboo. Use paperless ticketing, a reusable shopping bag and re-usable containers for toiletries that should be biodegradable.
- Pack rechargeable batteries, a battery charger and plug adapter. Single-use batteries are incredibly toxic and many countries do not have proper disposal facilities, so bring any used batteries back home.
- Take a reusable water bottle and use purification tablets, or decant from the largest bottles available locally to reduce waste from single-use plastic, disposable bottles.
- Book hotels that publish their environmental impact, employment and cultural policy. Newer hotels will be more energy efficient.
- Minimize transportation pollution and environmental impact by using alternative, fuel-efficient transport methods and offsetting your carbon emissions.
- Unplug your home and office appliances.

SURF RELATED CHARITIES

Surf AID is a non-profit humanitarian organisation whose aim is to improve the health, wellbeing and self-reliance of people living in isolated regions connected to us through surfing. *www.surfaidinternational.org*

Surfrider Foundation's mission statement is all about the protection and enjoyment of oceans, waves and beaches through a powerful activist network. It's a grassroots organisation engaged with a wide range of environmental issues that affect coastlines. www.surfrider.org

Waves 4 Water has developed a DIY volunteer program called Clean Water Couriers. Surfers traveling to third-world countries add some water filters to their luggage and either deliver them to local non-profits or install the simple systems in remote villages. *www.wavesforwater.org*

Save The Waves Coalition is a global nonprofit organization dedicated to protecting and preserving the coastal environment, with an emphasis on the surf zone and educating the public about its value. Focused on fighting against coastal development that destroys surf spots, STW has established the World Surfing Reserves program that proactively identifies, designates and preserves outstanding waves, surf zones and their surrounding environments, around the world. This global network of surfing reserves will create a UNESCO style list of the world's most sacred surf spots and will be recognized by the international surfing and environmental communities. *www.savethewaves.org*

Surfers for Cetaceans calls on surfers everywhere to support the conservation and protection of whales, dolphins and other marine wildlife, while protesting against whaling, the killing of threatened or endangered species and the constant polluting and degradation of our marine environment. *www.s4cglobal.org*

Surfers Against Sewage (SAS) campaign for clean, safe recreational water, free from sewage effluents, toxic chemicals, nuclear waste and marine litter. *www.sas.org.uk*

Sustainable Surf seeks to help transform the surf industry and community from its current unsustainable operating model to a global model of sustainability in action. *www.sustainablesurf.org*

Surfers Without Borders is a humanitarian aid organization dedicated to creating projects that teach environmental awareness, reduce ocean pollution, promote sustainable development, and foster good relations between surfers and coastal communities around the world. *www.surferswithoutborders.org*

Waves for Development create life-enriching experiences in coastal communities through educational surf programs. Cultural exchange, environmental conservation, life skills, social entrepreneurship and sustainable tourism are values this surf NGO wants to promote. *www.wavesfordevelopment.org*

WHILE TRAVELLING

- Engage in local culture. Eat local foods, shop in local markets and attend local festivals.
- Buy locally sourced products and services. Choose organic, ocean-friendly and sustainably sourced foods. Support locally owned businesses, community tour operators and artisans where your money will go directly to the local economy. Avoid buying products made from threatened natural resources and report poaching or other illegal activities to the local authorities.
- Refrain from over-aggressive bargaining and haggling over small change that could make a bigger difference to the vendor's life.
- Hire local guides who are knowledgeable about the destination.
- Tread lightly. Follow designated trails, respect signs, rules and caretakers and never remove archaeological or biological material from sites.
- Reduce, reuse, and recycle. Maintain normal environmental habits when traveling, including turning off lights and using less water. Turn off heating or air-con until you are in the room. Avoid excessive washing of sheets, towels and clothes in hotels. Opt for beverages in reusable glass bottles.
- Use the suggestion box to inform your hotel/hosts ideas on how to operate a more environmentally friendly business.

AFTER TRAVELLING

- Share your responsible travel tips on how to positively impact the World, while still having an amazing journey. Share or donate your travel guides, brochures and literature to minimize waste.
- Continue exploring and being involved with the issues or region that captured your attention. Fulfill any promises made on the road.
- Give back. Traveling often opens your eyes and heart to something new. Donate to a local charity.

Surf Brands have long been supporters of environmental causes and many have set up charitable or non-profit foundations to try and make a direct impact on issues that affect their customers. Quicksilver, O'Neill, Billabong, Hurley, Patagonia and even Kelly Slater (USA) have set up foundations or programs that give back to the surfing world.

OTHER ORGANISATIONS

Adventurers and Scientists for Conservation is an organisation that uses adventure athletes to gather scientific data and knowledge of the natural environment, while on a trip to a remote area. Data collection can be expensive, time consuming, and physically challenging, so this partnership enables outdoor ambassadors to acquire the relevant skills before heading out into the more difficult to reach corners of the world. ASC has utilized the unique skills of climbers, mountaineers, divers, paddlers and other adventurers to acquire this data.
www.adventureandscience.org

Greenpeace - Defending Our Oceans is committed to defending the health of the world's oceans and the plants, animals and people that depend upon them.
www.greenpeace.org/ international/en/campaigns/ oceans

Oceana is the largest international group focused 100% on protecting and restoring the world's oceans.
www.oceana.org

Reef Check are an international non-profit organisation aimed at protecting and rehabilitating reefs worldwide, dedicated to conservation of two ecosystems: tropical coral reefs and California rocky reefs.
www.reefcheck.org

WiLDCOAST set out to protect some of the most beautiful and biologically significant coastal areas in California and Latin America. Today, WiLDCOAST operates 4 main programs— Wildlife Conservation, Marine Life Conservation, Coastal Conservation, and Climate Change.
www.wildcoast.net

1% For the Planet aims to build and support an alliance of businesses financially committed to creating a healthy planet. They offer a simple, tangible and proactive way for the business community to be a part of the solution.
www.sustainablesurf.org

REGIONAL ORGANISATIONS
(Summary only)
- Surfrider Foundation USA, Australia, Brazil, Canada, Europe, Japan
- Surfers' Enviro. Alliance (USA)
- Sierra Club (USA)
- Ocean Institute (USA)
- KAHEA: The Hawaiian-Environmental Alliance (Hawaii)
- North Shore Community Land Trust (Hawaii)
- Surfing Education Association (Hawaii)
- LiVBLUE (USA & Mexico)
- Ocean Revolution (USA & Mexico)
- SurfEns (Mexico)
- DGCostera (Peru)
- Surfbreak Protection Soc. (NZ)
- Nat'l Surfing Reserves (Aus)
- Salvem o Surf (Portugal)

Packing List

PAPERWORK

- [ ] passport (min 3-6 months validity)
- [ ] visas
- [ ] tickets
- [ ] money/travellers cheques
- [ ] credit / debit cards
- [ ] travel insurance documents
- [ ] 2 x copies of passport photo page
- [ ] spare passport photos
- [ ] home and international driving licences
- [ ]

SURF EQUIPMENT

- [ ] boards
- [ ] boardbag
- [ ] fins
- [ ] leashes and spare string
- [ ] wax / traction pads
- [ ] wax comb
- [ ] ding repair/solarez
- [ ] duct tape
- [ ] fin keys /screwdriver
- [ ] spare fin screws / fin box plate
- [ ] straps / soft-racks / rope / string
- [ ] helmet
- [ ] ear plugs
- [ ] nose cones
- [ ] rash prevention

TROPICAL

- [ ] boardshorts
- [ ] reef boots
- [ ] surf hat
- [ ] vest / shortie
- [ ] long-sleeve rash vest
- [ ] snorkel mask and fins / flippers
- [ ] waterproof sunscreen / zinc
- [ ] mossie net
- [ ] insect repellant
- [ ] flip flops
- [ ] thin trousers / long sleeve shirt
- [ ] walk shorts
- [ ] rain coat / umbrella
- [ ]

TEMPERATE/COLD

- [ ] wetsuit
- [ ] wetsuit boots / gloves / hood
- [ ] shoes
- [ ] walking boots
- [ ] thermal top and bottoms
- [ ] thick trousers / jeans
- [ ] fleece jacket / gilet
- [ ] waterproof jacket and trousers
- [ ] beanie / balaclava
- [ ] scarf / gloves
- [ ]

CLOTHES

- [ ] towel
- [ ] t-shirts (short and long sleeve)
- [ ] socks
- [ ] underwear
- [ ] shoes / belt
- [ ] sunglasses / sun hat
- [ ]

TOILETRIES

- [ ] toothbrush / toothpaste / toothpicks / floss
- [ ] biodegradable soap / gel / shampoo
- [ ] razor and shaving cream / gel / oil
- [ ] sunscreen / aftersun
- [ ] tampons / condoms / q-tips
- [ ]

CAMPING

- [ ] tent
- [ ] sleeping bag / mat
- [ ] torch
- [ ] multi-tool
- [ ] compass
- [ ] binoculars
- [ ] water purifying tablets
- [ ] waterproof bag / shopping bag
- [ ] cooking stove / utensils
- [ ] lighter / matches
- [ ] water bottle

GADGETS / ELECTRICAL / BOOKS

- [ ] electrical outlet travel adapter
- [ ] phone / charger / car charger
- [ ] laptop / tablet / charger / 12v adapter
- [ ] ebook reader / charger
- [ ] camera / charger / data cable / data cards
- [ ] waterproof housing for phone / camera
- [ ] music player / radio / speakers
- [ ] solar charger
- [ ] rechargeable batteries
- [ ] reading books / magazines
- [ ] stormrider guides / maps
- [ ] stormrider playing cards
- [ ] stormrider surf journal
- [ ]

FIRST AID KIT (see over page)

- [ ]

PERSONAL ITEMS

- [ ]
- [ ]
- [ ]
- [ ]
- [ ]
- [ ]
- [ ]
- [ ]
- [ ]

Medical Packing List

Surfers should always travel with some sort of first aid kit. Lacerations from your board are the most common type of injury (followed by lacerations from someone else's board) along with abrasions from contact with the ocean floor. Being able to treat reef cuts is a major priority, as well as having remedies for ailments commonly experienced when travelling. Further reading and increasing your first aid knowledge is recommended. Below is a list of essentials plus some heavy duty kit for the more medically experienced surf trippers. We have avoided brand names as these vary from country to country but the basic treatment/compound is generally the same.

If a **C** follows the item then it is available off the shelf at a chemist / pharmacist.

If a **P** follows the item then a prescription is usually required.

If an **A** follows the item it denotes an alternative to the conventional treatment.

Always follow the manufacturers recommendations and use common sense when dealing with all medications. Make a record of all treatments. Never use out of date pharmaceuticals and use a hard case to protect bottles of solutions. Be open to local remedies, especially when dealing with localised ailments.

Surf specific first aid kits are available from *globalodyssi.com* who provided much of the first aid information in the appendix.

CLEANING WOUNDS

☐ hydrogen peroxide 3%

☐ povidone-iodine 10% solution

☐

TREATING WOUNDS

☐ antibiotic powder

☐ antibiotic cream

☐ erthromycin 500mg (general bacterial infections) **P**

☐ doxycycline 100mg capsules (specific bacterial infections) **P**

☐

WOUND DRESSINGS

☐ adhesive tape (1" wide and waterproof)

☐ band-aids / plasters (multi-sized waterproof)

☐ sterile gauze pads (multi-sized)

☐ steristrips / butterfly stitches

☐ bandages

☐

PAIN RELIEF

☐ aspirin, paracetemol

☐ ibuprofen (pain, fever, inflammation)

☐ acetaminophen (with 30 mg codeine for severe pain) **C**

☐ pseudoephedrine (nasal, sinus, ear conditions)

☐

☐

☐

☐

☐

GENERAL AILMENTS

- [ ] sulfacetamide sodium 10% (eye drops) **C**
- [ ] eye drops
- [ ] antibiotic ear drops (for infected surfers ear) **P**
- [ ] silver sulfediazine cream 1% (burns, skin infections) **P**
- [ ] lindane lotion (crabs, lice) **C**
- [ ] oral re-hydration kit (severe dehydration)
- [ ] laxative: cascara, senna, or castor oil
- [ ] diphynhydramine (itching, rash and allergic reactions)
- [ ] lopramide (acute diarrhoea)
- [ ] bismuth subsalicylate (nausea, diarrhoea)
- [ ] antacid/heartburn tablets
- [ ] trimethoprim / sulfamethoxazole (bladder infections) **P**
- [ ] anti-fungal cream (cystitis / thrush)
- [ ]

ALTERNATIVE TREATMENTS (all A)

- [ ] echinacea (boosts the immune system)
- [ ] garlic capsules (prevent general illness)
- [ ] cayenne capsules (prevent colds/flu)
- [ ] aloe vera gel (sunburn)
- [ ] royal jelly / bee pollen (burns, wounds)
- [ ] tea tree oil (a natural antiseptic good for coral cuts)
- [ ] arnica (bruising and shock)
- [ ] ginger root (chew for nausea, travel sickness)
- [ ] chamomile (itching, rash)
- [ ] hypericum / calendula (cuts, bites and stings)
- [ ] oil of cloves (tooth pain and mouth sores)

EQUIPMENT

- [ ] tweezers
- [ ] scissors/utility knife
- [ ] duct tape
- [ ] thermometer
- [ ] eyedropper
- [ ] safety pins / needle
- [ ] safety razor blades / scalpel
- [ ] sutre / syringe medickit
- [ ] lighter / matches
- [ ] torch
- [ ] cotton applicators / buds
- [ ] tongue blades
- [ ] mirror
- [ ] water filtrationstraw
- [ ] soap (small bar)
- [ ] gloves, latex or vinyl
- [ ]
- [ ]
- [ ]
- [ ]
- [ ]
- [ ]
- [ ]
- [ ]

First Aid

How to give CPR

- Place the heel of your hand 1-1.5"in (2.5-4cm) above the lower tip of the breastbone, which usually corresponds to directly between the patient's nipples.
- Place your other hand on top of the first. Bring your shoulders directly over the person's body, keeping your arms straight.
- **For adults:** Press down to depress the breastbone 1.5-2"in (4-5cm). Current recommendations are for 30 chest compressions, delivered at a rate of 100 compressions per minute, followed by two rescue breaths. Push hard, push fast and alternate compression sessions with another person to avoid exhaustion.
- Continue until patient has a return of pulse and is breathing or until EMS arrives.
- Check pulse after the first minute of CPR (slide index and middle finger into groove on either side of Adam's apple) and every few minutes after. If pulse returns, stop chest compressions and assess breathing.
- If no pulse, continue with 30 pumps and 2 breaths until help arrives.

Rescue Breaths

- Tilt the head back and listen for breathing. If you suspect a neck injury, do not twist the head or tilt the head back. Elevate the chin slightly to open the airway.
- If not breathing normally, pinch the nose shut, cover the mouth with yours and blow until you see the chest rise. Remove your mouth and allow person to exhale.
- For adults, allow 1.5-2 seconds for each breath.
- As you are administering breaths, watch for the chest to rise. If person's chest does not rise when air is forced in, the airway may be blocked. Recheck airway by re-tilting the head back and lifting the chin.
- Check for pulse, if there is a pulse, continue breaths at the following rate: For adults, 12 breaths per minute (one breath every 5 seconds).
- If there is no pulse, or victim is still not breathing, moving, or coughing, recommence chest compressions.

Average Pulse Rates

Adults	60-80 beats per minute
Children	70-150
Infants	100-160

Average Breathing Rates

Adults	12-20 breaths per minute
Children	18-40
Infants	30-60

BASIC LIFE SUPPORT
Primary Assessment

Recognising life-threatening emergencies like heart attack, cardiac arrest, stroke and airway obstruction is an important first aid skill. Primary assessment is the first evaluation of an injured or ill person and begins the order of steps to take in the "Cycle of Care", which can be remembered using the acronym "AB-CABS".

- Airway open?
- Breathing normally?
- Chest compressions
- Airway open
- Breathing for patient
- Serious bleeding, shock, spinal injury

Check for an open airway by gently tilting the head back and listening for regular breathing. If breathing is infrequent, slow, noisy gasps or patient is not breathing at all, then it may be necessary to administer CPR. Early CPR is the best treatment for cardiac arrest and doubles or triples the chance of survival. Compressions are more important in most heart or circulatory failure situations, while drowning victims will require rescue breaths to oxygenate the blood during CPR.

Treatment:

- Asses the scene for dangers
- Apply barriers (gloves, ventilation barrier)
- Check the victim for responsiveness, an open airway and normal breathing
- CALL FOR HELP - Call for Emergency Medical Services (EMS)
- Begin chest compressions
- Open airway
- Give rescue breaths
- Continue with CPR until help or an AED (defibrillator) arrives

SUBMERSION INJURIES (near-drowning)

Symptoms: A person is in the water with signs of distress. He or she can't stay above water, swims unevenly, signals for help, blue lips or ears, skin is cold and pale, bloated abdomen, vomiting, choking, confusion, lethargy, no response from victim or lack of breathing.

Treatment: The focus of the first aid for a near-drowning victim in the water is to get oxygen into the lungs without aggravating any suspected neck injury.

- If the victim's breathing has stopped, begin mouth-to-mouth rescue breathing as soon as you safely can. This could mean starting the rescue breaths in the water.
- Continue to breathe for the person every five seconds while moving the victim to the shore.

- If the airway is obstructed making breathing impossible, remove the obstruction or begin performing the Heimlich manoeuvre to clear it by hugging the victim from behind with your arms around the victim's stomach and using the thumb side of a closed fist with your other hand on top of the fist to pull in and up. Continue these thrusts until the airway is cleared.
- Chest compressions in the water are difficult to do without a flat surface that does not give way and are reserved until such a surface is available.
- Once on shore, reassess the victim's breathing and circulation (heartbeat and pulse). If there is breathing and circulation without suspected spine injury, place the person in recovery position (lying on the stomach, arms extended at the shoulder level and bent, head on the side with the leg on the same side drawn up at a right angle to the torso) to keep the airway clear and to allow the swallowed water to drain. If there is no breathing, begin CPR/Basic Life Support. Continue CPR (mouth-to-mouth breathing and chest compressions) until help arrives or the person revives.
- Keep the person warm by removing wet clothing and covering with warm blankets to prevent hypothermia. Remain with the recovering person until emergency medical personnel have arrived.

HYPOTHERMIA
Severe hypothermia
body temperature below 32°C/90°F
Mild hypothermia
body temperature lowered to 34°C/ 93°F

A patient suffering from severe hypothermia may be disoriented, confused, uncoordinated or completely unresponsive. Breathing and pulse will be at such low intensity that detection will be difficult so don't abandon resuscitation attempts until patient has been rewarmed. A patient suffering from mild hypothermia may be conscious and alert, yet shivering and displaying slightly impaired coordination.
Treatment: Treat hypothermia as a medical emergency. Do not move patient unless necessary to prevent further heat loss. Handling may cause irregular heartbeat. Gently remove wet clothing and cover with blankets or warm clothing. Monitor and record vital signs until EMS arrive. For mild cases, move to warm dry area, wrap in blankets/clothes and give warm non-alcoholic, non-caffeinated drinks.

HEAD INJURIES
Emergency medical personnel should immediately treat any serious or potentially serious head injury. If any of the following symptoms are present, seek immediate medical care: Severe head or facial bleeding, bleeding from the nose or ears, severe headache, change in level of consciousness for more than a few seconds, black and blue discoloration below the eyes or behind ears, cessation of breathing, confusion, loss of balance, weakness or an inability to use an arm or leg, unequal pupil size, repeated vomiting, slurred speech, seizures.
If severe head trauma occurs:
Keep the person still. Until medical help arrives, keep the injured person lying down and quiet, with the head and shoulders slightly elevated. Don't move the person unless necessary, and avoid moving the person's neck. Stop any bleeding. Apply firm pressure to the wound with sterile gauze or a clean cloth. But don't apply direct pressure to the wound if you suspect a skull fracture. Watch for changes in breathing and alertness. If the person shows no signs of circulation (breathing, coughing or movement), begin CPR.

FRACTURES
A fracture is a broken bone. It requires medical attention. If the broken bone is the result of major trauma or injury, call your local emergency number.
Treatment: Seek medical attention immediately. Call for EMS, or transport victim to emergency room after immobilizing affected area. Wait for EMS and **DO NOT** attempt to transport victim if you suspect head, back, or neck injury; if there's a visible deformity of bone; or if the victim cannot be splinted or transported without causing more pain. Don't move the person except if necessary to avoid further injury. Take these actions immediately while waiting for medical help:

- Stop any bleeding. Apply pressure to the wound with a sterile bandage, a clean cloth or a clean piece of clothing.
- Immobilize the injured area. Don't try to realign the bone or push a bone that's sticking out back in. If you've been trained in how to splint and professional help isn't readily available, apply a splint to the area above and below the fracture sites. Padding the splints can help reduce discomfort.
- Apply ice packs to limit swelling and help relieve pain until emergency personal arrive. Do not place ice pack directly on skin.
- Treat for shock. If the person feels faint or is breathing in short, rapid breaths, lay the person down with the head slightly lower than the trunk and, if possible, elevate the legs.

SUNBURN

Covering skin with high SPF waterproof sunscreen is the simplest preventative measure, however using SPF-rated lycra, a surf hat and avoiding midday exposure is more effective. The lips, ears, lower back, thighs, calves and behind the knees are problem areas requiring added attention.

Treatment: for sunburn and possible heat exhaustion includes slow rehydration with water or sports drinks to replace electrolytes, whether feeling thirsty or not. Cool showers, moisturizing creams and taking ibuprofen can lessen the severity of the symptoms. Do not peel, pick or burst blisters and seek medical attention if more than 20% of body is burned and symptoms like headache, dizziness, sleepiness, fevers or chills persist.

MALARIA

Widespread across the tropics, malaria parasites (Plasmodium) are transmitted by the Anopheles mosquito. Six Plasmodium species usually infect humans and the main killers are P. falciparum and P. vivax. Drug resistant strains exist and the risk varies regionally so consult a doctor before travelling. High-risk islands include eastern Indonesia, Solomons, Vanuatu, Hispaniola and Sao Tomé. Prevention is paramount by avoiding bites (mosquito nets, long clothing, repellent) and oral medication (prophylaxis).

Symptoms: May include fever, sweats, chills, convulsions, joint or back pain, headaches, dry cough, enlarged spleen, nausea or vomiting and can take anything from 8-40 days to appear (longer if taking prophylaxis). Many other conditions can present the same symptoms, so expert diagnosis (blood test) is crucial. P. falciparum can cause confusion, neurologic focal signs, respiratory difficulties and coma.

Treatment: Reliable prophylaxis is provided by mefloquine (Lariam), doxycycline (generic), and atovaquone-proguanil (Malarone), which is now coming off patent and expected to fall significantly in price. Side effects limit the usefulness of Larium in certain people. Fake malaria drugs are common in Asia and Africa, so source drugs before you travel. Effective treatment for malaria requires expert knowledge of drugs and correct dosage.

INFECTION

Tropical waters carry higher levels of bacteria than cooler water. This means that infections can occur very rapidly, even on the smallest of wounds. They should be treated immediately and constantly monitored for signs of infection, which include swelling, bruising, extreme pain, increasing redness, tenderness, warmth or drainage around the wound. Also, any flu-like symptoms, such as fever, exhaustion, and swollen glands could be signs of infection or a disease. If these are present, consult a doctor immediately. Keeping the wound covered and clean will ensure that it heals quickly and effectively.

Treatment: If infection is present, scrub the wound using gauze dipped in antiseptic. Once all the yellow pus is removed, re-apply antiseptic and dress appropriately.

Coral Cuts

Usually consist of an inflamed, swollen, red, tender wound that may develop into a sore or ulcer with infectious drainage. Redness around the skin of the wounded area suggests infection and requires immediate medical attention.

Treatment: Scrub with soap and water, then flush with fresh water. If the wound stings, rinse it with acetic acid (vinegar) or isopropyl alcohol. Flush the wound with a mixture of half water and half hydrogen peroxide to remove coral dust, then flush with fresh water. Rinse daily and apply an antibiotic ointment 3-4 times per day.

Fire Coral Cuts

Fire coral has a bright yellow-green and brown skeletal covering and are widely found in tropical and subtropical waters.

Symptoms: Within 5-30 minutes following skin contact with fire coral, a burning sensation or a stinging pain develops. A red rash with raised wheals or vesicles appears, and itching develops. Lymph glands may swell over time.

Treatment: Rinse with seawater. Avoid fresh water because it will increase pain. Apply topical acetic acid (vinegar) or isopropyl alcohol. Remove tentacles with tweezers. Immobilize the affected area because movement may cause the venom to spread. Apply hydrocortisone cream 2-3 times daily as needed for itching. Discontinue immediately if any signs of infection appear.

Reef Cuts

Rocky volcanic reefs carry many bacteria and cuts from them pose a high risk for infection.

Treatment: Scrub the wound to remove all debris and apply lime juice (this helps to stop the bleeding in a short amount of time) while scrubbing. Apply an antiseptic. Apply povidone-iodine solution (ie; betadine) twice a day to help keep the wound clean.

BITES AND STINGS

For all types of bites and stings: DO NOT attempt to suck out the venom with your mouth, apply a tourniquet, place ice directly on the bite or sting, administer alcohol, stimulants or aspirin.

Blue Bottle / Portuguese Man of War Sting

The tentacles of these jellyfish will cause a sharp, painful sting. Do not rub sting area with towel or wet sand to rub tentacles off – this may make the pain worse. **Treatment:** Prevent further stings. Using a stick or gloved fingers, carefully remove tentacles. Rinse the affected area with seawater. Do NOT use fresh water or vinegar, as these may cause the stinging cells to sting all at once! Do not scrub the affected area. Apply ice to reduce pain and swelling.

Sea Urchin Puncture, Stonefish, Scorpionfish, or Lionfish Stings

The spines from any of these sea creatures can cause redness, swelling, or numbness around the area. This may lead to severe pain or infection. Tissue shredding may occur. Throbbing pain may peak in 1-2hrs and last 12hrs. Seek immediate medical attention for stonefish, scorpionfish, or lionfish envenomation as anti-venom is needed. Death may occur. **Treatment:** Immerse the affected area for 30-90 minutes in water as hot as the injured person can tolerate. Repeat as necessary to control pain. Use tweezers to remove any large spines, but don't dig around wound. If black markings are present after 48 to 72 hours, seek medical attention, as spines may have been left in the wound. Remove sea urchin spines (the claw-shaped pedicellaria) by applying shaving cream and gently scraping with a razor, or use tweezers. Scrub wound with soap and water followed by extensive flushing with fresh water. Do not close the wound with tape or glue skin.

Shark Bites

Provide emergency care immediately. A medical healthcare provider should evaluate all shark bite victims. Control any bleeding by applying direct pressure to bite area. Keep the victim calm and warm. If only a minor wound is present, consider washing the wound with soap and water and cover it with a clean dressing until medical care arrives. If the wound appears serious, do not attempt to clean it yourself. If swelling, bruising, extreme pain, increasing redness (sometimes seen as streaks), tenderness, warmth or drainage around the bite area and any flu-like symptoms occur then seek medical help immediately.

SOFT TISSUE INJURIES

Soft tissue injuries such as bruises and sprains should be treated using the **R.I.C.E** Method:
Rest - Rest the patient where possible, ensuring they are comfortable.
Ice - Apply ice to the affected area.
Compression - Apply a compression bandage to the affected area.
Elevation - Elevate the affected area.

CUTS, SCRAPES, WOUNDS

The faster you can treat and manage your wounds effectively, the less chance for infection you will have. Use the following guidelines to treat most minor cuts, scrapes, or wounds.

1. Stop the bleeding

Before you clean the wound, try to the stop the bleeding. Put on medical gloves before applying direct pressure to the wound. In case of swelling, remove any clothing or jewelry from around the wound. Use a sterile gauze pad or other clean piece of cloth to place over the wound. Apply direct pressure on the wound for a full 15 minutes. Resist the temptation to check to see if the bleeding has stopped.

2. Clean the Wound

Wash hands thoroughly. Use medical gloves when cleaning the wound. Remove large pieces of dirt or other debris from the wound with sterilized tweezers. Do not dig tweezers deeply into the wound. Wash the wound under clean, fresh water (lots of it) to remove all the dirt, debris, and bacteria from the wound. Lukewarm water and mild soap are the best. Gently scrub with a washcloth or gauze pad. (Moderate scrubbing may be needed if the wound is very dirty.) Hard scrubbing may actually cause more damage to the tissue and increase the chance of infection. Scrubbing the wound will probably hurt and may increase bleeding, but it is necessary to clean the wound thoroughly. If some dirt or other debris remains in the wound, repeat the cleaning. Apply antiseptic to further aid in cleansing before bandaging.

3. Bandage the Wound

Most wounds heal better with less scaring if they are kept covered. Use an antibiotic ointment and non-stick dressing before applying a clean bandage to the wound. If a bandage is stuck to a scab, soak it in warm water to soften the scab and make the bandage easier to remove. Use adhesive steri-strips (butterfly stitches) to hold the edges of the wound together. Take the dressing off and leave it off whenever you are sure the wound will not become irritated or dirty. Stitches are only an option within a few hours of injury, as the risk of enclosing an infection becomes too great. A quick test to determine whether you need stitches is to stop the bleeding and wash the wound well, then pinch the sides of the wound together. If the edges of the wound come together and it looks better, you may want to consider getting stitches. If stitches may be needed, avoid using an antiseptic or antibiotic ointment until after a health professional has examined the wound.

Perpetual Calendar

YEAR	#
2014	4
2015	5
2016	13
2017	1
2018	2
2019	3
2020	11
2021	6
2022	7
2023	1
2024	9
2025	4
2026	5
2027	6
2028	14
2029	2
2030	3
2031	4
2032	12
2033	7
2034	1
2035	2
2036	10
2037	5
2038	6
2039	7
2040	8
2041	3
2042	4
2043	5
2044	13
2045	1
2046	2
2047	3
2048	11
2049	6
2050	7

How to use

The number opposite each of the years in the list to the left indicates which of the calendars on the following pages is to be used for that year, eg the number opposite 2025 is 4, so calendar 4 can be used as a 2025 calendar.

Leap Years

Years divisible exactly by four are leap years with 366 days instead of 365 (29 days in February instead of 28). However the last year of a century is not a leap year except when divisible by 400.

1

JANUARY
M 2 9 16 23 30
T 3 10 17 24 31
W 4 11 18 25
T 5 12 19 26
F 6 13 20 27
S 7 14 21 28
S 1 8 15 22 29

FEBRUARY
M   6 13 20 27
T   7 14 21 28
W 1 8 15 22
T 2 9 16 23
F 3 10 17 24
S 4 11 18 25
S 5 12 19 26

MARCH
M   6 13 20 27
T   7 14 21 28
W 1 8 15 22 29
T 2 9 16 23 30
F 3 10 17 24 31
S 4 11 18 25
S 5 12 19 26

APRIL
M 3 10 17 24
T 4 11 18 25
W 5 12 19 26
T 6 13 20 27
F 7 14 21 28
S 1 8 15 22 29
S 2 9 16 23 30

MAY
M 1 8 15 22 29
T 2 9 16 23 30
W 3 10 17 24 31
T 4 11 18 25
F 5 12 19 26
S 6 13 20 27
S 7 14 21 28

JUNE
M   5 12 19 26
T   6 13 20 27
W   7 14 21 28
T 1 8 15 22 29
F 2 9 16 23 30
S 3 10 17 24
S 4 11 18 25

JULY
M 3 10 17 24 31
T 4 11 18 25
W 5 12 19 26
T 6 13 20 27
F 7 14 21 28
S 1 8 15 22 29
S 2 9 16 23 30

AUGUST
M   7 14 21 28
T 1 8 15 22 29
W 2 9 16 23 30
T 3 10 17 24 31
F 4 11 18 25
S 5 12 19 26
S 6 13 20 27

SEPTEMBER
M   4 11 18 25
T   5 12 19 26
W   6 13 20 27
T   7 14 21 28
F 1 8 15 22 29
S 2 9 16 23 30
S 3 10 17 24

OCTOBER
M 2 9 16 23 30
T 3 10 17 24 31
W 4 11 18 25
T 5 12 19 26
F 6 13 20 27
S 7 14 21 28
S 1 8 15 22 29

NOVEMBER
M   6 13 20 27
T   7 14 21 28
W 1 8 15 22 29
T 2 9 16 23 30
F 3 10 17 24
S 4 11 18 25
S 5 12 19 26

DECEMBER
M   4 11 18 25
T   5 12 19 26
W   6 13 20 27
T   7 14 21 28
F 1 8 15 22 29
S 2 9 16 23 30
S 3 10 17 24 31

4

JANUARY
M   6 13 20 27
T   7 14 21 28
W 1 8 15 22 29
T 2 9 16 23 30
F 3 10 17 24 31
S 4 11 18 25
S 5 12 19 26

FEBRUARY
M 3 10 17 24
T 4 11 18 25
W 5 12 19 26
T 6 13 20 27
F 7 14 21 28
S 1 8 15 22
S 2 9 16 23

MARCH
M 3 10 17 24 31
T 4 11 18 25
W 5 12 19 26
T 6 13 20 27
F 7 14 21 28
S 1 8 15 22 29
S 2 9 16 23 30

APRIL
M 7 14 21 28
T 1 8 15 22 29
W 2 9 16 23 30
T 3 10 17 24
F 4 11 18 25
S 5 12 19 26
S 6 13 20 27

MAY
M   5 12   19 26
T   6 13   20 27
W   7 14   21 28
T 1 8 15   22 29
F 2 9 16   23 30
S 3 10 17 24 31
S 4 11 18 25

JUNE
M 2 9   16 23 30
T 3 10   17 24
W 4 11   18 25
T 5 12   19 26
F 6 13   20 27
S 7 14 21 28
S 1 8 15 22 29

JULY
M 7 14 21 28
T 1 8 15 22 29
W 2 9 16 23 30
T 3 10 17 24 31
F 4 11 18 25
S 5 12 19 26
S 6 13 20 27

AUGUST
M 4 11   18 25
T 5 12   19 26
W 6 13   20 27
T 7 14   21 28
F 1 8 15 22 29
S 2 9 16 23 30
S 3 10 17 24 31

SEPTEMBER
M 1 8 15 22 29
T 2 9 16 23
W 3 10 17 24
T 4 11 18 25
F 5 12 19 26
S 6 13 20 27
S 7 14 21 28

OCTOBER
M 6 13 20 27
T 7 14 21 28
W 1 8 15 22 29
T 2 9 16 23 30
F 3 10 17 24 31
S 4 11 18 25
S 5 12 19 26

NOVEMBER
M 3 10   17 24
T 4 11   18 25
W 5 12   19 26
T 6 13   20 27
F 7 14   21 28
S 1 8 15 22 29
S 2 9 16 23 30

DECEMBER
M 1 8 15   22 29
T 2 9 16   23 30
W 3 10 17   24 31
T 4 11 18   25
F 5 12 19   26
S 6 13 20 27
S 7 14 21 28

2

	JANUARY	FEBRUARY	MARCH	APRIL	MAY	JUNE	JULY	AUGUST	SEPTEMBER	OCTOBER	NOVEMBER	DECEMBER
M	1 8 15 22 29	5 12 19 26	5 12 19 26	2 9 16 23 30	7 14 21 28	4 11 18 25	2 9 16 23 30	6 13 20 27	3 10 17 24	1 8 15 22 29	5 12 19 26	3 10 17 24 31
T	2 9 16 23 30	6 13 20 27	6 13 20 27	3 10 17 24	1 8 15 22 29	5 12 19 26	3 10 17 24 31	7 14 21 28	4 11 18 25	2 9 16 23 30	6 13 20 27	4 11 18 25
W	3 10 17 24 31	7 14 21 28	7 14 21 28	4 11 18 25	2 9 16 23 30	6 13 20 27	4 11 18 25	1 8 15 22 29	5 12 19 26	3 10 17 24 31	7 14 21 28	5 12 19 26
T	4 11 18 25	1 8 15 22	1 8 15 22 29	5 12 19 26	3 10 17 24 31	7 14 21 28	5 12 19 26	2 9 16 23 30	6 13 20 27	4 11 18 25	1 8 15 22 29	6 13 20 27
F	5 12 19 26	2 9 16 23	2 9 16 23 30	6 13 20 27	4 11 18 25	1 8 15 22 29	6 13 20 27	3 10 17 24 31	7 14 21 28	5 12 19 26	2 9 16 23 30	7 14 21 28
S	6 13 20 27	3 10 17 24	3 10 17 24 31	7 14 21 28	5 12 19 26	2 9 16 23 30	7 14 21 28	4 11 18 25	1 8 15 22 29	6 13 20 27	3 10 17 24	1 8 15 22 29
S	7 14 21 28	4 11 18 25	4 11 18 25	1 8 15 22 29	6 13 20 27	3 10 17 24	1 8 15 22 29	5 12 19 26	2 9 16 23 30	7 14 21 28	4 11 18 25	2 9 16 23 30

3

	JANUARY	FEBRUARY	MARCH	APRIL	MAY	JUNE	JULY	AUGUST	SEPTEMBER	OCTOBER	NOVEMBER	DECEMBER
M	7 14 21 28	4 11 18 25	4 11 18 25	1 8 15 22 29	6 13 20 27	3 10 17 24	1 8 15 22 29	5 12 19 26	2 9 16 23 30	7 14 21 28	4 11 18 25	2 9 16 23 30
T	1 8 15 22 29	5 12 19 26	5 12 19 26	2 9 16 23 30	7 14 21 28	4 11 18 25	2 9 16 23 30	6 13 20 27	3 10 17 24	1 8 15 22 29	5 12 19 26	3 10 17 24 31
W	2 9 16 23 30	6 13 20 27	6 13 20 27	3 10 17 24	1 8 15 22 29	5 12 19 26	3 10 17 24 31	7 14 21 28	4 11 18 25	2 9 16 23 30	6 13 20 27	4 11 18 25
T	3 10 17 24 31	7 14 21 28	7 14 21 28	4 11 18 25	2 9 16 23 30	6 13 20 27	4 11 18 25	1 8 15 22 29	5 12 19 26	3 10 17 24 31	7 14 21 28	5 12 19 26
F	4 11 18 25	1 8 15 22	1 8 15 22 29	5 12 19 26	3 10 17 24 31	7 14 21 28	5 12 19 26	2 9 16 23 30	6 13 20 27	4 11 18 25	1 8 15 22 29	6 13 20 27
S	5 12 19 26	2 9 16 23	2 9 16 23 30	6 13 20 27	4 11 18 25	1 8 15 22 29	6 13 20 27	3 10 17 24 31	7 14 21 28	5 12 19 26	2 9 16 23 30	7 14 21 28
S	6 13 20 27	3 10 17 24	3 10 17 24 31	7 14 21 28	5 12 19 26	2 9 16 23 30	7 14 21 28	4 11 18 25	1 8 15 22 29	6 13 20 27	3 10 17 24	1 8 15 22 29

5

	JANUARY	FEBRUARY	MARCH	APRIL	MAY	JUNE	JULY	AUGUST	SEPTEMBER	OCTOBER	NOVEMBER	DECEMBER
M	5 12 19 26	2 9 16 23	2 9 16 23 30	6 13 20 27	4 11 18 25	1 8 15 22 29	6 13 20 27	3 10 17 24 31	7 14 21 28	5 12 19 26	2 9 16 23 30	7 14 21 28
T	6 13 20 27	3 10 17 24	3 10 17 24 31	7 14 21 28	5 12 19 26	2 9 16 23 30	7 14 21 28	4 11 18 25	1 8 15 22 29	6 13 20 27	3 10 17 24	1 8 15 22 29
W	7 14 21 28	4 11 18 25	4 11 18 25	1 8 15 22 29	6 13 20 27	3 10 17 24	1 8 15 22 29	5 12 19 26	2 9 16 23 30	7 14 21 28	4 11 18 25	2 9 16 23 30
T	1 8 15 22 29	5 12 19 26	5 12 19 26	2 9 16 23 30	7 14 21 28	4 11 18 25	2 9 16 23 30	6 13 20 27	3 10 17 24	1 8 15 22 29	5 12 19 26	3 10 17 24 31
F	2 9 16 23 30	6 13 20 27	6 13 20 27	3 10 17 24	1 8 15 22 29	5 12 19 26	3 10 17 24 31	7 14 21 28	4 11 18 25	2 9 16 23 30	6 13 20 27	4 11 18 25
S	3 10 17 24 31	7 14 21 28	7 14 21 28	4 11 18 25	2 9 16 23 30	6 13 20 27	4 11 18 25	1 8 15 22 29	5 12 19 26	3 10 17 24 31	7 14 21 28	5 12 19 26
S	4 11 18 25	1 8 15 22	1 8 15 22 29	5 12 19 26	3 10 17 24 31	7 14 21 28	5 12 19 26	2 9 16 23 30	6 13 20 27	4 11 18 25	1 8 15 22 29	6 13 20 27

6

	JANUARY	FEBRUARY	MARCH	APRIL	MAY	JUNE	JULY	AUGUST	SEPTEMBER	OCTOBER	NOVEMBER	DECEMBER
M	4 11 18 25	1 8 15 22	1 8 15 22 29	5 12 19 26	3 10 17 24 31	7 14 21 28	5 12 19 26	2 9 16 23 30	6 13 20 27	4 11 18 25	1 8 15 22 29	6 13 20 27
T	5 12 19 26	2 9 16 23	2 9 16 23 30	6 13 20 27	4 11 18 25	1 8 15 22 29	6 13 20 27	3 10 17 24 31	7 14 21 28	5 12 19 26	2 9 16 23 30	7 14 21 28
W	6 13 20 27	3 10 17 24	3 10 17 24 31	7 14 21 28	5 12 19 26	2 9 16 23 30	7 14 21 28	4 11 18 25	1 8 15 22 29	6 13 20 27	3 10 17 24	1 8 15 22 29
T	7 14 21 28	4 11 18 25	4 11 18 25	1 8 15 22 29	6 13 20 27	3 10 17 24	1 8 15 22 29	5 12 19 26	2 9 16 23 30	7 14 21 28	4 11 18 25	2 9 16 23 30
F	1 8 15 22 29	5 12 19 26	5 12 19 26	2 9 16 23 30	7 14 21 28	4 11 18 25	2 9 16 23 30	6 13 20 27	3 10 17 24	1 8 15 22 29	5 12 19 26	3 10 17 24 31
S	2 9 16 23 30	6 13 20 27	6 13 20 27	3 10 17 24	1 8 15 22 29	5 12 19 26	3 10 17 24 31	7 14 21 28	4 11 18 25	2 9 16 23 30	6 13 20 27	4 11 18 25
S	3 10 17 24 31	7 14 21 28	7 14 21 28	4 11 18 25	2 9 16 23 30	6 13 20 27	4 11 18 25	1 8 15 22 29	5 12 19 26	3 10 17 24 31	7 14 21 28	5 12 19 26

7

	JANUARY	FEBRUARY	MARCH
M	3 10 17 24 31	7 14 21 28	7 14 21 28
T	4 11 18 25	1 8 15 22	1 8 15 22 29
W	5 12 19 26	2 9 16 23	2 9 16 23 30
T	6 13 20 27	3 10 17 24	3 10 17 24 31
F	7 14 21 28	4 11 18 25	4 11 18 25
S	1 8 15 22 29	5 12 19 26	5 12 19 26
S	2 9 16 23 30	6 13 20 27	6 13 20 27

	APRIL	MAY	JUNE
M	4 11 18 25	2 9 16 23 30	6 13 20 27
T	5 12 19 26	3 10 17 24 31	7 14 21 28
W	6 13 20 27	4 11 18 25	1 8 15 22 29
T	7 14 21 28	5 12 19 26	2 9 16 23 30
F	1 8 15 22 29	6 13 20 27	3 10 17 24
S	2 9 16 23 30	7 14 21 28	4 11 18 25
S	3 10 17 24	1 8 15 22 29	5 12 19 26

	JULY	AUGUST	SEPTEMBER
M	4 11 18 25	1 8 15 22 29	5 12 19 26
T	5 12 19 26	2 9 16 23 30	6 13 20 27
W	6 13 20 27	3 10 17 24 31	7 14 21 28
T	7 14 21 28	4 11 18 25	1 8 15 22 29
F	1 8 15 22 29	5 12 19 26	2 9 16 23 30
S	2 9 16 23 30	6 13 20 27	3 10 17 24
S	3 10 17 24 31	7 14 21 28	4 11 18 25

	OCTOBER	NOVEMBER	DECEMBER
M	3 10 17 24 31	7 14 21 28	5 12 19 26
T	4 11 18 25	1 8 15 22 29	6 13 20 27
W	5 12 19 26	2 9 16 23 30	7 14 21 28
T	6 13 20 27	3 10 17 24	1 8 15 22 29
F	7 14 21 28	4 11 18 25	2 9 16 23 30
S	1 8 15 22 29	5 12 19 26	3 10 17 24 31
S	2 9 16 23 30	6 13 20 27	4 11 18 25

8

	JANUARY	FEBRUARY	MARCH
M	2 9 16 23 30	6 13 20 27	5 12 19 26
T	3 10 17 24 31	7 14 21 28	6 13 20 27
W	4 11 18 25	1 8 15 22 29	7 14 21 28
T	5 12 19 26	2 9 16 23	1 8 15 22 29
F	6 13 20 27	3 10 17 24	2 9 16 23 30
S	7 14 21 28	4 11 18 25	3 10 17 24 31
S	1 8 15 22 29	5 12 19 26	4 11 18 25

	APRIL	MAY	JUNE
M	2 9 16 23 30	7 14 21 28	4 11 18 25
T	3 10 17 24	1 8 15 22 29	5 12 19 26
W	4 11 18 25	2 9 16 23 30	6 13 20 27
T	5 12 19 26	3 10 17 24	7 14 21 28
F	6 13 20 27	4 11 18 25	1 8 15 22 29
S	7 14 21 28	5 12 19 26	2 9 16 23 30
S	1 8 15 22 29	6 13 20 27	3 10 17 24

	JULY	AUGUST	SEPTEMBER
M	2 9 16 23 30	6 13 20 27	3 10 17 24
T	3 10 17 24 31	7 14 21 28	4 11 18 25
W	4 11 18 25	1 8 15 22 29	5 12 19 26
T	5 12 19 26	2 9 16 23 30	6 13 20 27
F	6 13 20 27	3 10 17 24 31	7 14 21 28
S	7 14 21 28	4 11 18 25	1 8 15 22 29
S	1 8 15 22 29	5 12 19 26	2 9 16 23 30

	OCTOBER	NOVEMBER	DECEMBER
M	1 8 15 22 29	5 12 19 26	3 10 17 24 31
T	2 9 16 23 30	6 13 20 27	4 11 18 25
W	3 10 17 24 31	7 14 21 28	5 12 19 26
T	4 11 18 25	1 8 15 22 29	6 13 20 27
F	5 12 19 26	2 9 16 23 30	7 14 21 28
S	6 13 20 27	3 10 17 24	1 8 15 22 29
S	7 14 21 28	4 11 18 25	2 9 16 23 30

11

	JANUARY	FEBRUARY	MARCH
M	6 13 20 27	3 10 17 24	2 9 16 23 30
T	7 14 21 28	4 11 18 25	3 10 17 24 31
W	1 8 15 22 29	5 12 19 26	4 11 18 25
T	2 9 16 23 30	6 13 20 27	5 12 19 26
F	3 10 17 24 31	7 14 21 28	6 13 20 27
S	4 11 18 25	1 8 15 22 29	7 14 21 28
S	5 12 19 26	2 9 16 23	1 8 15 22 29

	APRIL	MAY	JUNE
M	6 13 20 27	4 11 18 25	1 8 15 22 29
T	7 14 21 28	5 12 19 26	2 9 16 23 30
W	1 8 15 22 29	6 13 20 27	3 10 17 24
T	2 9 16 23 30	7 14 21 28	4 11 18 25
F	3 10 17 24	1 8 15 22 29	5 12 19 26
S	4 11 18 25	2 9 16 23 30	6 13 20 27
S	5 12 19 26	3 10 17 24 31	7 14 21 28

	JULY	AUGUST	SEPTEMBER
M	6 13 20 27	3 10 17 24 31	7 14 21 28
T	7 14 21 28	4 11 18 25	1 8 15 22 29
W	1 8 15 22 29	5 12 19 26	2 9 16 23 30
T	2 9 16 23 30	6 13 20 27	3 10 17 24
F	3 10 17 24 31	7 14 21 28	4 11 18 25
S	4 11 18 25	1 8 15 22 29	5 12 19 26
S	5 12 19 26	2 9 16 23 30	6 13 20 27

	OCTOBER	NOVEMBER	DECEMBER
M	5 12 19 26	2 9 16 23 30	7 14 21 28
T	6 13 20 27	3 10 17 24	1 8 15 22 29
W	7 14 21 28	4 11 18 25	2 9 16 23 30
T	1 8 15 22 29	5 12 19 26	3 10 17 24 31
F	2 9 16 23 30	6 13 20 27	4 11 18 25
S	3 10 17 24 31	7 14 21 28	5 12 19 26
S	4 11 18 25	1 8 15 22 29	6 13 20 27

12

	JANUARY	FEBRUARY	MARCH
M	5 12 19 26	2 9 16 23	1 8 15 22 29
T	6 13 20 27	3 10 17 24	2 9 16 23 30
W	7 14 21 28	4 11 18 25	3 10 17 24 31
T	1 8 15 22 29	5 12 19 26	4 11 18 25
F	2 9 16 23 30	6 13 20 27	5 12 19 26
S	3 10 17 24 31	7 14 21 28	6 13 20 27
S	4 11 18 25	1 8 15 22 29	7 14 21 28

	APRIL	MAY	JUNE
M	5 12 19 26	3 10 17 24 31	7 14 21 28
T	6 13 20 27	4 11 18 25	1 8 15 22 29
W	7 14 21 28	5 12 19 26	2 9 16 23 30
T	1 8 15 22 29	6 13 20 27	3 10 17 24
F	2 9 16 23 30	7 14 21 28	4 11 18 25
S	3 10 17 24	1 8 15 22 29	5 12 19 26
S	4 11 18 25	2 9 16 23 30	6 13 20 27

	JULY	AUGUST	SEPTEMBER
M	5 12 19 26	2 9 16 23 30	6 13 20 27
T	6 13 20 27	3 10 17 24 31	7 14 21 28
W	7 14 21 28	4 11 18 25	1 8 15 22 29
T	1 8 15 22 29	5 12 19 26	2 9 16 23 30
F	2 9 16 23 30	6 13 20 27	3 10 17 24
S	3 10 17 24 31	7 14 21 28	4 11 18 25
S	4 11 18 25	1 8 15 22 29	5 12 19 26

	OCTOBER	NOVEMBER	DECEMBER
M	4 11 18 25	1 8 15 22 29	6 13 20 27
T	5 12 19 26	2 9 16 23 30	7 14 21 28
W	6 13 20 27	3 10 17 24	1 8 15 22 29
T	7 14 21 28	4 11 18 25	2 9 16 23 30
F	1 8 15 22 29	5 12 19 26	3 10 17 24 31
S	2 9 16 23 30	6 13 20 27	4 11 18 25
S	3 10 17 24 31	7 14 21 28	5 12 19 26

9

JANUARY
M	1 8 15 22 29
T	2 9 16 23 30
W	3 10 17 24 31
T	4 11 18 25
F	5 12 19 26
S	6 13 20 27
S	7 14 21 28

FEBRUARY
M	5 12 19 26
T	6 13 20 27
W	7 14 21 28
T	1 8 15 22 29
F	2 9 16 23
S	3 10 17 24
S	4 11 18 25

MARCH
M	4 11 18 25
T	5 12 19 26
W	6 13 20 27
T	7 14 21 28
F	1 8 15 22 29
S	2 9 16 23 30
S	3 10 17 24 31

APRIL
M	1 8 15 22 29
T	2 9 16 23 30
W	3 10 17 24
T	4 11 18 25
F	5 12 19 26
S	6 13 20 27
S	7 14 21 28

MAY
M	6 13 20 27
T	7 14 21 28
W	1 8 15 22 29
T	2 9 16 23 30
F	3 10 17 24 31
S	4 11 18 25
S	5 12 19 26

JUNE
M	3 10 17 24
T	4 11 18 25
W	5 12 19 26
T	6 13 20 27
F	7 14 21 28
S	1 8 15 22 29
S	2 9 16 23 30

JULY
M	1 8 15 22 29
T	2 9 16 23 30
W	3 10 17 24 31
T	4 11 18 25
F	5 12 19 26
S	6 13 20 27
S	7 14 21 28

AUGUST
M	5 12 19 26
T	6 13 20 27
W	7 14 21 28
T	1 8 15 22 29
F	2 9 16 23 30
S	3 10 17 24 31
S	4 11 18 25

SEPTEMBER
M	2 9 16 23 30
T	3 10 17 24
W	4 11 18 25
T	5 12 19 26
F	6 13 20 27
S	7 14 21 28
S	1 8 15 22 29

OCTOBER
M	7 14 21 28
T	1 8 15 22 29
W	2 9 16 23 30
T	3 10 17 24 31
F	4 11 18 25
S	5 12 19 26
S	6 13 20 27

NOVEMBER
M	4 11 18 25
T	5 12 19 26
W	6 13 20 27
T	7 14 21 28
F	1 8 15 22 29
S	2 9 16 23 30
S	3 10 17 24

DECEMBER
M	2 9 16 23 30
T	3 10 17 24 31
W	4 11 18 25
T	5 12 19 26
F	6 13 20 27
S	7 14 21 28
S	1 8 15 22 29

10

JANUARY
M	7 14 21 28
T	1 8 15 22 29
W	2 9 16 23 30
T	3 10 17 24 31
F	4 11 18 25
S	5 12 19 26
S	6 13 20 27

FEBRUARY
M	4 11 18 25
T	5 12 19 26
W	6 13 20 27
T	7 14 21 28
F	1 8 15 22 29
S	2 9 16 23
S	3 10 17 24

MARCH
M	3 10 17 24 31
T	4 11 18 25
W	5 12 19 26
T	6 13 20 27
F	7 14 21 28
S	1 8 15 22 29
S	2 9 16 23 30

APRIL
M	7 14 21 28
T	1 8 15 22 29
W	2 9 16 23 30
T	3 10 17 24
F	4 11 18 25
S	5 12 19 26
S	6 13 20 27

MAY
M	5 12 19 26
T	6 13 20 27
W	7 14 21 28
T	1 8 15 22 29
F	2 9 16 23 30
S	3 10 17 24 31
S	4 11 18 25

JUNE
M	2 9 16 23 30
T	3 10 17 24
W	4 11 18 25
T	5 12 19 26
F	6 13 20 27
S	7 14 21 28
S	1 8 15 22 29

JULY
M	7 14 21 28
T	1 8 15 22 29
W	2 9 16 23 30
T	3 10 17 24 31
F	4 11 18 25
S	5 12 19 26
S	6 13 20 27

AUGUST
M	4 11 18 25
T	5 12 19 26
W	6 13 20 27
T	7 14 21 28
F	1 8 15 22 29
S	2 9 16 23 30
S	3 10 17 24 31

SEPTEMBER
M	1 8 15 22 29
T	2 9 16 23 30
W	3 10 17 24
T	4 11 18 25
F	5 12 19 26
S	6 13 20 27
S	7 14 21 28

OCTOBER
M	6 13 20 27
T	7 14 21 28
W	1 8 15 22 29
T	2 9 16 23 30
F	3 10 17 24 31
S	4 11 18 25
S	5 12 19 26

NOVEMBER
M	3 10 17 24
T	4 11 18 25
W	5 12 19 26
T	6 13 20 27
F	7 14 21 28
S	1 8 15 22 29
S	2 9 16 23 30

DECEMBER
M	1 8 15 22 29
T	2 9 16 23 30
W	3 10 17 24 31
T	4 11 18 25
F	5 12 19 26
S	6 13 20 27
S	7 14 21 28

13

JANUARY
M	4 11 18 25
T	5 12 19 26
W	6 13 20 27
T	7 14 21 28
F	1 8 15 22 29
S	2 9 16 23 30
S	3 10 17 24 31

FEBRUARY
M	1 8 15 22 29
T	2 9 16 23
W	3 10 17 24
T	4 11 18 25
F	5 12 19 26
S	6 13 20 27
S	7 14 21 28

MARCH
M	7 14 21 28
T	1 8 15 22 29
W	2 9 16 23 30
T	3 10 17 24 31
F	4 11 18 25
S	5 12 19 26
S	6 13 20 27

APRIL
M	4 11 18 25
T	5 12 19 26
W	6 13 20 27
T	7 14 21 28
F	1 8 15 22 29
S	2 9 16 23 30
S	3 10 17 24

MAY
M	2 9 16 23 30
T	3 10 17 24 31
W	4 11 18 25
T	5 12 19 26
F	6 13 20 27
S	7 14 21 28
S	1 8 15 22 29

JUNE
M	6 13 20 27
T	7 14 21 28
W	1 8 15 22 29
T	2 9 16 23 30
F	3 10 17 24
S	4 11 18 25
S	5 12 19 26

JULY
M	4 11 18 25
T	5 12 19 26
W	6 13 20 27
T	7 14 21 28
F	1 8 15 22 29
S	2 9 16 23 30
S	3 10 17 24 31

AUGUST
M	1 8 15 22 29
T	2 9 16 23 30
W	3 10 17 24 31
T	4 11 18 25
F	5 12 19 26
S	6 13 20 27
S	7 14 21 28

SEPTEMBER
M	5 12 19 26
T	6 13 20 27
W	7 14 21 28
T	1 8 15 22 29
F	2 9 16 23 30
S	3 10 17 24
S	4 11 18 25

OCTOBER
M	3 10 17 24 31
T	4 11 18 25
W	5 12 19 26
T	6 13 20 27
F	7 14 21 28
S	1 8 15 22 29
S	2 9 16 23 30

NOVEMBER
M	7 14 21 28
T	1 8 15 22 29
W	2 9 16 23 30
T	3 10 17 24
F	4 11 18 25
S	5 12 19 26
S	6 13 20 27

DECEMBER
M	5 12 19 26
T	6 13 20 27
W	7 14 21 28
T	1 8 15 22 29
F	2 9 16 23 30
S	3 10 17 24 31
S	4 11 18 25

14

JANUARY
M	3 10 17 24 31
T	4 11 18 25
W	5 12 19 26
T	6 13 20 27
F	7 14 21 28
S	1 8 15 22 29
S	2 9 16 23 30

FEBRUARY
M	7 14 21 28
T	1 8 15 22 29
W	2 9 16 23
T	3 10 17 24
F	4 11 18 25
S	5 12 19 26
S	6 13 20 27

MARCH
M	6 13 20 27
T	7 14 21 28
W	1 8 15 22 29
T	2 9 16 23 30
F	3 10 17 24 31
S	4 11 18 25
S	5 12 19 26

APRIL
M	3 10 17 24
T	4 11 18 25
W	5 12 19 26
T	6 13 20 27
F	7 14 21 28
S	1 8 15 22 29
S	2 9 16 23 30

MAY
M	1 8 15 22 29
T	2 9 16 23 30
W	3 10 17 24 31
T	4 11 18 25
F	5 12 19 26
S	6 13 20 27
S	7 14 21 28

JUNE
M	5 12 19 26
T	6 13 20 27
W	7 14 21 28
T	1 8 15 22 29
F	2 9 16 23 30
S	3 10 17 24
S	4 11 18 25

JULY
M	3 10 17 24 31
T	4 11 18 25
W	5 12 19 26
T	6 13 20 27
F	7 14 21 28
S	1 8 15 22 29
S	2 9 16 23 30

AUGUST
M	7 14 21 28
T	1 8 15 22 29
W	2 9 16 23 30
T	3 10 17 24 31
F	4 11 18 25
S	5 12 19 26
S	6 13 20 27

SEPTEMBER
M	4 11 18 25
T	5 12 19 26
W	6 13 20 27
T	7 14 21 28
F	1 8 15 22 29
S	2 9 16 23 30
S	3 10 17 24

OCTOBER
M	2 9 16 23 30
T	3 10 17 24 31
W	4 11 18 25
T	5 12 19 26
F	6 13 20 27
S	7 14 21 28
S	1 8 15 22 29

NOVEMBER
M	6 13 20 27
T	7 14 21 28
W	1 8 15 22 29
T	2 9 16 23 30
F	3 10 17 24
S	4 11 18 25
S	5 12 19 26

DECEMBER
M	4 11 18 25
T	5 12 19 26
W	6 13 20 27
T	7 14 21 28
F	1 8 15 22 29
S	2 9 16 23 30
S	3 10 17 24 31

Translations

ENGLISH	FRENCH	SPANISH	PORTUGUESE	INDONESIAN
big	gros/grand	grande	grande	besar
beach	plage	playa	praia	pantai
boat	bateau	barco	barco	perahu
bottom	fond	fondo	fundo	dasar
channel	chenal	canal	canal	saluran
cliff	falaise	acantilado	penhasco	jurang
coast	côte	costa	costa	pesisir
cold	froid	frío/fria	frio	dingin
coral reef	récif de corail	arrecifes de coral	recife de coral	karang
current/rip	courant	corriente	agueiro or corrente	arus laut
dangerous	dangereux	peligroso	perigoso	bahaya
deep water	eau profonde	aguas profundas	águas profundas	laut dalam
fast	vite	rápido	rápido	cepat
harbour	port	puerto	porto	pelabuhan
high pressure	haute pression	alta presión/anticiclón	alta pressão	tekanan tinggi
high tide	marée haute	marea alta	maré alta	air pasang
help!	A l'aide!	¡ayuda!	ajuda!	tolong!
hot	chaud	caliente	quente	panas
island	île	isla	ilha	pulau
jellyfish	méduse	medusa	alforreca	ubur ubur
lava	lave	lava	lava	lahar
left	gauche	izquierda	esquerda	kiri
low pressure	basse pression	baja presión/borrasca	baixa pressão	tekanan rendah
low tide	marée basse	marea baja	baixa-mar	air surut
moon	lune	luna	lua	bulan
ocean	océan	océano	oceano	lautan
offshore	offshore	viento terral	offshore	angin darat
onshore	onshore	viento del mar	onshore	angin laut
point	pointe	lugar, pico	pico	tanjung
rain	pluie	lluvia	chuva	hujan
right	droite	derecha	direito	kanan
rivermouth	emboucheure	desembocadura (de ria)	boca do rio	maura sungai
rocks	rocher	rocas	rochas	batu
sand	sable	arena	areia	pasir
shallow	peu profond	poco profundo	pouco profundo	dangkal
shark	requin	tiburón	tubarão	hiu
sheltered	abri	abrigado	protegido	terlindung
slow	lent	lento	lento	pelan
small	petit	pequeño	pequeno	kecil
storm	tempête	tormenta	yempestade	badai
sun	soleil	sol	sol	matahari
surfboard	planche de surf	plancha de surf	prancha de surfe	papan selancar
surfing	surf	surf	surfar	main ski/berselancar
swell	houle	marejada	swell	gelombang
tube/barrel	barrique	tubo	tubo	lengkung
urchins	oursins	erizos	erizos	bulu babi
water	eau	agua	água	air
wave	vague	ola	onda	ombak
wax	wax	parafina	wax	lilin
wind	vent	viento	vento	angin
north	nord	norte	norte	utara
south	sud	sur	sul	selatan
east	est	este	leste	timur
west	ouest	oeste	oeste	barat

ENGLISH	FRENCH	SPANISH	PORTUGUESE	INDONESIAN
yes	oui	sí	sim	ya
no	non	no	não	tidak
hello	bonjour	hola	olá	halo
goodbye	au revoir	adiós	adeus	selamat jalan
sorry	pardon	perdón	desculpe	ma'af
thank you	merci	gracias	obrigado	terima kasih
please	s'il vous plait	por favor	por favor	tolong
good	bon	bueno	bom	bagus
bad	mauvais	malo	mau	tidak bagus
today	aujourd'hui	hoy	hoje	hari ini
tomorrow	demain	mañana	amanhã	besok
yesterday	hier	ayer	ontem	kemarin
night	nuit	noche	noite	malam
morning	matin	mañana	manhã	pagi
police	la police	policía	polícia	polisi
ambulance	ambulance	ambulancia	ambulância	ambulans
doctor	médecin	médico	médico	dokter
broken bone	os cassé	hueso roto	osso quebrado	patah tulang
fever	fièvre	fiebre	febre	deman
pharmancy	pharmancie	farmacia	farmácia	apotik
hospital	hôpital	hospital	hospital	rumah sakit
infection	infection	infección	infecção	infeksi
diarrhoea	diarrhée	diarrea	diarreia	diare
toothache	mal aux dents	dolor de muelas	dor de dente	sakit gigi
vomit	vomir	vomitar	vomitar	muntah
please help	s'il vous plaît aider moi	por favor ayuda	por favor ajude-me	tolong bantu
taxi	taxi	taxi	táxi	taksi
aeroplane	avion	avión	avião	pesawat
train	train	tren	comboio	kereta api
open	ouvert	abierto	abrir	buka
closed	fermé	cerrado	fechado	tutup
toilet	toilettes/wc	baño	casa de banho	kamar kecil
shop	magasin	tienda	loja	toko
lost	perdu	perdido	perdido	tersesat
one	un	uno	um	satu
two	deux	dos	dois	dua
three	trois	tres	três	tiga
four	quatre	cuatro	quatro	empat
five	cinq	cinco	cinco	lima
six	six	seis	seis	enam
seven	sept	siete	sete	tujuh
eight	huit	ocho	oito	delapan
nine	neuf	nueve	nove	sembilan
ten	dix	diez	dez	sepuluh
twenty	vingt	veinte	vinte	dua puluh
thirty	trente	treinta	trinta	tiga puluh
forty	quarante	cuarenta	quarenta	empat puluh
fifty	cinguant	cincuenta	cinqüenta	lima puluh
sixty	soixante	sesenta	sessenta	enam puluh
seventy	soisante-dix	setenta	setenta	tujuh puluh
eighty	quatre-vingt	ochenta	oitenta	delapan puluh
ninety	quatre-vingt-dix	noventa	noventa	sembilan puluh
hundred	cent	cien	trinta	seratus
thousand	mille	mil	mil	seribu

World Swell Heights

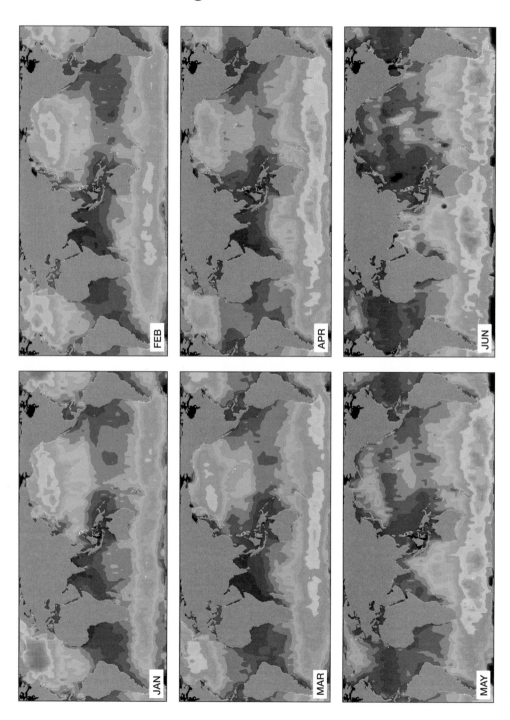

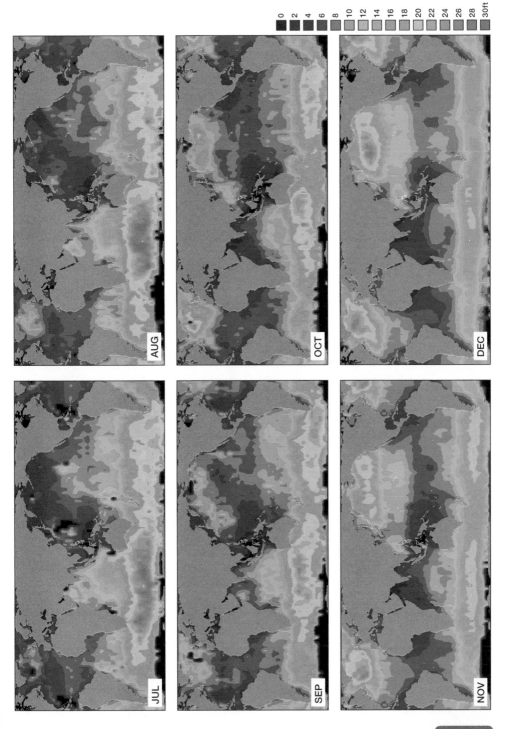

World Weather

EUROPE

WATER TEMPS (°C)

Location	J-F	M-A	M-J	J-A	S-O	N-D
SÃO MIGUEL **AZORES**	16	17	18	22	22	19
LANZAROTE **CANARY IS.**	18	18	19	22	22	20
CORNWALL **ENGLAND**	9	10	12	16	14	11
BRITTANY **FRANCE**	10	10	13	16	15	12
LANDES **FRANCE**	12	13	17	21	18	15
COTE BASQUE **FRANCE**	12	13	17	21	18	14
NW **GREECE**	15	16	20	24	23	19
REYKJANES PEN. **ICELAND**	5	7	8	11	9	8
DONEGAL BAY **IRELAND**	8	9	12	16	13	10
TEL AVIV **ISRAEL**	18	19	23	27	25	21
SARDINIA **ITALY**	13	14	19	24	22	16
CENTRAL **ITALY**	13	14	19	24	22	17
MADEIRA	16	17	19	22	21	19
MALTA AND GOZO	15	16	20	25	23	18
NETHERLANDS	5	6	12	16	15	9
LOFOTEN **NORWAY**	5	6	7	10	9	7
PENICHE **PORTUGAL**	13	14	16	18	17	15
ALGARVE **PORTUGAL**	15	16	18	21	19	17
CAITHNESS **SCOTLAND**	5	6	10	15	12	8
PAIS VASCO **SPAIN**	12	13	15	19	17	14
ASTURIAS **SPAIN**	12	13	15	19	17	14
GALICIA **SPAIN**	12	13	15	18	17	14
BLACK SEA **TURKEY**	7	9	14	24	20	13
GOWER **WALES**	9	10	12	16	14	11

RAINFALL (mm)

Location	J-F	M-A	M-J	J-A	S-O	N-D
SÃO MIGUEL AZORES	110	85	50	27	95	110
LANZAROTE CANARY IS.	37	22	3	0	18	55
CORNWALL ENGLAND	90	63	62	75	87	115
BRITTANY FRANCE	115	83	63	70	98	145
LANDES FRANCE	132	126	105	84	130	134
COTE BASQUE FRANCE	132	126	105	84	130	161
NW GREECE	133	81	24	15	114	179
REYKJANES PEN. ICELAND	78	59	42	53	80	78
DONEGAL BAY IRELAND	82	57	62	87	100	100
TEL AVIV ISRAEL	142	33	2	0	14	140
SARDINIA ITALY	50	37	19	5	42	67
CENTRAL ITALY	67	54	42	18	81	111
MADEIRA	82	58	12	2	55	95
MALTA AND GOZO	75	27	7	4	46	101
NETHERLANDS	54	41	46	68	72	65
LOFOTEN NORWAY	61	51	41	59	101	89
PENICHE PORTUGAL	90	80	30	4	31	100
ALGARVE PORTUGAL	60	50	12	1	35	65
CAITHNESS SCOTLAND	48	40	50	80	60	57
PAIS VASCO SPAIN	105	82	78	75	125	140
ASTURIAS SPAIN	105	83	78	75	125	143
GALICIA SPAIN	99	80	50	38	75	130
BLACK SEA TURKEY	70	65	42	35	71	87
GOWER WALES	100	70	75	100	115	135

MIN / MAX TEMPS (°C)

Location	J-F min	J-F max	M-A min	M-A max	M-J min	M-J max	J-A min	J-A max	S-O min	S-O max	N-D min	N-D max
SÃO MIGUEL AZORES	11	17	11	18	14	21	17	26	16	23	13	19
LANZAROTE CANARY IS.	14	21	15	23	18	25	21	29	20	27	16	23
CORNWALL ENGLAND	4	8	5	11	9	16	13	19	11	17	6	10
BRITTANY FRANCE	4	9	6	12	9	17	13	20	10	17	6	11
LANDES FRANCE	5	12	7	15	12	20	16	24	13	22	6	14
COTE BASQUE FRANCE	5	12	7	15	12	20	16	24	13	22	6	14
NW GREECE	6	14	9	18	18	28	23	33	17	27	10	17
REYKJANES PEN. ICELAND	-2	3	0	5	5	11	8	14	4	11	-1	3
DONEGAL BAY IRELAND	3	8	4	10	8	14	12	17	9	14	5	9
TEL AVIV ISRAEL	9	19	12	24	18	28	24	31	21	31	14	23
SARDINIA ITALY	7	14	10	18	16	25	21	30	17	25	10	18
CENTRAL ITALY	5	12	8	17	15	25	20	30	15	24	7	15
MADEIRA	13	18	13	19	16	21	19	25	18	24	15	21
MALTA AND GOZO	10	15	12	17	17	24	22	29	20	26	14	18
NETHERLANDS	1	5	4	11	11	18	14	21	11	17	4	8
LOFOTEN NORWAY	-4	2	-3	4	5	12	11	15	4	9	-1	3
PENICHE PORTUGAL	8	15	11	19	14	23	17	28	15	25	9	16
ALGARVE PORTUGAL	9	16	12	19	16	24	20	28	17	24	11	18
CAITHNESS SCOTLAND	1	6	3	9	8	15	11	18	8	14	3	8
PAIS VASCO SPAIN	7	12	9	15	12	19	16	22	13	19	9	14
ASTURIAS SPAIN	7	12	9	15	12	19	16	22	14	20	9	14
GALICIA SPAIN	7	13	8	16	12	19	15	23	13	21	8	14
BLACK SEA TURKEY	3	10	5	14	14	21	18	26	14	23	7	15
GOWER WALES	3	6	7	9	12	15	15	18	11	14	6	11

AFRICA

WATER TEMPS (°C)

Location	J-F	M-A	M-J	J-A	S-O	N-D
LUANDA & BENGO **ANGOLA**	26	26	24	21	23	25
SAL **CAPE VERDE**	21	21	24	26	27	25
NORTH **GABON**	27	28	25	23	24	26
GOLD COAST **GHANA**	27	28	27	25	24	26
IVORY COAST	27	28	27	25	24	26
KENYA	26	28	27	25	26	27
NORTHWEST **LIBERIA**	27	27	28	26	27	28
CENTRAL **MOROCCO**	16	17	19	22	21	18
INHAMBANE **MOZAMBIQUE**	25	25	23	21	22	24
SKELETON COAST **NAMIBIA**	21	19	17	16	16	17
SWAKOPMUND **NAMIBIA**	20	18	15	13	14	16
SAO TOME	28	28	27	25	26	27
ALMADIES PEN. **SENEGAL**	17	17	21	26	27	22
CAPE PEN. **S. AFRICA**	16	16	15	14	15	16
GARDEN ROUTE **S. AFRICA**	22	22	19	18	19	20
ST. FRANCIS BAY **S. AFRICA**	21	19	17	15	16	19
WILD COAST **S. AFRICA**	22	21	19	18	19	21
DURBAN **SOUTH AFRICA**	25	25	23	20	22	23
TOGO & BENIN	27	28	27	24	25	27
WESTERN SAHARA	18	18	19	21	22	20

RAINFALL (mm)

Location	J-F	M-A	M-J	J-A	S-O	N-D
LUANDA & BENGO ANGOLA	30	113	10	1	4	30
SAL CAPE VERDE	3	0	0	10	30	16
NORTH GABON	248	330	143	6	233	338
GOLD COAST GHANA	33	145	487	117	140	150
IVORY COAST	33	145	487	117	140	150
KENYA	27	118	191	72	81	85
NORTHWEST LIBERIA	44	156	744	685	758	183
CENTRAL MOROCCO	40	20	3	1	13	35
INHAMBANE MOZAMBIQUE	128	83	28	13	43	138
SKELETON COAST NAMIBIA	3	6	0	2	0	0
SWAKOPMUND NAMIBIA	3	6	1	1	0	0
SAO TOME	94	140	81	0	66	103
ALMADIES PEN. SENEGAL	1	0	5	135	105	2
CAPE PEN. S. AFRICA	10	30	82	77	37	14
GARDEN ROUTE S. AFRICA	53	60	64	65	70	58
ST. FRANCIS BAY S. AFRICA	35	47	62	57	62	50
WILD COAST S. AFRICA	127	115	48	47	94	121
DURBAN SOUTH AFRICA	125	102	47	32	75	122
TOGO & BENIN	33	121	310	64	101	36
WESTERN SAHARA	32	20	3	0	115	44

MIN / MAX TEMPS (°C)

Location	J-F min	J-F max	M-A min	M-A max	M-J min	M-J max	J-A min	J-A max	S-O min	S-O max	N-D min	N-D max
LUANDA & BENGO ANGOLA	24	30	24	31	22	28	18	25	21	28	23	29
SAL CAPE VERDE	19	23	19	24	20	25	22	27	23	26	21	25
NORTH GABON	24	31	23	31	24	30	22	28	23	29	24	30
GOLD COAST GHANA	23	32	24	32	24	30	23	28	23	28	23	31
IVORY COAST	23	32	24	32	24	30	23	28	23	28	23	31
KENYA	23	31	24	31	22	29	21	27	21	29	23	30
NORTHWEST LIBERIA	21	31	22	31	22	30	23	26	22	28	21	30
CENTRAL MOROCCO	9	21	11	22	15	24	18	27	16	26	10	21
INHAMBANE MOZAMBIQUE	22	30	20	30	15	26	15	26	17	28	21	29
SKELETON COAST NAMIBIA	15	23	14	24	10	23	8	21	10	19	13	22
SWAKOPMUND NAMIBIA	15	23	14	23	10	23	8	20	10	19	13	22
SAO TOME	23	30	23	30	21	28	21	28	21	29	21	29
ALMADIES PEN. SENEGAL	17	25	18	24	21	28	24	30	24	30	22	26
CAPE PEN. S. AFRICA	16	26	13	24	9	19	7	18	10	20	14	24
GARDEN ROUTE S. AFRICA	17	25	15	24	9	21	8	20	11	21	15	23
ST. FRANCIS BAY S. AFRICA	16	25	14	24	9	21	7	20	11	21	14	23
WILD COAST S. AFRICA	20	25	18	24	15	23	13	21	16	22	18	23
DURBAN SOUTH AFRICA	20	28	19	27	11	23	11	22	16	23	18	26
TOGO & BENIN	24	28	26	28	23	27	23	26	23	27	24	28
WESTERN SAHARA	10	20	12	21	15	23	17	25	16	25	10	23

INDIAN OCEAN

Location	|	WATER TEMPS (°C)						|	RAINFALL (mm)						| MIN	MAX	MIN	MAX	MIN	MAX	MIN	MAX	MIN	MAX	MIN	MAX TEMPS (°C)
	J-F	M-A	M-J	J-A	S-O	N-D	J-F	M-A	M-J	J-A	S-O	N-D	J-F		M-A		M-J		J-A		S-O		N-D	
ANDHRA PRADESH **INDIA**	26	28	29	28	28	27	9	18	82	138	190	37	19	30	25	34	28	36	26	33	25	32	23	31
ANDAMAN ISLANDS **INDIA**	27	28	29	28	27	27	30	40	420	400	380	190	23	28	25	30	26	29	25	27	25	27	25	28
KERALA/TAMIL NADU **INDIA**	27	29	28	27	27	27	15	78	451	546	261	102	22	31	25	32	23	30	23	29	23	30	23	31
BALUCHISTAN **IRAN**	23	25	29	29	28	25	18	9	5	55	8	7	12	25	19	31	26	36	29	35	24	33	14	29
VEZO REEFS **MADAGASCAR**	27	27	25	23	24	26	70	24	15	4	12	45	23	32	21	32	16	28	15	27	17	29	21	31
SE **MADAGASCAR**	25	25	22	21	21	23	242	130	10	10	30	200	23	30	21	29	18	24	17	25	17	27	21	30
NORTH MALÉ **MALDIVES**	27	28	27	26	27	27	32	40	240	212	172	113	23	29	25	31	25	31	24	29	24	29	23	29
THAA & LAAMU **MALDIVES**	28	29	29	28	28	28	32	40	240	212	172	113	25	30	25	31	25	31	25	31	24	30	24	30
HUVADHOO **MALDIVES**	28	29	29	28	28	28	34	44	242	206	183	112	25	30	25	31	25	31	25	31	24	30	24	30
MAURITIUS	27	26	24	22	23	25	205	174	81	61	38	82	23	30	21	29	17	26	17	24	17	26	19	29
OMAN	22	23	25	24	23	23	3	3	3	3	2	7	24	26	26	31	29	35	30	31	28	31	25	28
WEST MAKRAN **PAKISTAN**	24	26	29	29	28	25	9	4	4	73	9	4	16	27	23	31	29	35	29	33	26	33	18	30
WEST **RÉUNION**	28	27	26	24	25	26	240	225	77	60	45	247	23	30	22	29	16	27	17	25	18	26	21	28
SEYCHELLES	28	28	27	25	26	27	334	180	121	103	172	245	25	30	28	31	28	30	26	28	26	29	25	30
SOUTHEAST **SRI LANKA**	27	28	28	27	27	27	115	53	49	79	164	361	24	28	25	31	26	33	25	33	24	32	24	28
SOUTHWEST **SRI LANKA**	27	28	28	28	27	27	92	190	282	132	255	250	22	31	23	31	25	31	25	29	24	29	22	30
PHUKET **THAILAND**	27	27	29	28	28	28	31	89	306	283	360	121	22	31	24	32	24	30	25	30	24	29	23	29
YEMEN	25	27	29	25	26	26	3	2	0	4	0	3	22	28	24	31	28	36	28	36	26	35	23	29

EAST ASIA

Location	WT J-F	WT M-A	WT M-J	WT J-A	WT S-O	WT N-D	RF J-F	RF M-A	RF M-J	RF J-A	RF S-O	RF N-D	MIN J-F	MAX J-F	MIN M-A	MAX M-A	MIN M-J	MAX M-J	MIN J-A	MAX J-A	MIN S-O	MAX S-O	MIN N-D	MAX N-D
HAINAN **CHINA**	24	26	29	29	29	25	7	21	150	180	240	25	19	24	21	27	24	32	25	32	24	31	20	25
SIMEULUE & BANYAKS **INDO**	27	28	28	27	27	28	120	110	130	130	200	220	23	30	23	31	23	31	24	31	23	30	23	29
NIAS & HINAKO ISL. **INDO**	29	28	28	27	28	28	115	117	150	160	235	237	22	30	22	32	23	32	23	32	22	31	22	29
MENTAWAI ISLANDS **INDO**	29	28	28	27	28	28	112	117	155	155	235	238	22	30	22	32	22	32	22	32	22	30	22	30
LAMPUNG **INDONESIA**	28	28	28	27	28	28	320	300	230	220	310	430	23	30	23	30	23	31	23	30	23	30	23	30
KAMPAR RIVER **INDONESIA**	27	27	28	28	28	28	114	118	141	151	223	237	22	29	23	30	24	31	24	32	24	31	23	30
WEST JAVA **INDONESIA**	29	28	28	27	28	28	300	117	105	55	77	172	23	29	23	31	23	31	23	31	23	30	23	30
BALI **INDONESIA**	29	28	28	27	28	28	300	177	105	55	77	172	23	29	23	31	23	31	23	31	23	30	23	30
LOMBOK **INDONESIA**	29	28	28	27	27	28	310	150	70	35	65	220	25	30	25	30	25	29	24	28	25	29	25	30
WEST SUMBAWA **INDO**	29	28	28	27	28	28	300	177	105	55	77	172	23	29	23	31	23	31	23	31	23	30	23	30
SUMBA **INDONESIA**	29	29	28	26	27	29	340	140	20	5	10	150	24	28	24	30	24	31	23	30	24	32	25	31
SAVU & ROTE **INDONESIA**	29	29	27	26	27	29	340	140	20	5	10	150	24	28	24	30	24	31	23	30	24	32	25	31
NORTHERN MALUKU **INDO**	28	28	29	28	28	29	123	207	577	501	198	123	24	31	24	30	23	28	23	27	23	28	24	31
CHIBA PREFECTURE **JAPAN**	13	15	18	21	19	17	67	117	155	145	215	80	-2	9	5	15	15	23	21	29	16	24	3	14
SHIKOKU **JAPAN**	17	16	22	27	25	20	95	190	352	282	267	85	3	12	8	18	16	25	23	30	18	26	6	16
OKINAWA **JAPAN**	19	21	25	28	26	22	130	165	290	240	160	130	13	18	17	22	22	27	25	30	23	28	16	22
EAST **MALAYSIA**	29	31	31	29	28	27	203	150	172	206	246	548	22	29	23	32	23	33	23	33	22	32	23	30
SANDAUN/EAST SEPIK **PNG**	28	28	29	28	28	28	130	170	210	170	210	160	23	29	23	30	23	30	22	30	23	30	23	30
KAVIENG **PNG**	28	28	28	27	28	28	434	368	169	154	178	283	24	30	23	31	23	31	23	30	23	30	24	31
CATANDUANES **PHIL.**	24	24	24	26	25	24	460	380	141	154	220	524	23	29	23	31	24	31	24	31	24	31	23	29
EASTERN SAMAR **PHIL.**	23	23	24	25	24	23	550	290	240	160	260	590	22	28	23	30	23	32	23	32	23	31	22	30
NW LUZON **PHILIPPINES**	24	26	26	27	26	25	10	45	270	450	250	45	22	30	24	33	26	32	25	31	25	31	23	30
SIARGAO **PHILIPPINES**	24	24	24	25	24	24	460	380	141	154	220	524	23	29	23	31	24	31	24	31	24	31	23	29
JEJU DO **SOUTH KOREA**	12	13	18	24	23	17	60	82	130	227	119	66	3	8	6	16	14	24	23	29	15	25	5	15
TAIWAN	23	24	27	29	28	25	15	48	244	381	195	42	13	23	17	27	22	30	23	31	21	30	15	26
DA NANG **VIETNAM**	23	24	28	29	28	25	65	15	45	110	490	215	20	25	22	29	25	34	25	34	24	30	21	26

AUSTRALASIA — WATER TEMPS (°C)

	J-F	M-A	M-J	J-A	S-O	N-D
NORTHWEST **W.A.**	26	26	24	22	22	23
SOUTHWEST **W.A.**	19	21	19	17	16	18
SYDNEY NORTH **NSW**	21	20	18	15	16	19
CENTRAL COAST **NSW**	22	21	19	17	19	21
SOUTH COAST **NSW**	20	20	17	15	16	17
BYRON BAY **QUEENSLAND**	25	24	21	19	20	23
GOLD COAST **QUEENSLAND**	25	24	21	19	20	23
SUNSHINE COAST **QLD.**	26	24	23	21	22	24
ADELAIDE **SOUTH AUS.**	19	18	15	13	14	17
HOBART **TASMANIA**	15	13	11	11	11	13
GREAT OCEAN ROAD **VIC.**	18	19	16	13	14	16
PHILLIP ISLAND **VICTORIA**	17	17	14	12	13	15
KAIKOURA **NEW ZEALAND**	16	14	13	12	11	13
MAHIA PEN. **NEW ZEALAND**	18	16	13	12	12	15
GISBOURNE **NEW ZEALAND**	19	18	16	14	14	17
TARANAKI **NEW ZEALAND**	18	17	15	13	15	16

AUSTRALASIA — RAINFALL (mm)

	J-F	M-A	M-J	J-A	S-O	N-D
NORTHWEST	19	13	40	30	6	3
SOUTHWEST	21	52	200	195	95	32
SYDNEY NORTH	103	125	129	92	75	84
CENTRAL COAST	129	148	120	78	76	100
SOUTH COAST	110	134	96	65	82	96
BYRON BAY	178	197	175	97	98	132
GOLD COAST	185	170	114	66	72	118
SUNSHINE COAST	160	120	70	50	60	110
ADELAIDE	20	35	70	65	50	25
HOBART	45	45	50	50	55	55
GREAT OCEAN ROAD	37	66	74	92	86	60
PHILLIP ISLAND	50	55	55	50	65	60
KAIKOURA	65	70	90	90	70	70
MAHIA PEN.	75	75	87	93	56	60
GISBOURNE	80	80	110	50	70	50
TARANAKI	80	87	225	125	97	97

AUSTRALASIA — MIN | MAX TEMPS (°C)

	J-F MIN	J-F MAX	M-A MIN	M-A MAX	M-J MIN	M-J MAX	J-A MIN	J-A MAX	S-O MIN	S-O MAX	N-D MIN	N-D MAX
NORTHWEST	22	32	20	30	14	25	12	22	15	25	20	28
SOUTHWEST	14	24	12	23	10	18	8	16	9	18	12	22
SYDNEY NORTH	18	26	15	23	10	19	8	18	12	22	16	25
CENTRAL COAST	19	26	16	24	11	19	9	17	13	19	17	21
SOUTH COAST	16	26	14	24	9	18	7	17	10	21	14	24
BYRON BAY	21	27	18	26	13	21	12	20	15	23	19	26
GOLD COAST	20	28	18	27	12	22	9	21	14	24	18	28
SUNSHINE COAST	21	29	18	27	12	22	10	21	15	26	19	29
ADELAIDE	17	30	14	25	9	18	8	16	10	21	14	27
HOBART	12	22	10	19	6	13	5	12	7	16	10	20
GREAT OCEAN ROAD	14	24	13	21	9	16	8	14	9	16	12	21
PHILLIP ISLAND	14	26	12	22	8	16	6	14	9	18	12	21
KAIKOURA	13	21	10	18	5	13	4	11	8	16	10	19
MAHIA PEN.	14	24	11	21	6	16	5	14	8	18	12	22
GISBOURNE	13	24	11	21	6	15	5	14	7	17	11	22
TARANAKI	13	21	11	18	7	14	6	12	8	15	11	18

PACIFIC OCEAN — WATER TEMPS (°C)

	J-F	M-A	M-J	J-A	S-O	N-D
RAROTONGA **COOK ISL.**	26	26	25	23	23	25
MAMANUCAS **FIJI**	28	27	26	25	25	26
TAHITI & MOOREA **FR. POLY.**	27	27	26	25	26	27
TUAMOTU **FR. POLY.**	27	28	27	26	27	27
GALAPAGOS ISLANDS	23	24	22	21	20	21
KAUAI **HAWAII**	24	24	25	26	27	25
OAHU NTH SHORE **HAWAII**	24	24	25	26	27	25
POHNPEI **MICRONESIA**	28	28	29	29	29	29
SOUTH PROV. **NEW CAL.**	26	25	23	21	22	24
RAPA NUI	24	23	21	20	20	22
SAVAI'I & UPOLU **SAMOA**	28	28	29	27	27	28
TONGATAPU **TONGA**	26	26	24	22	23	24

PACIFIC OCEAN — RAINFALL (mm)

	J-F	M-A	M-J	J-A	S-O	N-D
RAROTONGA	238	226	170	109	114	187
MAMANUCAS	300	320	105	60	72	170
TAHITI & MOOREA	300	170	95	67	75	195
TUAMOTU	200	130	95	70	110	170
GALAPAGOS ISLANDS	57	60	9	4	7	6
KAUAI	75	50	15	65	35	65
OAHU	90	55	17	18	35	65
POHNPEI	283	411	463	427	427	417
SOUTH PROV.	110	135	95	83	47	60
RAPA NUI	110	110	110	80	80	120
SAVAI'I	397	300	152	100	162	315
TONGATAPU	210	287	102	107	112	120

PACIFIC OCEAN — MIN | MAX TEMPS (°C)

	J-F MIN	J-F MAX	M-A MIN	M-A MAX	M-J MIN	M-J MAX	J-A MIN	J-A MAX	S-O MIN	S-O MAX	N-D MIN	N-D MAX
RAROTONGA	23	29	22	28	20	26	18	25	19	26	21	27
MAMANUCAS	23	30	23	30	21	28	20	26	21	28	22	30
TAHITI & MOOREA	23	30	23	30	21	29	20	28	21	29	23	30
TUAMOTU	23	25	23	26	22	25	21	24	22	25	23	25
GALAPAGOS ISLANDS	23	30	23	30	21	28	19	25	18	25	20	27
KAUAI	16	26	17	27	18	29	20	31	20	31	17	27
OAHU	19	26	19	27	21	29	23	29	22	30	20	27
POHNPEI	24	30	24	30	23	30	23	31	23	31	23	31
SOUTH PROV.	23	29	22	27	19	24	17	23	18	25	21	28
RAPA NUI	21	29	19	29	16	27	13	25	15	26	17	29
SAVAI'I	24	30	23	30	23	29	23	29	23	29	23	30
TONGATAPU	22	29	22	29	19	26	18	26	18	26	21	28

NORTH AMERICA — WATER TEMPS (°C)

	J-F	M-A	M-J	J-A	S-O	N-D
VANCOUVER ISLAND **CAN.**	7	9	11	15	14	10
NOVA SCOTIA, **CANADA**	1	3	9	15	12	4
GREAT LAKES **USA/CAN.**	3	5	10	18	14	6
SITKA **ALASKA, USA**	6	6	9	13	12	8
SAN FRAN/SAN MATEO **USA**	12	12	13	14	14	13
SANTA CRUZ COUNTY **USA**	13	13	14	15	15	14
SANTA BARB/VENTURA **USA**	14	14	16	17	16	15
LOS ANGELES COUNTY **USA**	14	15	16	19	19	16
SAN DIEGO COUNTY **USA**	15	15	17	19	18	17
CENTRAL FLORIDA **USA**	16	20	24	26	24	21
OUTER BANKS, N.C. **USA**	9	11	19	25	20	14
OREGON **USA**	9	10	12	13	12	11
RHODE ISLAND **USA**	4	5	13	20	17	9
TEXAS **USA**	18	19	24	27	26	21

NORTH AMERICA — RAINFALL (mm)

	J-F	M-A	M-J	J-A	S-O	N-D
VANCOUVER ISLAND	183	106	67	37	119	217
NOVA SCOTIA	120	120	100	105	120	140
GREAT LAKES	50	55	75	80	84	72
SITKA	289	256	222	252	510	341
SAN FRAN/SAN MATEO	95	55	10	0	15	70
SANTA CRUZ COUNTY	95	52	8	0	11	72
SANTA BARB/VENTURA	85	49	3	0	11	52
LOS ANGELES COUNTY	75	50	5	0	10	50
SAN DIEGO COUNTY	50	28	5	3	6	37
CENTRAL FLORIDA	50	80	175	175	225	57
OUTER BANKS	122	99	101	142	134	119
OREGON	220	150	65	25	110	260
RHODE ISLAND	90	110	80	75	85	110
TEXAS	40	40	80	60	110	40

NORTH AMERICA — MIN | MAX TEMPS (°C)

	J-F MIN	J-F MAX	M-A MIN	M-A MAX	M-J MIN	M-J MAX	J-A MIN	J-A MAX	S-O MIN	S-O MAX	N-D MIN	N-D MAX
VANCOUVER ISLAND	0	6	3	12	9	20	12	23	8	16	3	8
NOVA SCOTIA	-9	0	-3	6	7	17	13	23	7	7	-3	5
GREAT LAKES	-13	-2	-7	11	5	23	12	26	4	18	-8	4
SITKA	-7	-2	-2	8	5	16	8	18	4	12	-3	2
SAN FRAN/SAN MATEO	6	14	8	17	11	20	12	22	11	22	7	16
SANTA CRUZ COUNTY	5	14	7	17	10	20	12	22	11	22	7	15
SANTA BARB/VENTURA	6	18	8	19	11	21	14	24	12	23	6	20
LOS ANGELES COUNTY	8	19	9	20	13	22	16	28	13	26	9	21
SAN DIEGO COUNTY	8	17	11	19	16	22	17	23	15	23	10	20
CENTRAL FLORIDA	14	25	17	28	22	31	24	32	23	30	16	26
OUTER BANKS	3	11	8	17	17	25	22	29	17	24	7	15
OREGON	2	9	4	12	9	16	11	20	8	18	3	10
RHODE ISLAND	-5	3	1	10	11	20	17	26	11	20	1	8
TEXAS	8	19	15	25	22	31	23	33	20	30	11	22

CENT AM/CARIB	WATER TEMPS (°C) J-F	M-A	M-J	J-A	S-O	N-D	RAINFALL (mm) J-F	M-A	M-J	J-A	S-O	N-D	MIN MAX TEMPS (°C) J-F		M-A		M-J		J-A		S-O		N-D	
ABACO/ELEUTHERA BAH.	22	23	25	27	26	24	40	60	130	130	170	50	18	24	20	26	22	29	24	31	23	30	20	26
BARBADOS	25	26	27	28	27	26	47	34	85	147	174	150	21	28	21	30	23	31	23	31	23	31	22	29
BRITISH VIRGIN ISLANDS	25	25	26	27	28	26	40	60	85	85	110	100	22	28	23	29	25	30	25	31	24	30	23	29
GUANACASTE COSTA RICA	26	27	28	27	27	26	4	18	205	202	270	70	23	35	23	35	22	33	23	32	23	32	22	31
GOLFO DE NICOYA CR.	26	27	28	27	27	26	5	20	200	200	270	75	23	35	23	35	23	33	23	32	23	32	22	32
GULFO DULCE COSTA RICA	26	27	28	27	27	26	4	18	205	202	270	70	23	35	23	35	22	33	23	32	23	32	22	31
LIMÓN COSTA RICA	26	26	27	27	27	27	260	240	280	350	180	390	20	30	21	30	22	31	22	30	22	30	21	30
CUBA	25	26	28	29	29	27	58	52	142	130	161	68	18	26	20	28	22	31	24	32	23	31	20	27
AMBER COAST DOM REP.	25	26	27	28	28	27	170	140	90	75	110	280	21	27	22	27	24	29	25	30	24	30	22	28
COSTA BALSAMO EL SAL.	27	27	28	28	28	27	4	34	255	260	272	22	20	30	21	31	23	29	23	29	24	28	21	27
ORIENTE SALVAJE EL SAL.	26	27	28	28	28	27	7	28	226	306	227	26	20	30	22	31	23	30	22	30	21	29	20	29
GUADELOUPE	25	25	27	28	28	26	75	95	152	197	245	175	19	28	20	29	22	30	23	31	22	31	20	30
GUATEMALA	27	28	29	28	28	27	5	50	280	310	350	35	19	31	21	32	22	31	22	31	22	30	20	31
JAMAICA	27	28	28	29	29	28	19	33	97	85	143	60	19	30	20	31	22	32	23	33	23	32	21	31
MARTINIQUE	25	25	28	28	28	26	95	80	160	240	240	170	21	27	22	28	23	29	24	29	24	30	23	29
NORTHERN BAJA MEXICO	15	16	18	20	20	16	51	28	50	3	5	38	8	17	11	19	14	21	17	24	15	23	10	20
CENTRAL BAJA MEXICO	11	13	16	20	20	17	35	15	5	15	75	30	10	21	12	24	16	27	20	30	20	28	17	24
LOS CABOS MEXICO	23	23	25	28	28	26	15	0	2	25	150	20	12	24	13	29	17	33	22	35	21	33	15	27
NAYARIT MEXICO	23	23	25	28	28	26	25	40	100	160	230	75	16	26	18	27	23	30	24	32	24	32	19	28
COLIMA/MICHOACAN MEX.	27	26	28	29	29	28	4	1	158	254	254	18	22	31	22	32	25	33	25	33	24	32	22	32
WEST OAXACA MEXICO	27	27	28	28	28	27	4	0	147	177	180	8	22	29	23	31	25	32	25	32	24	31	22	30
EAST OAXACA MEXICO	26	26	28	29	28	26	4	1	165	197	181	14	21	30	23	32	25	33	24	32	23	31	21	30
RIVAS PROV. NICARAGUA	26	27	28	28	27	26	10	5	200	170	300	50	21	33	23	35	24	34	23	31	22	31	21	31
BOCAS DEL TORO PANAMA	26	26	27	27	27	27	200	170	215	250	120	300	20	30	21	30	22	31	22	30	22	30	21	30
SOUTHWEST PANAMA	26	27	28	28	27	27	110	67	315	387	365	510	24	29	25	30	24	31	24	31	24	31	24	29
NORTHWEST PUERTO RICO	25	26	27	28	28	26	65	75	132	137	150	127	21	28	22	29	23	31	24	31	24	31	22	30
ST MARTIN & ST BARTS	25	25	26	28	28	26	50	50	75	90	110	95	23	28	24	29	25	30	25	30	25	31	24	29
TRINIDAD & TOBAGO	26	26	27	28	28	27	55	50	147	232	181	154	20	31	20	32	22	32	22	31	22	32	21	32

SOUTH AMERICA	WATER TEMPS (°C) J-F	M-A	M-J	J-A	S-O	N-D	RAINFALL (mm) J-F	M-A	M-J	J-A	S-O	N-D	MIN MAX TEMPS (°C) J-F		M-A		M-J		J-A		S-O		N-D	
MAR PLATA ARGENTINA	18	17	12	9	10	15	70	70	60	50	55	65	15	25	12	22	6	15	5	13	7	17	12	22
SANTA CATARINA BRAZIL	23	22	20	17	17	21	105	92	112	130	125	100	22	28	19	27	14	22	13	21	16	22	20	26
RIO DE JANEIRO BRAZIL	24	25	22	20	20	23	110	120	85	55	90	130	23	30	22	29	20	26	19	26	20	26	22	28
FERNANDO DO NOR. BRAZ.	27	27	27	26	26	26	70	190	270	203	45	26	25	30	24	29	23	28	22	27	23	28	24	29
ARICA CHILE	20	19	18	16	17	18	0	0	0	0	0	0	18	27	17	25	14	21	13	19	14	21	16	24
IQUIQUE CHILE	19	19	18	16	17	18	0.5	0	0	0	0	0	18	27	17	25	14	21	13	19	14	21	16	24
ANTOFAGASTA CHILE	18	17	16	15	16	17	0	0	1	2	1	0	16	24	14	21	12	19	10	16	12	18	14	21
PICHELEMU CHILE	16	15	14	13	13	15	18	62	230	210	82	37	12	27	9	25	7	18	5	17	7	21	11	26
CARIBBEAN COLOMBIA	26	26	27	27	28	27	2	13	110	117	185	82	23	30	24	31	25	31	25	31	25	31	24	30
NORTHERN ECUADOR	25	25	23	22	21	22	100	110	40	15	10	15	23	27	24	28	23	27	23	27	23	27	23	27
GUAYAS/MANABI ECUADOR	24	24	22	21	22	23	244	196	18	18	2	27	21	31	22	32	20	31	18	29	19	31	20	31
NORTH PIURA PERU	24	25	23	22	21	22	3	4	0	0	0	1	23	30	23	31	21	30	20	28	20	29	21	29
SOUTH PIURA PERU	22	22	19	18	17	19	10	10	0	0	0	0	23	32	22	31	19	28	17	26	17	28	19	30
CHICAMA PERU	21	21	18	17	17	18	3	4	0	0	0	1	21	29	20	29	18	25	16	22	16	23	17	25
COSTA VERDE PERU	20	21	19	17	18	19	1	1	1	2	1	0	19	26	18	25	16	21	14	18	15	20	17	23
PUNTA HERMOSA PERU	19	20	16	24	15	17	1	0	5	8	5	2	19	26	18	25	15	21	14	18	14	20	16	23

World Champions

YEAR	MEN	WOMEN	LONGBOARD MEN	LONGBOARD WOMEN
1976	Peter Townend (Australia)			
1977	Shaun Tomson (South Africa)	Margo Oberg (Hawaii)		
1978	Wayne Bartholomew (Australia)	Lynne Boyer (Hawaii)		
1979	Mark Richards (Australia)	Lynne Boyer (Hawaii)		
1980	Mark Richards (Australia)	Margo Oberg (Hawaii)		
1981	Mark Richards (Australia)	Margo Oberg (Hawaii)		
1982	Mark Richards (Australia)	Debbie Beacham (USA)		
1983	Tom Carroll (Australia)	Kim Mearig (USA)		
1984	Tom Carroll (Australia)	Freida Zamba (USA)		
1985	Tom Curren (USA)	Freida Zamba (USA)		
1986	Tom Curren (USA)	Freida Zamba (USA)	Nat Young (Australia)	
1987	Damien Hardman (Australia)	Wendy Botha (South Africa)	Stuart Entwistle (Australia)	
1988	Barton Lynch (Australia)	Freida Zamba (USA)	Nat Young (Australia)	
1989	Martin Potter (GB)	Wendy Botha (Australia)	Nat Young (Australia)	
1990	Tom Curren (USA)	Pam Burridge (Australia)	Nat Young (Australia)	
1991	Damien Hardman (Australia)	Wendy Botha (Australia)	Martin McMillan (Australia)	
1992	Kelly Slater (USA)	Wendy Botha (Australia)	Joey Hawkins (USA)	
1993	Derek Ho (Hawaii) (Hawaii)	Pauline Menczer (Australia)	Rusty Keaulana (Hawaii)	
1994	Kelly Slater (USA)	Lisa Andersen (USA)	Rusty Keaulana (Hawaii)	
1995	Kelly Slater (USA)	Lisa Andersen (USA)	Rusty Keaulana (Hawaii)	
1996	Kelly Slater (USA)	Lisa Andersen (USA)	Bonga Perkins (Hawaii)	
1997	Kelly Slater (USA)	Lisa Andersen (USA)	Dino Miranda (Hawaii)	
1998	Kelly Slater (USA)	Layne Beachley (Australia)	Joel Tudor (USA)	
1999	Mark Occhilupo (Australia)	Layne Beachley (Australia)	Colin Mcphillips (USA)	
2000	Sunny Garcia (Hawaii)	Layne Beachley (Australia)	Beau Young (Australia)	
2001	C.J Hobgood (USA)	Layne Beachley (Australia)	Colin McPhillips (USA)	
2002	Andy Irons (Hawaii)	Layne Beachley (Australia)	Colin McPhillips (USA)	
2003	Andy Irons (Hawaii)	Layne Beachley (Australia)	Beau Young (Australia)	
2004	Andy Irons (Hawaii)	Sofia Mulanovich (Peru)	Joel Tudor (USA)	
2005	Kelly Slater (USA)	Chelsea Georgeson (Australia)	N/A	
2006	Kelly Slater (USA)	Layne Beachley (Australia)	Josh Constable (Australia)	Schuyler McFerran (USA)
2007	Mick Fanning (Australia)	Stephanie Gilmore (Australia)	Phil Rajzman (Brazil)	Jennifer Smith (USA)
2008	Kelly Slater (USA)	Stephanie Gilmore (Australia)	Bonga Perkins (Hawaii)	Joy Monahan (Hawaii)
2009	Mick Fanning (Australia)	Stephanie Gilmore (Australia)	Harley Ingleby (Australia)	Jennifer Smith (USA)
2010	Kelly Slater (USA)	Stephanie Gilmore (Australia)	Duane Desoto (Hawaii)	Cori Schumacher (USA)
2011	Kelly Slater (USA)	Carissa Moore (Hawaii)	Taylor Jensen (USA)	Lindsay Steinriede (USA)
2012	Joel Parkinson (Australia)	Stephanie Gilmore (Australia)	Taylor Jensen (USA)	Kelia Moniz (Hawaii)
2013	Mick Fanning (Australia)	Carissa Moore (Hawaii)	Picolo Clemente (Peru)	Kelia Moniz (Hawaii)
2014				
2015				
2016				
2017				
2018				
2019				
2020				
2021				
2022				
2023				
2024				
2025				

JUNIOR BOYS	JUNIOR GIRLS	TRIPLE CROWN	BODYBOARD MEN	YEAR
				1976
				1977
				1978
				1979
				1980
				1981
			Daniel Kaimi (USA Hawaii)	1982
		Michael Ho (Hawaii)	Mike Stewart (USA Hawaii)	1983
		Derek Ho (Hawaii)	Mike Stewart (USA Hawaii)	1984
		Michael Ho (Hawaii)	N/A	1985
		Derek Ho (Hawaii)	Ben Severson (USA Hawaii)	1986
		Gary Elkerton (Australia)	Mike Stewart (USA Hawaii)	1987
		Derek Ho (Hawaii)	Mike Stewart (USA Hawaii)	1988
		Gary Elkerton (Australia)	Mike Stewart (USA Hawaii)	1989
		Derek Ho (Hawaii)	Mike Stewart (USA Hawaii)	1990
		Tom Carroll (Australia)	Mike Stewart (USA Hawaii)	1991
		Sunny Garcia (Hawaii)	Mike Stewart (USA Hawaii)	1992
		Sunny Garcia (Hawaii)	Michael Eppelstun (Australia)	1993
		Sunny Garcia (Hawaii)	Guilherme Tamega (Brazil)	1994
		Kelly Slater (USA)	Guilherme Tamega (Brazil)	1995
		Kaipo Jaquias (Hawaii)	Guilherme Tamega (Brazil)	1996
		Mike Rommelse (Australia)	Guilherme Tamega (Brazil)	1997
Andy Irons (Hawaii)		Kelly Slater (USA)	Andre Botha (South Africa)	1998
Joel Parkinson (Australia)		Sunny Garcia (Hawaii)	Andre Botha (South Africa)	1999
Pedro Henrique (Brazil)		Sunny Garcia (Hawaii)	Paulo Barcellos (Brazil)	2000
Joel Parkinson (Australia)		Myles Padaca (Hawaii)	Guilherme Tamega (Brazil)	2001
N/A		Andy Irons (Hawaii)	Miguel Cervantes (Spain)	2002
Adriano De Souza (Brazil)		Andy Irons (Hawaii)	Damian King (Australia)	2003
Pablo Paulino (Brazil)		Sunny Garcia (Hawaii)	Damian King (Australia)	2004
Kekoa Bacalso (Hawaii)	Jessi Miley-Dyer (Australia)	Andy Irons (Hawaii)	Ben Player (Australia)	2005
Jordy Smith (South Africa)	Nicola Atherton (Australia)	Andy Irons (Hawaii)	Jeff Hubbard (USA Hawaii)	2006
Pablo Paulino (Brazil)	Sally Fitzgibbons (Australia)	Bede Durbidge (Australia)	Ben Player (Australia)	2007
Kai Barger (Hawaii)	Pauline Ado (France)	Joel Parkinson (Australia)	Uri Valadao (Brazil)	2008
Maxime Huscenot (Reunion Isl)	Laura Enever (Australia)	Joel Parkinson (Australia)	Jeff Hubbard (USA Hawaii)	2009
Jack Freestone (Australia)	Alizee Arnaud (France)	Joel Parkinson (Australia)	Amaury Lavernhe (France)	2010
Caio Ibelli (Brazil)	Leila Hurst (Hawaii)	John Florence (Hawaii)	Pierre-Louis Costes (France)	2011
Jack Freestone (Australia)	Nikki Van Dijk (Australia)	Sebastian Zietz (Hawaii)	Jeff Hubbard (USA Hawaii)	2012
Gabriel Medina (Brazil)	Ella Williams (New Zealand)	Jeremy Flores (France)	Ben Player (Australia)	2013
				2014
				2015
				2016
				2017
				2018
				2019
				2020
				2021
				2022
				2023
				2024
				2025

Further information about Surfers, Events, Schedules and results can be found at the following links:

www.aspworldtour.com
vanstriplecrownofsurfing.com
ibaworldtour.com

Index

Contributors

Publishers Bruce Sutherland, Dan Haylock, Ollie Fitzjones

Editor Bruce Sutherland

Design and Production Dan Haylock

Everything Else Ollie Fitzjones

Research Antony "YEP Been There" Colas

Accounts Andrea Fitzjones

Research and Forecasting Content Partners

YEP magicseaweed

Photographers

Wesley Allison	Alfredo Escobar	Baby Marmotte	Steve Ryan
Javier Amezaga	Jason Feast	Greg Martin	Pedro Salinas
Baja Surf Adventures	Marc Fenies	Laurent Masurel	Cory Scott
Don Balch	Juan Fernandez	Ray Max	David Seri
Gonzalo Barandiaran	Javier Fernandez	Emilliano Mazzoni	Olivier Servaire
Bliss/surf-martinique	Ollie Fitzjones	Dick Meseroll	Roger Sharp
Jamie Bott	Steve Fitzpatrick	James Metyko	Andrew Shield
Rod Braby	Gecko	Jørgen Michaelson	Sully
Ricardo Bravo	Thierry Gibaud	Louise Millais	Surfbanyak
Chris Burkard	Rob Gilley	Stéphane Mira	Bruce Sutherland
Stuart Butler	Kevin Griffin	Moonwalker	Bernard Testemale
John Callahan	Alan Van Gysen	Bill Morris	Ben Thouard
Tom Carey	Warren Hawke	Laurent Nevarez	Tostee
Emiliano Cataldi	Dan Haylock	Tim Nunn	Patrice Touhar
Sylvain Cazenave	Georg Hilmarsson	Kristen Pelou	Yannick Le Touquin
Chagas	Phil Holden	Peruecosurf	Seth Tyler
Pierrede Champs	Dustin Humphries	Damien Poullenot	Willy Uribe
Philippe Chevodian	Timo Jarvinen	David Pu'u	Flavio Vidigal
Antony YEP Colas	Paul Kennedy	Geoff Ragatz	Waidroka
Christophe 'Kiki' Commarieu	Michael Kew	Ben Rak	Doug Waters
Dean Dampney	Mike Knott	Jason Reposar	Alex Williams
De Marsan	Bob Ledbetter	Jelle Rigole	Jeremy Wilmotte
Jeff Divine	Chris Van Lennup	Stéphane Robin	Peter 'Joli' Wilson
Easydrop	Obdulio Luna	Garth Robinson	

The Stormrider Surf Journal

First published in 2014 by LOW PRESSURE LTD©
Tel/Fax +33 (0)5 58 77 76 85   enquiries@lowpressure.co.uk

Creation of all maps, graphic arrangement,
pictograms, text and index © Low Pressure Ltd 2014

A catalogue reference for this book can be obtained from the
British Library. ISBN Softback: 978-1-908520-39-5

Printed by Hong Kong Graphics and Printing using
50% chlorine-free paper stock from managed forests
and 50% recycled wood-free cartridge.